D0762350

PURITAN
ISLAM

PURITAN
ISLAM

*The Geoexpansion
of the
Muslim World*

BARRY A. VANN

 Prometheus Books

59 John Glenn Drive
Amherst, New York 14228–2119

Published 2011 by Prometheus Books

Jacket design by Grace M. Conti-Zilsberger
Cover Images courtesy of Barry A. Vann and Dover Publications, Inc.

Inquiries should be addressed to
Prometheus Books
59 John Glenn Drive
Amherst, New York 14228–2119
VOICE: 716–691–0133
FAX: 716–691–0137
WWW.PROMETHEUSBOOKS.COM

15 14 13 12 11   5 4 3 2 1

Library of Congress Cataloging-in-Publication Data

Vann, Barry.
    Puritan Islam : the geoexpansion of the Muslim world / by Barry A. Vann.
        p. cm.
    Includes bibliographical references and index.
    ISBN 978–1–61614–517–0 (cloth : alk. paper)
    ISBN 978–1–61614–518–7 (ebook)
    1. Islam 2. Islamic fundamentalism. 3. Salatiyah 4. Religion and geography.
5. Human geography. I. Title.

BP163.V36 2011
297.09—dc23

                                                                        2011019047

I would like to dedicate this book to Amy, Sarah, and Preston Vann, but I am especially indebted to my brother Richard "Rick" Jared Jones, as well as Charles and Lillie Evans. They know well the deepest meaning of this book.

Contents

Qur'anic Geotheology and Other Perspectives of Islam

Overview

The Islamic Republic of Iran is a simmering cauldron of instability sandwiched between the contested spaces of Afghanistan and Iraq. It is led by a cadre of mullahs and elected officials who have geopious visions for their country's place in sacred history. With nearly seventy million Shia (followers of Ali), it is the world's largest fundamentalist Islamic country. Its large size and unique place in Islam, (meaning "submission to Allah,") has geopolitical implications for regional and, indeed, world peace. Consider what might happen if the United States were to completely withdraw from Iraq, which also has a Shia majority. The two countries might form a political union based in large measure on a common geotheological vision of the world. Such a union, however, would not change the unfolding demographic challenges facing the region. On the contrary, religious fundamentalism associated with Abrahamic religions is inextricably linked to high fertility rates because of the culture's stress on patriarchy. Fundamentalists place a premium on traditional gender roles that invite higher fertility among women.

With a current natural increase rate (the percentage by which a population grows in a year) of around 1.12, the number of Iranians will double to 140 million in little less than seventy-two years.[1] Iraq's population, too, will double in less than thirty years.[2] Making matters worse for political stability in the near future, neither country's economic growth will likely keep pace with its expanding population. Unemployed Iranians and Iraqis will move to other countries in search of a sustainable life. If current demographic patterns in the Middle East and Asia continue, many residents will likely take part in Zelinskian migration scenarios, named for geographer Wilbur Zelinsky, who advanced a theory of migration called mobility transition. Zelinskian migration scenarios would create waves of emigrants moving across and out of Muslim countries.[3] Impoverished conditions encourage many young Muslims to seek explanations for their plight among the geotheological imaginings of Islamic fundamentalism. In other words, Muslims want to know what roles they each play, with respect to the worship of the divine and with respect to spaces, including nature and nations. Unbridled population growth and increasing poverty, as well as a related rise in fundamentalism, will jeopardize global political and economic stability.

While some observers of Middle Eastern affairs lean toward cultural and military interventions in the region as an unspoken means to reign in the regional population explosion, others argue against any American and European involvement. As I will soon show, a number of writers reason that conflicts and protests involving Muslims living in the Middle East, Southeast Asia, and Europe are minor and discrete examples of sectarian violence resulting from nationalistic responses to the penetration of Western symbols and to modes of production associated with European and American imperialism.[4] The presence of armed American and European soldiers as well as the potentially corrupting influence of a flood of American dollars in Muslim countries certainly fuel anxieties of fundamentalists, or as Khaled Abou El Fadl, scholar of Islamic jurisprudence, refers to them, puritan Muslims,[5] who fear that their culture is being corrupted by unbelievers. As this book will show, such a situation will make Muslim-on-Muslim violence worse, but upon closer inspection, it is actually fundamentalist-on-moderate violence that will increase. To the fundamentalist, countrymen who compromise the precepts of the true faith with non-Muslims are likewise regarded as unbelievers, no matter their self-identity, and are potentially culpable in inviting God's wrath on the entire nation. To outsiders, violent actions seem senseless. But in the Islamic puritans' minds, where an active deity punishes and rewards human actions, they believe that their resistance will stop the spread of unbelief and, therefore, save the entire nation from a more frightful *geotheokolasis* (God uses nature to punish).[6]

Regardless of one's views on America's involvement in those countries, it is nonetheless important to understand the thought processes of Islamic puritans. To get "inside the heads" of puritans, it is important to go to the Qur'an, the source of Islam's geotheology.[7] Qur'anic geotheology is important to consider because it involves mental imagery that has implications for understanding how puritans view the concepts of community (*umma*) and nation; to the puritan, membership in community and nation is contingent upon adherence to the faith in public spaces. Geotheology also includes landscapes and other features and forces of nature, as well as human efforts to govern societies and their lands in response to the perceived expectations of the deity. Just as it is logical to associate rigid Jewish and Christian beliefs with literal interpretations of the Torah and the Bible, it makes sense to do the same with Islam and its Qur'an.[8]

A Place Close to the Heart of the Creator

The fear of geotheokolasis has affected the history of all Abrahamic religions. Religious fundamentalists from the three Abrahamic faiths have historically battled each other for a perceived place close to the heart of the creator. The battle for the Abrahamic God among the three major monotheistic religions has been waged for nearly 1,400 years. The seeds of this long-lasting conflict, though, were planted much earlier. The causes of the ancient and continuing battle began innocently enough as a domestic dispute somewhere between 2100 and 1800 BCE when a jealous wife named Sarah (*Sarai*) convinced her husband to banish his young concubine named Hagar and her son, Ishmael, whom he had fathered. Ironically, it was Sarah, an elderly, barren woman, who had planned and encouraged her husband's relationship with Hagar in the first place. Her change of heart happened when Sarah conceived and delivered her own son. His name was Isaac (*Yitzchak*). The sons born in this blended family became fathers of two distinct lines of descent, but the looming family dispute over inheriting Abraham's place in the heart of the creator grew when centuries later a Galilean named Jesus (in Hebrew,

Yahshua), a descendant of Isaac, invited others, including non-Semites, into Abraham's family. Later, in the seventh century, a desert-dwelling man—a descendant of Ishmael—named Muhammad, claimed that he was the last prophet of the God of Abraham. A strict monotheist, Muhammad, who claimed to have received the word of God from the angel Gabriel, authored the Qur'an, the holy book of Islam.

It has been nearly four thousand years since the seeds of religious conflict were planted, and, after jihads in the seventh and eighth centuries, crusades through the thirteenth century, and our own wars in Iraq and Afghanistan, adversaries are no closer to a victory today than the ancients were during the time of Abraham. However, with rapid growth in Muslim populations coupled with a persistent demographic decline in the historically Christian countries of Europe and North America, Islam will soon emerge, perhaps before midcentury, as the world's largest religion.[9] Along with a growth in the sheer numbers of Muslim adherents, there will also be an increasing presence of their religious symbols in heretofore secular, public spaces.

Through the creation of real and imagined landscapes, personal identity, and community affiliation, Muslims express their submission to Allah ("the god"). Just as Abram demonstrated his submission to God by changing his name to Abraham, many Muslim converts change their names to show their personal submission to Allah. American boxer Mohammad Ali, formerly Cassius Clay, American basketball player Lou Alcindor, who changed his name to Kareem Abdul-Jabbar, and British musician Cat Stevens, now known as Yusuf Islam, provide recent notable examples.

Like all Muslims, Western converts to Islam must pray facing the Saudi Arabian city of Mecca, and, while on the surface this may seem a mere ritual, it has deeper political implications for international alliances. Furthermore, Muhammad declared that the angel Gabriel gave him the Qur'an in Arabic, his native tongue. As the Muslim holy book declares, "We [have] revealed it, a true judgment in Arabic."[10] By acknowledging the sanctity of an Arab city, adherents demonstrate a geopious sentiment (the emotional side of religion tied to space, including political units such as countries, cities, and towns). Adherents are further encouraged to nurture geopiety toward Arabs and their culture by acknowledging the sanctity of the Arabic tongue.

Unlike many Christians who believe that Israel and its Jewish inhabitants deserve a sacred commitment from Western countries, most Muslims do not share that sentiment. They are more likely to believe that the Arab and the non-Arab Muslim world legitimately warrant greater respect and supportive relationships with the West. As global demographic patterns continue to favor Muslim countries, these religiously inspired "geographies of the imagination" could lead to new diplomatic relationships and international alliances that break from the Judeo-Christian tradition of supporting Israel and Judaic institutions.

From a review of the writings on the faith, it is hard to appreciate the geographic implications associated with the rise of Islam. Most writers either celebrate Islam as a religion of peace or demonize it as an inherently violent worldview. It is my contention that by applying concepts developed in the subfield of religious geography, scholars can better understand Islam's relationship to the demographic trends and political forces that are shaping the cultural landscape of the entire world. To accomplish that goal, it is important to survey how other writers perceive Islam; despite their best efforts, most such writers can be placed into one of two camps: the apologists and the critics. I attempt to dig deeper into Islam to identify its subparts, including gender, regional traditions in jurisprudence, and how puritans deviate from moderate Muslims. While I use geographic concepts like region, diffusion, and geotheology, among others, I go deeper into the immaterial and synergistic aspects of religion, economics, and demography.

A Religion of Peace

There are clear political and intellectual signs in the United States that a softening of attitudes toward Muslim countries is occurring. While it is obvious that President Barack Obama has adopted a conciliatory policy toward Muslim countries, some Republicans like Ron Paul, a member of the US House of Representatives from Texas, declared in May 2007 that events like that of September 11, 2001, were invited by the interventionist policies of the United States.[11] As this book shows, Representative Paul and others like him envision a rethinking of American foreign affairs. The realignment of American foreign policy away from Israel and toward Muslim countries is supported by a number of intellectuals who argue that Islam is the religion of peace, social justice, and respect for the other. One can look to the works of Seyyed Hossein Nasr, a prolific writer in the field of Islamic studies and a noted scholar with a particular expertise in Islamic history, for an example. His book *The Heart of Islam: Enduring Values for Humanity* attempts to show how radical Muslims do not represent the true history and core values of Islam.[12] Nasr's book, which also endeavors to show common ground with Christianity and Judaism, provides only a partial and perhaps biased history of Islamic jurisprudence and its tradition of interpreting and enforcing Islamic laws (*sharia*). Nasr does not adequately explain historic and contemporary divisions among Islamic jurists (*mullahs*).

Huston Smith, a former professor of religion at the University of California, shares Nasr's view. In *The World's Religions: Our Great Wisdom Traditions*, which, according to Michael Joseph Gross, a book reviewer for the *New York Times*, has been the standard introductory text on religion since its original printing, Smith focuses on positive interactions between Muslims and people of other faiths.[13] He, like Nasr, argues that Jesus and Muhammad were of one mind. He offers no negative judgments of Islam in his book. Christianity, however, is a different matter. In Smith's opinion, Jesus would have become more like Muhammad had his career lasted longer. He writes, "If Jesus had had a longer career, or if the Jews had not been so socially powerless at the time [they were made that way by Western imperialists from Rome], Jesus might have systematized his teachings more. As it was, his work was left unfinished. It was reserved for another Teacher to systemize the laws of Morality." "The Koran," according to Smith, "is this later Teacher."[14] Smith's identification of Jesus hence supports the Muslim view of the Nazarene as a prophetic figure and not the propitiation for humanity's sin and the source of eternal salvation.

A number of scholars cast Islam in a way that allows them to situate the religion into their imagined world of accepting, multicultural societies.[15] Noted scholars of religion, such as Karen Armstrong, Kelly Knauer, Adnan A. Musallam, and S. Sayyid, certainly depict Islam in such a manner.[16] These writers see modern Islamism or radical Islam as a recent development, a sociological response to threats from a colonizing and secular West. To Armstrong, it is simply a manifestation of a global rise in fundamentalism shared by all religions. In contrast to the view of Armstrong, it could be that the West is witnessing a rise in secularism set against the ways of life among highly religious people who have not changed. When secular writers see this cultural contrast, especially as it occurs in remote reaches of the world made available through images projected in the print media, radio broadcasts, and on television, they conclude that the world is witnessing a new rise in fundamentalism. In other words, highly religious people peacefully go about their daily lives, but, when they are confronted with challenges to their worldviews and lifestyles, they react in ways that are highly contrastive with the images of cerebral, secular society.

When non-Muslim scholars write about Islam, they often do so in comparative terms, which allow them to avoid theological areas in which there are no real bases for comparison. According to cultural geographer Roger W. Stump, comparative studies reduce difficulties associated with the imprecision of defining the concept of religion.[17] The avoidance of controversial issues involving theological imaginings suggesting ways to govern space is also apparent in many academic works. As I will show in the next section of this chapter, popular writers are not so inclined. Perchance they hope to capitalize on people's fear of Islamic terrorists. Nevertheless, academic writers who touch on controversial aspects of Islam often frame the discussion in comparative terms. For example, in Ronald Johnstone's well-written *Religion in Society: A Sociology of Religion*, Islam is introduced as follows: "Major religions, such as Islam and Buddhism, have . . . actively courted nonmembers, not infrequently using force and political means when ordinary persuasion was insufficient. In fact, in Islam the political-military and religious motivations are so mixed as to be impossible to separate, which is true throughout the history of Christianity also, of course."[18]

From reading Johnstone's introduction to Islam, it is easy to believe that Islam diffused from the Saudi Peninsula the same way that Buddhism spread from India. Peaceful Buddhist missionaries carried their faith from its hearth on the Indian subcontinent to the east, especially early on to nearby Sri Lanka (formerly Ceylon). In a similar manner to both Islam and Buddhism,

Christianity spread through Europe during the *Pax Romana* (two hundred years of Roman peace). Emperors Nero and Diocletian, from the first and third centuries, respectively, certainly did not intertwine their governance of the empire with Christianity. Indeed, the two were known for being especially harsh to Christians. Such simplistic comparisons as the one put forth by Johnstone are perhaps used to avoid the appearance of picking on a particular religion. While it may be politically expedient to follow that pattern, it is simply not true to history when one uses such inaccurate comparisons.

Not all Muslims nor, indeed, many Christians and Jews agree with Nasr that Islam and the other Abrahamic religions share common ground on theological matters, let alone on themes such as the governance of space, which refers to nature, and the governance of people and lands. As noted by Islamic juristic scholar Khaled Abou El Fadl, mentioned above, many Muslims (puritans) embrace a literal reading of the Qur'an, so they feel that voices like Nasr's represent an unsatisfactory departure from the true religion established by Muhammad in the seventh century.[19] The modern incarnation of Islam is hence a complex and diverse religion; yet, the idea that Islam is a ubiquitous religion of peace is on the ascendancy among many Western secularists and scholars.

Critical and Objective Depictions of Islam

A number of mostly popular authors have written accusatory and even inflammatory articles and books on Islam.[20] In a more useful manner, others have published solid, critical work on aspects of the faith that embody notions of space, a concept that J. K. Wright called geotheology. Khaled Abou El Fadl, for instance, describes how Islamic jurisprudence has been divided in identifying sacred and profane spaces and what is required of Muslims in response to perceived violations of their lands, people, and institutions. According to El Fadl, Muslim jurists have tended to divide the world into three spheres of imagined spaces: the abode or space of Islam, the abode of war or contested space, and the abode of peace or nonbelligerence.[21] Jonathan Brockopp, associate professor of history and religious studies at Penn State University, similarly identifies these spaces as the abode of Islam, the abode of treaty, and the abode of war.[22] El Fadl contends that Muslim jurists have long disagreed over the exact location of these spaces. They have also disagreed on what constitutes legal justification for fighting non-Muslims. As is shown in chapter 3, there is ample reason to believe that a puritan Muslim could read the holy text and conclude that sectarian differences in Islam itself could provide situational justification to act violently against other self-identified Muslims, as well as against unbelievers such as Jews, Christians, Buddhists, or atheists and agnostics. Unfortunately, writes El Fadl, "Islamic civilization has crumbled, and the traditional institutions that once sustained the juristic discourse (no doubt a moderating influence) have all but vanished."[23] To make matters worse, puritan Muslims of today have been inspired by eighteenth- and nineteenth-century Wahhabism and Salafism (discussed later in this introduction), and, as participants in fundamentalist movements bent on repelling secular and therefore evil forces, they are "uninterested in critical historical inquiry and [have] responded to the challenge of modernity by escaping to the secure haven of the text . . . [where] they came to consider intellectualism and rational moral insight to be inaccessible and, thus, corruptions of the purity of the Islamic message."[24] This is, however, only part of what drives puritan Islam. As is shown later in this book, purity is also sought to reap divine blessings while avoiding Allah's wrath.

Advocates of democratic reform in the Middle East have not neglected the study of Islam either. In their *Triumph of Democracy over Militant Islamism*, Colonel B. Wayne Quist, a retired air force colonel who served in Saudi Arabia, and David F. Drake, the physician, author, and the current director for the Center of Democracy and Human Rights in Saudi Arabia, take a similar view to that of Peter R. Demant, history professor at the Universidale de São Paulo. These men argue that the current issues involving radical Islam should be recognized as a regional or "in-house" problem.[25] Specifically, Quist and Drake argue that al Qaeda is a Saudi problem and that the attacks of 9/11 stem from America's oil interests and entanglements with the Saudi government. They go on to argue that the Bush administration's wars in Afghanistan and Iraq were pursued to plant the seeds of freedom and democracy in the Middle East. Democracy, they believe, is the antidote to militant Islam. However, with Shia making up the majority of the Iraqi population and having suffered greatly under the Sunni government of Saddam Hussein, true democracy will empower the formerly oppressed Shia community in Iraq. No doubt much of the civil unrest in Iraq is the result of interfaith conflict. With neighboring Iran the center of the Shiite world, which was also a target of Saddam Hussein's military forces during the Iran-Iraq war in the 1980s, how could any American administration not expect Iran to get involved in the sectarian violence that continues to plague Iraqi city streets and countryside?

Feminists have also added their thoughts on the gendered spaces of Islam, and, oddly, few of them have issued public criticisms against the patriarchal aspects of the religion. In discussing gendered spaces in Islam, Mervat Hatem, a political science professor at Howard University, argues that Islamic women have sought to develop and "use their intellectual skills to interpret the Islamic texts from a gender perspective. The result is a new space for women within the Islamic tradition."[26] In establishing this point, Hatem points to Omaima Abou Bakr, a professor of English and literature at Cairo University, Konca Kuris from Turkey, and Farida Banani of Morocco as examples of women creating public places in the Islamic world where women are permitted to perform jobs and activities that may be construed by some observers as male-only practices. In the case of Omaima Abou Bakr, this means working as a professor. While little can be said to fault her conclusion, she excludes millions of women in places like Saudi Arabia, Afghanistan, and Iraq. Clearly Morocco, Egypt, and Turkey, each with longstanding ties with Europe as well as more liberal juristic traditions, have more ambiguous spaces that permit public displays of liberal religious views than do countries in which a stricter reading of the Islamic texts is the rule.

The point that some places within the Muslim world allow for female spaces to form outside the role of housekeeper and child bearer deserves further discussion. In Islam, there are diverse juristic schools that break from a strict Qur'anic worldview. Within the Sunni realm, there are four schools of jurisprudence: Hanafi, Hanbali, Maliki, and Shafii. Named for the ninth-century scholar Ahmad Ibn Hanbal, Hanbali is the most literal of the four traditions. As an outgrowth of this literal tradition, conservative Wahhabism gained traction in the eighteenth century. Wahhabism is a theological school founded by Muhammad ibn 'Abd al-Wahhab. It stresses the unity and uniqueness of God while seeking to rid Islam of the corruptions that its followers believe have crept into the faith. The Hanbali school, found in Saudi Arabia, Kuwait, and Bahrain, holds that the Qur'an provides sufficient basis for judging legal matters, and Hanbali is, hence, a more patriarchal juristic tradition.[27] Public expressions of feminism are not well tolerated in these places. On the other hand, in places like Turkey (Hanafi), Egypt (Shafii) and Morocco (Maliki), allowances are made for local customs and/or other sources of Islamic law, so there could be opportunities for women to express their views in public spaces in the countries identified by Mervat Hatem.[28] Just as critics of Islam like to portray the entire faith with broad descriptions, the same can be said for Islamic apologists. Regional traditions and immaterial aspects of imagined worlds make sweeping generalizations about Islam— including declarations that all Muslims are terrorists or that all Muslims are lovers of peace—virtually meaningless.

Figure 1. This Muslim woman on a street in Dearborn, Michigan, appears to be from a conservative Hanbali region. (Photo courtesy of the author.)

Unlike most overly defensive or critical books discussed earlier in the text, *Islamic Ethics of Life: Abortion, War, and Euthanasia* is a welcome addition to an intelligent, nonpolemic or politically motivated discourse on Islam, despite social and cultural influences from distant lands over the centuries. The book examines three highly controversial topics: abortion, war, and euthanasia. In the book, Jonathan E. Brockopp and a number of Islamic scholars weave together a highly readable collection of essays that examine how Muslim leaders have viewed these three issues by drawing on classical sources (i.e., the Qur'an and Hadith), *fatwas* (a ruling on an issue by a recognized leader in the Islamic world) published in newspapers, booklets, periodicals, and compiled volumes, and other fatwas delivered via electronic media. Each essay is written with respect to understanding how Islamic ethics interfaces with the modern world.

In some places, *Islamic Ethics of Life* tells the story of how jurists (*muftis*, or legal experts empowered to render rulings on religious matters) have been influenced by external social and cultural movements. For example, Vardit Rispler-Chaim, a professor in the Department of Arabic Language and Literature at the University of Haifa, discusses abortion and shows how some Western ethicists who hold the view that the unborn have the right not to be born have influenced Islamic discourse in recent years.[29] By adopting such a view, Islamic societies would necessarily embrace the notion that those fetuses that face a life of hardship resulting from physical or mental impediments as well as adverse economic and social circumstances can be justifiably aborted. Rispler-Chaim shows how Islam has dealt with these external influences in a balanced and pragmatic way. *Islamic Ethics of Life* is a valuable collection of works on these salient ethical issues and often richly employs case studies to illustrate how Islamic jurists make decisions regarding *fatwas*.

This approach is worthy and its scholarship is impressive, but it seems in some ways to minimize the role of the Qur'an in setting the precedence for the puritan's understanding of all ethical issues facing humans. With that stated, however, issues like euthanasia and abortion are perhaps not adequately discussed in the Qur'an. This necessarily invites pragmatic Islamic jurists to decide how Muslims are to view these practices. Curiously, the issue of gay marriage, which has gained currency in recent years in the West, is not included in *Islamic Ethics of Life*. It is also interesting that geotheology (the relationship between the worship of the divine and the use/possession of geographic space), which is clearly a factor in defining contested spaces, is also not discussed in even the chapters on war. Admittedly this geographic concept, which was coined by the older American geographer John K. Wright, nearly disappeared from the literature before it was recently resurrected by the likes of Avihu Zakai, a professor of history at Hebrew University, and Barry A. Vann, a professor of geography at the University of the Cumberlands and author of *In Search of Ulster Scots Land: The Birth and Geotheological Imaginings of a Transatlantic People*, 1603–1703.[30]

Because puritan Islam, which has been shown to be militant, dismisses juristic discourse and seeks refuge in the Qur'an, it is important to explore what the sacred text says about geotheological concepts like people, lands, and governance. Although one cannot argue that these material and immaterial aspects of culture completely explain conflicts, it is within their interplay that many contests over spaces arise.

The Qur'anic Basis of Islamic Geotheology

There are a number of reasons for using the Qur'an[31] as the primary source in a quest to understand Islamic fundamentalism and how it will interface, and indeed is interfacing, with the secular world. First, unlike the Christian Bible, the Qur'an was written by Muhammad (or his surrogates) alone, which he claimed was revealed to him by the angel Gabriel (*Jibreel*). Also, unlike the Bible, the Qur'an was written over a much shorter period of time. Whereas the Christian holy book was compiled from the writings of more than forty authors whose discrete works were penned over a period of time spanning a dozen or more centuries, Muhammad wrote his book in about twenty-two years. These facts, together with the clear, concise style of writing used in the Qur'an, leave little room to debate the meaning of most of its passages, although some may read contradictions into certain sections. Nonetheless, Muhammad did not intend for there to be any ambiguity in his depiction of the true religion. As the Qur'an declares of itself in the first verse of Surah 11, "*Alif Lam Ra* [this is] a book, whose verses are made decisive, then are they made plain, from the Wise." Further, the entire Qur'an must be embraced and practiced. For Muhammad warned that "surely those who conceal any part of the Book that Allah has revealed and take for it a small price, they eat nothing but fire into their bellies, and Allah will not speak to them on the day of resurrection, nor will He purify them, and they shall have a painful chastisement."[32] Passages in the Qur'an allow observers to see how anyone who is prone to be fundamental in her beliefs can see herself, society, others, governance, and conflict.

The limited range of interpretations of Qur'anic passages encourages some sense of solidarity in the Muslim world. Unlike Christianity, which has splintered into hundreds of denominations and sects stemming from three main branches (Eastern Orthodox, Roman Catholic, and Protestant), if we exclude the autonomous Coptic and Syriac churches, Islam has only two principal divisions, Sunni and Shiite. Their split occurred in the seventh century and centered on who would be the Prophet's successor (*caliph*), and not necessarily on interpretations of the Qur'an.[33] As SUNY Albany geography professor Roger W. Stump writes, "Most importantly, the canonical form of the Qur'an was widely accepted at an early date, as were many of the basic components of Islamic orthodoxy. The rapid articulation of Islam as a religious system therefore precluded to some degree the sorts of theological and philosophical debates that emerged during the early centuries of Buddhism and Christianity."[34] Conflicts over the leadership of the umma also led to a schism in which a much smaller group called the Seceders (*Kharijites*) were formed.[35] Nevertheless, the two main divisions of Islam are Sunni and Shiite. Regardless of whether a person is a Sunni or a Shiite, she regards the Qur'an as the primary source of information about Allah, his followers, and his natural creation. This is the essence of geotheology.

Framing a Geographic Perspective on the Emerging World of Muhammad

Many modern historians and social scientists, the nineteenth century's Karl Marx and August Comte before them, often start from the premise that all religions are human concoctions, so the social scientists are seldom able or willing to get inside the heads of religious people to see how their beliefs shape their sense of place, community, nation, and, more important, their perception of reality. Geographers and historians such as Avihu Zakai, John K. Wright, Yi Fu Tuan, and, most recently, Barry A. Vann have given considerable attention to these aspects of geotheology, but few writers have applied geotheological concepts to Islam.[36] Roger Stump recently included notions of Islamic spatiality and contextuality in his *Geography of Religion*, but he avoids geotheology as a means of appreciating contextuality (the place and time that a religious practice took place).

To date, writers have not employed adequate nomenclature to capture the ways through which God may be viewed as using the forces of nature to dispense rewards or punishments on faithful or wayward humans. In the spirit of John K. Wright, who subdivided geotheology into geopiety, geoeschatology, and geoteleology, this work adds *geotheokolasis* (earth, God, punishment) and *geotheomisthosis* (earth, God, reward or payment) to fill the void in the lexicon of religious geography. The concepts of these terms, along with geotheology, will be addressed fully in chapter 4.

These concepts are needed because puritans form their perceptions of space and the forces of nature from the Qur'an, and, since the Muslim holy book has much to say about geography with implications for defining relationships to it, it is important to ask, "What does the Qur'an teach about Allah's creation?" How does it perceive natural events such as gentle rain, violent storms, and earthquakes? Are they connected to humans through, for example, payment for sins? On the other hand, are better lands given as blessings to the good? Answering these questions explains more about the Qur'an's imaginings of the world, and, perhaps more important, it gives observers a glimpse into how puritans think about the human habitat and how its resources are to be used and governed, which are topics taken up in later chapters. For now, it is necessary to further frame a paradigm for creating a Qur'anic depiction of space and how the Qur'an views it.

Geographers and sociologists have also explored how ethnic groups carve out spaces for themselves that some writers refer to as ethnic enclaves.[37] Ethnic enclaves help preserve both material and immaterial aspects of culture. Ideologies, musical tastes, belief systems, and other immaterial aspects of culture are carried with migrants just like the clothes on their backs and the bags in their hands. With most immigrants, regardless of legal status, coming into new lands with others from their communities back home, the chain migration model theoretically explains that they will most likely settle into places already "marked," as it were, with members from their original culture areas. This "ethnic status" model, in which one's ethnic status serves as a force to bind these immigrants psychologically and geographically together, leads to ethnic segregation and a true ethnic salad bowl—we can see each piece of lettuce, tomato, or carrot in the salad bowl, just as we can see each ethnicity in society. These enclaves retain their essence as distinct parts of the country's cultural mosaic. As described by sociologist William Schwab,

> The model argues that ethnic status alone can account for residential dissim-
> ilarity among [various] ethnic groups. In short, one's desire to maintain a par-
> ticular ethnic identity may be translated into a preference to live near others
> with similar ethnic backgrounds. Once an enclave is formed, a critical mass
> of ethnics supports an institutional structure of schools, churches (mosques),
> stores, and associations. In turn, these institutions provide the enclave with
> a means to recruit and hold members and to socialize the young into the
> ethnic subculture—a means of perpetuating the community.[38]

Schwab's comments are consistent with the writings of retired Columbia University sociology professor Herbert Gans, whose seminal study of Italian Americans living in the West End of Boston showed how the residents viewed and felt about their community.[39] Of course, in Gans's study, most of the socialization they experienced was with others from their home country, so old ideas were reinforced through contact with like-minded people.

Few geographers or sociologists, including Schwab and Gans, have taken a look at socialization in ethnic enclaves from a humanist psychology per-spective, although Chris Philo, professor of historical geography at the Uni-versity of Glasgow, Dan Montello, professor of geography at the University of California at Santa Barbara, and others have developed a related specialty area called behavioral geography. This area of geography incorporates psy-chological theories that relate individual and collective behaviors to specific places. Few, however, have drawn upon Maslow's hierarchy of needs, which progresses through physiological, safety and security, love and belonging-ness, self-esteem, and self-actualization needs, and applies it to Muslim enclaves. In my incarnation of humanistic geography, much is owed to the insights of Abraham Maslow, a twentieth-century professor of humanistic psychology, and his famous hierarchy of needs.[40] Maslow argued that people are deficiency motivated, striving to gain what they lack. As is typical in a chain migration scenario, over time, Muslim immigrants will arrive with lower levels of education than the founding members of their enclaves. Thus, they will be less able to find an economic niche outside the enclave in the secular spaces of Europe and North America. Whereas early on in the chain-migration process, it was the most secular and mobile members of the Muslim world who were able to make long-distance relocations, future immigrants arriving in Europe and North America will have the help of others who have paved the way for them. They will settle into enclaves pre-viously established by the pioneering members of their community.

Figure 2. An Islamic school (*madrasah*) in Dearborn, Michigan. (Photo courtesy of the author.)

Upon arrival, Muslim immigrants will be made aware of how to provide for their basic physiological needs (clothing, food, and water). Next, they will be shown how to obtain a safe and secure place to live. Such a place will be within the spaces marked by the community itself. Then, they will find love and acceptance in the established institutions, which are centered on religion and systemically connected to the "old country." Through religious affiliations, they will likely find ways to fulfill their need for what Maslow called belongingness, or feeling like an accepted member of a group or community.[41] In the context of the rewards and punishments proscribed by the Qur'an, the community will help the immigrant shape his opinions regarding himself, assimilation with others, space, the divine, and governance. Compliance with the teachings of the faith and its leaders will help the newcomers build a sense of personal esteem. Once they have reached this stage, according to Maslow's hierarchy, they will be able to move into the stage that he called self-actualization, at which point one possesses the ability to look beyond oneself and sees the needs of others. For devoted Muslims, serving the cause of Allah in propagating and protecting the faith among unbelievers is clearly a reasonable way to demonstrate that they are self-actualized. It is important to note that as immigrants settle into their new residences, although among people from a similar culture, they will most likely find that the religious imagery found in the Qur'an will, as nineteenth-century French sociologist Émile Durkheim observed with respect to Christianity in France, be the cohesive glue that binds their society.[42] We must recognize that, as with any religion, fundamentalist Islam explains reality and offers its adherents a prescription for optimizing life. Uncertainties associated with international relocations make some people seek peace and understanding in familiar surroundings. Religious institutions, modeled on the old country, are certainly capable of satisfying those social and psychological needs for familiarity. As we have witnessed in places like Northern Ireland, Palestine, and even in the American South, large and dissimilar racial and ethnic groups living in close proximity to one another embrace religiosity and its espousing organizations as a way to cope with concerns over a possible loss of their ethnic identity and political self-determination.

Summary

While the more developed countries in the West are witnessing a decline in their populations, which is a topic further explored in chapter 1, Muslim countries are growing rapidly. What is more important to consider is the fact that surplus Muslim populations are forming in those countries, and while it is inviting to think that peace in the Middle East will encourage people to stay in their homelands, the Qur'an makes it clear that Muslims are to move to other suitable places if the quality of life is better there.[43] In the imagined landscapes of the Qur'an, the bounty of other places is the product of Allah's benevolence as he rewards his devoted and submissive followers, a concept that I call *geotheomisthosis* (earth, God, reward). To puritans, their prosperity in other lands is not the result of hardworking, well-educated Westerners; it is their rightful reward for submission and service to Allah.

Given the complexity of juristic traditions and the growth of Muslim populations in virtually every Islamic country, one must ask, "What does the future hold for the increasingly secular West as it comes into contact with people who embrace the fundamentalist beliefs of Islam's spatially nebulous puritan community?" To answer that question, one is compelled to seriously consider the geotheological forces influencing population growth and mass population flows, for these are increasingly likely to occur. For now, the next step is to take a look at the geography of the emerging Muslim world.

Chapter 1

An Emerging Muslim World

Introduction

I n certain American cities, the impact of recent immigrants on the urban
landscape stands in contrast to the cultural impress of rural settlements
spread out across the traditional American hinterland. Urban and suburban
areas in the American heartland, Western places far removed from the sacred
lands of Muhammad, are rapidly changing. From calls to prayer heard across
public spaces in the suburban town of Hamtramck, Michigan, to prohibitions against carrying alcohol in taxi cabs driven by Muslims in Minneapolis,
Minnesota, formerly secular spaces are now contested by new standards for
religiously inspired behaviors. Other micro spaces are also being altered to
accommodate the emerging Muslim population in the United States. In
2007, wash benches for Muslim taxi drivers were installed at the Kansas City
International Airport. These benches enable drivers to clean their feet in
preparation for prayers. Also, because Muslims must pray facing Mecca five
times per day, international flights between countries like the United States
and the United Kingdom now boast maps on airline movie screens that show
the direction to Mecca. More recently, in 2008, Harvard University decided
to set aside six hours of gym time for Muslim women in a move that could
be construed as preferential treatment for one religious expression over all
others. Clearly, some of the West's secular spaces are being contested by new
religious meanings and uses. In light of these cultural changes, it is important to know that the economic and demographic processes shaping the
West's future are already at work. Furthermore, there are few signs that the
Near Eastern fountain of humanity—the birthplace of all non-Africans
living throughout the world[1]—is not drying up any time soon.[2]

Figure 3. A mosque rising from a Midwestern cornfield. (Photo courtesy of the author.).

Because of a decline in births coupled with an aging population, the future does not bode well for secular Europe. Let us consider the changes that are occurring in the European population. There were 186 million people living in Western Europe in 2005, but, based on demographic trends, that number could potentially drop to 183 million by 2050.[3] Southern Europe will also see a drop in population. The projected number of 141 million for 2050 reflects a 6.6 percent decline from 2005 figures. The situation is even worse in Eastern Europe. The present population of 297 million will drop to 232 million by the middle of the twenty-first century. Meanwhile, in predominantly Muslim countries, the opposite trend is occurring. For instance, in southwestern Asia, where we find countries like Kuwait, Turkey, and Saudi Arabia, the current population of 214 million will climb to 400 million. In North Africa, the 2005 population will climb from 193.8 million to 323.6 million by midcentury. Later, we will take a closer look at growth among all Muslim majority countries. Suffice it to say, these trends are nearly universal across the Muslim world.

What these statistics do not tell us is that the changes in population represent growth among some of the world's most disadvantaged people, while more affluent and better educated countries are aging and ultimately dying. Secularism, which characterizes the social environment of the latter, produces a declining demographic profile that acts like a cancer. It eats away at the most developed societies, creating a need to recruit foreign workers to fill less desirable employment niches.

Demographic and economic factors have indeed set the current migration scenario in motion. As Europe rebounded from the devastation leveled on it during World War II, economic expansion coupled with a decline in population over time in a number of countries created a labor shortage. By the 1960s, a number of Western European countries openly recruited guest workers from Spain, Portugal, and Italy. Over time, as that supply of relatively cheap labor dried up and labor shortages continued to vex their economies, European companies began to recruit workers from the Muslim areas of Yugoslavia, Turkey, and North Africa.[4] By the late 1970s, Western Europe contained eleven million foreign-born residents, representing about 5 percent of the population. The vast majority of Muslim immigrants settled into the older sections of existing urban centers like Brussels, Paris, and Berlin. Before onset of the 1980s, Muslim populations in those cities were 16 percent, 12 percent, and 18 percent of the cities' totals, respectively.[5] More recently in France, population data published in the mid 1990s show that 90 percent of the nation's population was at least nominally Roman Catholic and the Muslim population was less than 2 percent.[6] By 2006, the Roman Catholic population had dropped to 83 percent while 10 percent of the population was reported as Muslim.[7] In 2001, some 27 percent of London's population was born outside of the UK, and nearly one-third of Londoners were identified as nonwhite.[8] In London, particularly in Newham and Tower Hamlets, there are sizable clustered settlements of Muslims.[9]

Any surplus wealth in developing Muslim countries will be consumed to take care of the young and elderly or increase the wealth of the elites. These countries' economies will likely experience little, if any, expansion, or, more important, diversification. Their inability to employ more people will result in a steady stream of immigrants, first to Europe, and then, in a step-wise fashion, to the Americas—a process that is likely to continue for decades.[10]

In the absence of any major cultural transformation, which would necessarily have to radically change the role played by women in the workplace and the home, there is no end in sight to the increase in the number of Muslim people.

With fewer Europeans being born and able to fill employment niches to support their aging populations, there will be hardly any economic reasons to keep able-bodied workers out of their continent. There is, of course, no way of knowing who among the immigrants are, or will become, radical Muslims or followers of Islamism. Like the Romans before them, a good portion of modern-day Europeans who dismiss religion as an antiquated mindset, believe that immigrants will become imbued with secular ideas through contact with charter residents. Some social scientists and most multiculturalists, despite their recognition that modern societies are like ethnic salad bowls, subscribe to the possibility that some have called the melting pot model.[11] This point deserves further explanation. The melting pot model includes diverse ethnic groups that merge together to form a larger identity and way of life. Multiculturalists embrace an imagined world or global society in which people share a common interest in celebrating diversity. If a puritan Muslim wanted to accomplish this, however, he would have to sacrifice his strongly-held beliefs articulating a path to "the right way," all for the sake of tolerance and mutual celebration. In other words, only the benign aspects of diversity—the material products of culture found in food, dress, and language—can be maintained. Multiculturalists often argue that when large ethnic groups fail to share in the prosperity and material products of the country, it is because these immigrant communities are victims of racist policies. In these situations, multiculturalists blame the immigrants' plight on macro forces such as economic structures, government attitudes, and institutionalized racism. The solution, which reveals a Marxist orientation, is to change society's opportunity structure to ensure a "level playing field." This notion, however, assumes that all cultures have the same values, family structures, life styles, and needs. If the outcomes or goals of life among diverse ethnicities are the same, where is the cultural diversity? In the long run, the multiculturalists' idea would lead to a melting pot society.

With respect to Muslim immigrants and their interest in assimilating into the broader culture, information is now becoming available. The Pew Research Center estimated that in 2007 there were 2.35 million Muslims living in the United States. Other published estimates put the number higher, at nearly five million.[12] While the Pew report portrays American Muslims as middle class and mostly mainstream, hence the report's title: "Muslim Americans: Middle Class and Mostly Mainstream," there are figures in the report that reveal that many of America's Muslims resist secular assimilation. According to the report, 1.53 million Muslims in the United States (some 65 percent of the total) were born outside of the country. Only 43 percent believe that they should adopt American customs. Of America's Muslims, some 117,500 of them have a favorable view of al Qaeda, and over 300,000 believe that suicide bombing to protect Islam is acceptable. The proportion of Muslims who support violent resistance to social and political change is stronger among those under the age of thirty. Indeed, one in four younger US Muslims truly believes that suicide bombing to protect Islam is acceptable. The report does not explore the idea that there are a number of opinions on what constitutes a threat to Islam.

Figure 4. A Dearborn, Michigan, women's boutique caters to a middle-class clientele. (Photo courtesy of the author.)

According to Professors Barry A. Kosmin and Egon Mayer at the Graduate Center of the City University of New York, who reported data on American religious affiliation generated from surveys they conducted in 1995 and again in 2001, the Muslim population more than doubled in just six years.[13] In 1995, there were approximately 527,000 Muslim Americans, but in 2001, there were 1,104,000. In other words, during each of those six years, the United States added an average of 96,166 new residents who claim adherence to Islam, which happens to approximate the population of the suburban town of Dearborn, Michigan, in 2006. However, since 2001, the Muslim population has grown by 207,666 people per year. That number is two times the size of Burbank, California, or Green Bay, Wisconsin, and some-what larger than Iowa's capital city, Des Moines. If the doubling time continues at the current rate of six years, which is a valid demographic premise, by the year 2052 there will be over 300 million Muslims living in the United States, and, if they continue to live in ethnic enclaves, more American spaces will adopt laws inspired by the Islamic laws and codes of conduct, or sharia.

As the twenty-first century unfolds, more and more of non-US-born Muslims will live outside the mainstream. If nearly 50 percent of the current population of non-US-born Muslims wants to adopt American ways of life, it is uncertain how future immigrants will feel about assimilating into Western culture. Their opinions of American culture will likely be even lower because of their lack of marketable skills and position in the social hierarchy. (As we saw with the chain migration model, those with the most valuable skills lead the way in settling in new lands, making it easier to relocate for those who follow and have more humble vocational backgrounds.) As a result, these future immigrants will have a lower entry position in society, thereby filling lower positions in the social hierarchy. The socialization Muslim immigrants encounter in their new enclaves is not likely to foster favorable relations with charter residents.

Islam, like all religions, can serve to fill a psychological need of impoverished people who want to know why they are suffering and how they might improve their situation. Puritan Islam is no exception to that assumption. Few places today offer us a glimpse into this type of situation quite like

Uzbekistan, a landlocked part of the former Union of Soviet Socialist Republics (USSR) located in Central Asia. Made up of mostly non-Arab people, the country of twenty-six million souls is economically stressed. Once a land situated on the Silk Road connecting Asian suppliers with European markets, it has seen better times. With the advent of ocean-going commercial vessels, the area declined in economic power. In 1924, the region was absorbed, without the people's consent, into the Soviet Union. Since the collapse of the USSR in 1990,

> Uzbekistan, like other Central Asian countries, has a socio-economic environment favorable to the spread of the ideas of Islamism [militant Islam]: the decline of living standards resulting from the collapse of the relatively well-functioning state-centered economy and the lingering transition to a market economy . . . a significant part of the population which formerly identified itself as the middle class suddenly found itself among the "new poor." Many of the new poor come from the impoverished intelligentsia, who may be more receptive to Islamist ideas than others.[14]

For the time being, Uzbekistan shows few signs of anti-Western sentiments. This situation may change in the near future. Within thirty years, if current growth trends in the population continue, the number of Uzbeks will double to fifty-two million. Growth in its population is occurring simultaneously with an increasing economic dissimilarity across the landscape. Urban elites, who have taken over the economy, are focusing development on urban places. With traditional ways of life still maintained in the impoverished rural environs, population growth will continue to outpace what little, if any, economic wealth comes their way. As the country approaches the year 2050, urban secularists will no doubt witness an acceleration of highly religious people leaving rural settlements to relocate to urban areas. As early French sociologist Émile Durkheim witnessed in France during its Industrial Revolution in the eighteenth and nineteenth centuries, religion will be instrumental in providing these immigrants with a mental framework to bond with others of similar religious backgrounds.

Both domestic and international Islamist organizations are already at work in Uzbekistan. In addition to al Qaeda, Pakistani organizations like the warriors of Muhammad (*Sepa-e Sahaba*), the party of allies (*Harakat-ul Ansor*), the warriors of the healer (*Sepa-e Tabibi*), and the party of liberation (*Hizb-ut-Tahrir*), among others, are operating there.[15] It is important to recall that although Pakistan is a nuclear-armed ally of the United States and at least publicly supports the war on terror, its western provinces are located along the border of Afghanistan. When the Soviet Union invaded Afghanistan in 1979 with some 115,000 troops, five million Afghans fled as refugees. Three million went to the highlands of western Pakistan and the remaining two million fled to the Shiite lands of Iran.[16] By the mid-1990s, the high natural increase rate of population that characterized the refugee camps made the Afghan refugees' numbers rise and become a fertile source of recruits for those Islamist organizations, augmenting grass-roots efforts of the Islamic Movement Uzbekistan (IMU) and perhaps even al Qaeda.

It is also important to point out that contemporary Islamist movements, including the IMU, are affected by the theological teachings of an eighteenth-century evangelist named Muhammad ibn 'Abd al-Wahhab and late nineteenth-century reformers named Muhammad 'Abduh, Jamal-al-Din al Afghani, and Rashid Rida. Together, the movements created by these influential Muslims have created a desire for puritan Islam.[17] Abd al-Wahhab founded a theological school called Wahhabism, which seeks to rid Islam of the corruptions that its followers believe have crept into the faith. Muhammad Abduh, al Afghani, and Rashid Rida founded a movement that teaches Muslims to follow the precedents set by the Prophet Muhammad and his companions (*al-salaf al-salih*). This theology is called Salafism. In their original forms, Wahhabism was less tolerant of diversity and Qur'anic interpretations than Salafism, yet the latter was founded by nationalists. Both theologies maintain imagined worlds in which Islam experienced a golden age, a time before tradition and jurists corrupted their religion.[18] The founders and proponents of both movements have maintained that, on all matters, Muslims should return to the Qur'an and the precedent of the Prophet. Clearly, understanding what the Qur'an says about secular society is important to consider, for it is the primary source of the theologies that are flourishing among many young Muslims, including those who are migrating to more secular places.

While many of these immigrants are relocating to Western cities with a willingness to assimilate into the existing culture and social structures, others may be inspired by geotheological imaginings depicted in the Qur'an. Such imaginings discourage Muslims from socializing with charter residents possibly as a way to avoid what they believe will be a divine punishment Allah has planned for the unbelievers in the secular world. Furthermore, some of the resistance to assimilation into American culture, as seen in the Pew Research Center report, is a reflection of the manifestations of geopiety among Muslim immigrants. They are relocating to take advantage of the bounty that Allah has provided them through those countries. As Muhammad wrote, "Surely [as for] those whom the angels cause to die while they are unjust to their souls, they say: In what state were you? They shall say: Was not Allah's earth spacious, so that you should have migrated therein? So these it is whose abode is hell, and it is an evil resort."[19] Muslims are further assured that it is Allah's will for them to move to other places when the need presents itself. As recorded in the Qur'an, "And whoever flies in Allah's way, he will find in the earth many a place of refuge and abundant resources; and whoever goes forth from his house flying to Allah and His Apostle, and then death overtakes him, his reward is indeed with Allah and Allah is Forgiving, Merciful."[20] "[Also], with respect to those who fly after they are persecuted, then they struggle hard and are patient, most surely your Lord after that is Forgiving, Merciful."[21] With a divine mandate to migrate, these passages could lessen some of the anxiety caused by resettling in a foreign place.

Secular officials in Central Asia, Europe, and North America will most likely continue to seek a middle ground to accommodate the newcomers. In doing so, they will innocently present the wrong image to puritans. Well-meaning officials will no doubt try to seem open, accepting, and tolerant of Muslim beliefs. Without knowing it, they fulfill a Qur'anic declaration that identifies them as disbelievers: "Surely those who disbelieve in Allah and His apostles and [those who] desire to make a distinction between Allah and His apostles and say: we believe in some and disbelieve in others; and desire to take a course between [this and] that."[22] Puritan Islam has no tolerance for "taking the middle ground" on matters of religion. Part of the fuel that fires fundamentalists in Uzbekistan and elsewhere is the knowledge that their religious leaders in the past had made numerous compromises with communist regimes or Western capitalists.[23]

Muslim leaders of the West's expanding fundamentalist community will not endorse "bridge-building" with the natives, for the Qur'an tells them not to make friends of them: "O you who believe! Do not take the unbelievers for friends rather than the believers; do you desire that you should give to Allah a manifest proof against yourselves?"[24] The Qur'an further points out that "indeed He has revealed to you in the Book that when you hear Allah's communication disbelieved in and mocked at; do not sit with them until they enter into some other discourse; surely then you would be like them; surely Allah will gather together the hypocrites and the unbelievers all in hell."[25]

In the fall of 2005, American and European secularists were surprised and frightened by the sight of European Muslims protesting and burning effigies over cartoons depicting Muhammad. Public denunciations and protests are supported in the Qur'an: "Allah does not love the public utterance of hurtful speech, unless [it is] by one to whom injustice has been done; and Allah is Hearing, Knowing."[26] Failure to react to perceived wrongdoings against the faithful invites Allah's condemnation. Officials and nongovernment secularists will endeavor to create a social climate in which fundamentalists will not feel slighted. There will likely be increasing pressure on other religions, including mainstream Christianity and Judaism, to restrict religious expressions to private spaces. If restrictions impact fundamentalists, their theocratic vision of social order will be threatened. On the other hand, if restrictions leave out limitations on public expressions of the Islamic faith, then fundamentalists will perceive, and perhaps rightly so, that their desire for a world order centered on the literal teachings of the Qur'an is unfolding.

As overpopulation in Muslim countries continues to characterize life within them, more spaces in Western countries will become contested as increasingly perceptible streams of Muslim immigrants settle there.

Shia and Sunnis

Various groups of Sunni and Shia Muslims, scattered across dozens of countries, carry on an old struggle for political and religious power. Holding power is the key to propagating each group's competing vision of society. Just as there are juristic subdivisions in Sunni Islam (Hanafi, Hanbali, Maliki, and Shafti, which were briefly discussed in the introductory chapter), there are differing juristic traditions in the Shiite world, including the Alawite or Alawi sect. This particular group maintains a special reverence for Ali, Muhammad's cousin and son-in-law. The Asad family that rules Syria adheres to the Alawite expression of Shia Islam. Recognizing the spatial extent of Shia Islam, King Abdullah of Jordan (a moderate Sunni) called the lands that stretch from Lebanon, through Syria, across Iraq, and into Iran the "Shia Crescent."[27] The Asad family and the Islamic political and paramilitary organization based in Lebanon called Hezbollah are already allied to the government of Iran. With increasing power in the hands of democratically elected Shiite leaders in Iraq, it, too, may develop stronger ties with a theocratic Iran. Moderate Muslim leaders such as King Abdullah are concerned about regional peace because Shia in Lebanon, Syria, and Iraq form a culture area that could be united under the domination of a potentially nuclear-armed Iran.

While it is tempting to assume that Shia are the most likely Muslims to embrace puritanism due to their conservative traditions, they are certainly not alone in hatching groups determined to bring about a fundamentalist Islamic revival. The Egyptian Muslim Brotherhood and al Qaeda grew out of Sunni Islam, which was perhaps encouraged by Egypt's and Turkey's greater contact with the increasingly secular states of the West. It follows that devoted Sunni Muslims perceive these cultural influences in their sacred lands as evil and, hence, a threat to Islam. Herein lay a significant problem when trying to put a spatial fix on Islamism, for it is not contained within the specific boundaries of a city or country. It is perhaps better to appreciate Islamism as a theological foundation for the creation of an imagined, amorphous community made up of potentially highly mobile, like-minded believers.[28] Still, it is not likely that puritan Muslims are going to give up their vision of a sacred life without resistance. Although the Qur'an does provide ample support for migrating to places where Allah's bounty may be better utilized, it does not grant permission to do so when Islam is threatened. Assaults against the true religion, as per instructions in the Qur'an, must be met with force.[29] For now, though, let us concern ourselves with building a demographic and mobility model that shows that the world is beginning to experience perhaps the greatest population flows in recorded history. While these flows are not necessarily a bad thing, it must be recognized that hidden among those masses of people will be unknown numbers of immigrants psychologically linked together, and the basis for that linkage will be puritan Islam and its vision of a society living in submission to puritan rules.

Forces behind International Migrations

The reasons why humans move have received a good deal of attention from scholars, and, since mobility involves space, geographers have been keen to join them. The latter, who are especially interested in spatial issues, have developed some good theories that have relevance in explaining the evolving Muslim migration flows. It is not surprising that in the wake of the Industrial Revolution in western Europe, which caused an unprecedented flow of rural residents into urban areas in search of work, geographers and other social scientists at the time were interested in explaining those movements and their consequences on the lives of charter residents and immigrants. Early giants in the field of sociology, such as the nineteenth century's Auguste Comte, Émile Durkheim, and Karl Marx, and the next generation of sociologists, such as Ferdinand Tönnies, were keenly interested in the social consequences and underlying causes of movements within their respective societies. As one would expect from sociologists at the time, their interests were built on assumptions about why people had moved, which were generally relegated to simple, and presumably obvious, economic factors such as getting a job. Geographers, whose interests were limited to spatial aspects of measurable or observable phenomena such as the decline of population in one area and an increase in the numbers of people moving into another area, also developed a niche.[30] One geographer in particular established his career and legacy on what he called "laws of migration." Nineteenth-century geographer E. G. Ravenstein based his laws on patterns he observed in Europe during the 1870s and 1880s.[31] Some of his laws have not sustained the test of time, but five have proven reliable statements for us in the twenty-first century. They are as follows:

1. Most migrants move only a short distance.
2. Long distance migrations favor big city destinations.
3. Most migrations proceed in a step-by-step fashion.
4. Most migration flows are from rural to urban areas.
5. Migrations produce a counter flow.

We should add that international migrations typically occur among the best educated members of a society, which often results in a "brain drain" problem for the home country; the loss of the skilled and educated is a loss to society.[32] For example, among the one million Asian Indians living in America, close to three-quarters of them possess bachelor's degrees. A British government study found a similar pattern among African immigrants who hold at least high school diplomas.[33] What is not known from this data is the length of time in residence for the immigrant. It is reasonable to expect that as the best educated and most able immigrants become established in a new enclave, even if that enclave is in another country, others less able to market themselves will follow and fill lower social niches in the new enclave. These new social environments, therefore, become increasingly stratified by members of the home country. Here, we should reinsert Ravenstein's fifth law that states that migrations produce counter flows. However, for various reasons, a majority of the immigrants will remain in the host country, so counter flows are smaller than the original waves of immigrants.[34] As Nil Demet Güngör and Aysit Tansel, economists at Middle East Technical University in Ankara, Turkey, found in their study of Turkish Muslims, wage differentials, instability in the Turkish economy, work experience in Turkey, and a favorable opinion of host country lifestyles played major roles in deciding whether immigrants would return to the country of their birth.[35]

It is interesting to note that little attention is given to the strength of the new community in the host nation, which is based on the community in the "old country." If all economic factors that propel people to go in search of sustenance are equal, and if the new enclave looks, smells, and feels like home, why return? Clearly, government policies that help immigrants preserve their old culture and community in their new enclaves will increase the likelihood that they will feel at home in the host country. Multiculturalism as a political policy will certainly reduce the intensity of Ravenstein's law declaring a counter flow. Contact with the old country can be maintained through social networks held together by the Internet and other communication technologies. The importation of goods from the old country, which can enrich the host country with more variety in cuisine, music, and even personal dress, also serves to make immigrants feel at home in an unfamiliar land. However, just as tantalizing and appealing aspects of culture can be diffused into the host country, so can the bad. As less able-bodied and talented members of a home country join the immigrant flow, the likelihood is that those negative aspects of cultural diffusion will increase and be felt in the host country.

Since we have already addressed the economic reasons for moving into large cities, let us take a look at the step-by-step process of migration. In this law, we can expect that Muslim families and individuals will first relocate to European cities before making a transatlantic leap. Through social networks already established during the initial flows of immigrants into American cities, European Muslims can learn how to make the transatlantic resettlement. For decades, American universities have welcomed Muslims onto their campuses where many undertook studies in the sciences and engineering. In places like Dearborn, Michigan, large Muslim communities from various Middle Eastern countries have established themselves and their institutions. These American Muslim enclaves are socially tied to similar communities in Europe and the Middle East, making the movement of people and ideas among these continents a relatively easy process. It also makes it simple for networks of puritan Muslims to stay in touch with each other. The issues that bind them together are not linked to the wonders of the secular world, such as science, medicine, and entertainment. Religion provides them with ideas, beliefs, and symbols that serve as centripetal social forces. For American and European societies accustomed to Judeo-Christian religious sounds and visual expressions, Muslim symbols and practices in public spaces can become centrifugal or disuniting social forces among charter residents. Likewise, Muslims, who come from countries in which only Islamic religious symbols are experienced in public spaces, will likely feel a sense of separation when confronted with Christian symbols, including those that are prominently displayed in commercial spaces at Christmas time. Nonetheless, at the heart of both centripetal and centrifugal forces are issues, mental concepts, and material objects that are tied to deeply held and, oftentimes, sacred beliefs.

In the final analysis of the forces behind migration, economics is the bait that pulls people across international boundaries. The hook that keeps them in the host country is the comfort level they experience while in residence. Ethnic enclaves provide immigrants with a way to minimize the shock of long-distance migrations. In such places, immigrants see, feel, and smell the old country. If the immigrant is able to find an acceptable economic niche, she is not likely to return to the home country.

Carrying Capacity in Traditional Muslim Countries

It is reasonable to wonder why people who hold the opinion that the ground on which they trod is holy would want to leave such a place. Even during Muhammad's time, it was understood that life in the dry desert region was harsh. It is not surprising then that the Qur'an has much to say about environs and migration. A puritan believes in the literal meaning of the Qur'an, which certainly does not prohibit migrating for economic reasons. On the contrary—it encourages it. As we saw earlier in this chapter, whoever migrates out of economic or political need will find that the earth contains many places of refuge that are blessed with more than adequate resources for supporting life.[36] In case an immigrant were to think that his migration would be temporary, the Qur'an tells him that "The first of the migrants from Makkah [Mecca] and the people from Medina, and those who followed them in goodness, Allah is well pleased with them and they are well pleased with

Him, and He has prepared for them a garden beneath which rivers flow, to abide in them forever; that is a mighty achievement."[37] As the purported creator of all things, Allah has provided whatever bounty there may be across the earth as blessings for the believer's benefit and enjoyment. A believing Muslim is not discouraged by the lack of resources in her home country because she can move to more lush environs.

Qur'anic concepts like natural bounties, flowing rivers, and gardens suggest attributes of a place well suited to sustain human life in an agrarian society. What would happen to a people if their environment were no longer able to support the level of population living in it? Wilbur Zelinsky, an American geographer, attempted to answer that important question in his 1971 article on mobility transition.[38] He logically concluded that migration would take some of the pressure off of the local environment as people leave in search of a means of survival. Over a decade later, a Scottish geographer named Huw Jones refined Zelinsky's model by infusing it with a loose conflict perspective.[39] Jones believes that a modern society has a number of employment sectors, and, invariably, one may become saturated with too many workers while other employment sectors may have unfilled positions. Such a situation creates a surplus of labor specific to a segment of the economy, and, as a result, a number of people shift about in search of suitable employment. Jones argues that these people are the most likely to relocate in order to fill similar occupations in other places. It should also be pointed out that people with specialized skills or advanced educational levels are more likely to move further from home in order to find suitable work. This helps explain why many Asian and Middle Eastern immigrants in the United States are generally well educated and fill highly technical positions. On the other hand, Mexican immigrants, whose home country is right next door, tend to fill low-wage jobs.

At this point, it would be helpful to insert the concept of carrying capacity into Jones's model to more fully explain his views. The term carrying capacity is borrowed from ecology, but, with respect to humans who modify the environment, we need to consider economic structure. A robust, diversified economy is capable of absorbing many more people than an economy based on one or a few industries. Let us consider what could happen to a country that has an economy based primarily on tourism and complimentary industries like food services and hospitality if a major energy crisis were to occur. Clearly, it would seriously dampen the flow of visitors whose purchases and rental payments keep the economy running smoothly. For example, in Europe, an energy crisis could cost jobs and create social instability in many cities and nations. Likewise, if Middle Eastern, oil-rich countries have surplus populations relative to their rather limited employment sectors, they run the risk of political upheavals. Revolutions are much more likely if large numbers of young adults and adolescents are idle. It behooves both European and oil-producing states to allow and, indeed, encourage population flows between them, especially if it would alleviate pressure felt by the Middle East and fill low-wage service sector occupations in Europe with Middle Eastern and Asian workers. Here we can see that it is somewhat functional for this exchange of human beings to take place. It shifts the population away from places where the carrying capacity is restricted and moves surplus people into places where there are economic niches for them to fill. As we will see in the next section, changes in the demographic profiles of Muslim countries, combined with declining populations in Europe, suggest that the density of migration flows into Europe is likely to increase over the next few decades. There are signs that some of these Muslim countries already have too many people. Indeed the population densities of some countries rival those of urban places in the United States.

Now that we have looked at the concept of carrying capacity and the forces underlying migration decisions, it is possible to make better sense out of the data reflecting demographic transitions in Muslim countries. Projections for the year 2050 show that most of Europe will experience negative population growth, creating a population vacuum that is sure to pull in Muslims from the Middle East.[40] It is unclear what will happen to the natural increase rate of population among immigrants who recently arrived in Europe, but we can expect that a reduction in their growth rate will take at least a generation or two. If E. G. Ravenstein's step-by-step law is valid, a similar type of growth will soon occur in North America. The limited data collected thus far certainly suggest that America is proof of Ravenstein's law. These movements of people are predicated on sustained population growth in places that have limited capacity to absorb more people. It is difficult to know at what point population in Muslim enclaves in European and, indeed,

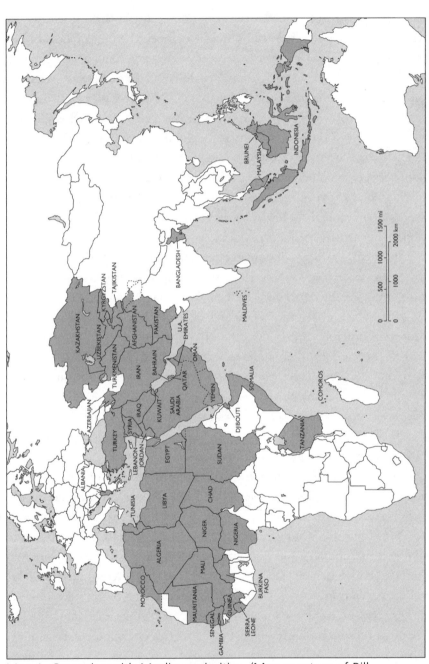

Map 1. Countries with Muslim majorities. (Map courtesy of Bill Nelson.)

American urban areas will exceed their carrying capacity, but, with no end in sight to the current natural increase rate in Muslim countries (see table 1), there can be little doubt that such will be the case in the not-so-distant future.

Table 1: Demographic and Economic Profile of Muslim Countries[41]

Country N = 46	2009 Population	2009 Population Density (people/sq. mile)	Doubling Time (years)	2009 Literacy Rate (%)	2009 Per Capita GDP (USD)
Afghanistan	32,738,376	131	27	36	800
Albania	3,619,778	342	72	86.5	4,900
Algeria	33,769,669	36	58	70	6,600
Azerbaijan	7,911,974	237	73	97	3,800
Bahrain	718,306	2,797	55	89	19,200
Bangladesh	153,546,901	2,969	34	43.1	2,000
Brunei	381,371	187.4	48	94	23,600
Burkina-Faso	15,264,735	144.4	23	28.7	1,300
Chad	10,111,337	20.8	24	47.5	1,600
Comoros	731,775	873.4	26	56.5	700
Djibouti	506,221	57.1	37	67.9	1,300
Egypt	81,713,517	212.6	42	57.7	4,200
Gambia	1,735,464	449.5	27	40.1	1,800
Guinea	9,806,509	103.3	27	35.9	2,100
Indonesia	237,512,355	336.8	55	87.9	3,500
Iran	65,875,223	104.3	64	79.4	7,700
Iraq	28,221,181	169.1	28	40.4	2,100
Jordan	6,198,677	174.6	41	91.3	4,500
Kazakhstan	15,340,533	14.9	102	98.4	7,800
Kuwait	2,596,799	377.4	37	83.5	21,300
Kyrgyzstan	5,356,869	72.5	44	97	1,700
Lebanon	3,971,941	1005.6	62	87.4	5,000
Libya	6,173,579	9.1	32	82.6	6,700
Malaysia	25,274,133	199.2	41	88.7	9,700
Maldives	385,925	3,331.8	64	97.2	900
Mali	12,324,029	26.2	22	46.4	900
Mauritania	3,364,940	8.5	25	41.7	1,800
Morocco	34,343,219	199.3	46	51.7	4,200
Niger	13,272,679	27.1	24	68	1,000
Nigeria	146,255,306	415.9	35	68	1,000
Oman	3,311,640	40.4	23	75.8	13,100
Pakistan	172,800,051	574.7	35	54.9	2,600
Palestine	3,907,883	1,627	No data	No data	No data
Qatar	824,789	186.4	55	82.5	23,200
Saudi Arabia	28,146,657	33.9	27	78.6	12,000
Senegal	12,853,259	174.3	28	40.2	1,700
Sierra Leone	6,294,774	227.6	32	31.4	600
Somalia	9,558,666	39.5	26	37.8	600
Sudan	40,218,455	43.8	35	61.1	1,900
Syria	19,747,586	277.9	33	76.9	3,400
Tajikistan	7,211,884	130.9	36	99.4	1,100
Tanzania	40,213,162	117.6	32	78.2	700
Tunisia	10,383,577	173.1	70	74.2	7,100
Turkey	71,892,807	241.6	71	86.5	7,400
Turkmenistan	5,179,571	27.5	38	98	5,700
United Arab Emirates	4,621,399	143.2	52	77.9	25,200
Uzbekistan	27,345,026	166.5	57	99.3	1,800
Yemen	20,013,376	112.9	21	50.2	800

The numbers in table 1 show some interesting patterns. While Albania, Azerbaijan, Kazakhstan, Lebanon, Tunisia, and Turkey require little more than six decades for their populations to double, Afghanistan will double its population in only twenty-seven years, despite its rather protracted political entanglements with relatively developed countries. These anomalies can be at least partially explained. In the case of Kazakhstan, its recent history as part of the Soviet Union surely impacted its attitudes and infrastructure to support large families. Contact with the highly secular West, especially in the tourism industry, no doubt influences fertility in Tunisia. Tourism creates a more diversified economy in Tunisia that makes it easier for women to find work outside the roles of homemaker and mother. In the case of Maldives, it draws low-wage workers from neighboring countries to fill positions in the tourism industry.[42] Beyond these considerations, though, much can be said about economic and environmental stresses on all Muslim countries.

Being situated in the Sahara Desert region of North Africa, one would not expect to see high population density in Libya, Algeria, and Sudan, so their current population data are not too surprising. In contrast, Egypt claims 212 people per square mile, a figure that in just forty-two years will climb to 424. The human resource potential is great in Egypt, but with a less than 60 percent literacy rate in its highly clustered and poor population living in the Nile corridor, residents who cannot find a niche will move away. The situation is even worse in Bangladesh. In less than thirty-five years, that country will have nearly six thousand people per square mile. With a mostly impoverished and illiterate population now, it will only get worse in the next three decades and no doubt beyond. To give this data some scope, consider that North American cities like Cleveland and Cincinnati have smaller population densities than Bahrain and Bangladesh. The population density in Maldives is already similar to Madison, Wisconsin. By 2031, Comoros will have a population density greater than Nashville, Tennessee, or Louisville, Kentucky. Also, in just thirty-five years, Pakistan, currently the second most populous Muslim nation, will have a similar population density to these US cities. Even Lebanon, with its relatively low population growth, is as dense as Jacksonville, Florida, and is already denser than Lexington, Kentucky. With an annual per capita gross domestic product (GDP) of only $5,000, the average person in Lebanon, which attracts a sizable wealthy tourist population from nearby Europe and the United States, must sense a great deal of relative deprivation. Keep in mind that when we exclude oil-producing nations and former Soviet countries, data for GDP and literacy, which are critical factors in calculating a human development index (HDI) as a measure of quality of life, suggest that populations in these countries are already stressing their carrying capacities.[43]

The countries King Abdullah included in the Shia Crescent are also growing faster than Western nations. Data are not readily available on the Hezbollah community in Lebanon, though Syria, Iraq, and Iran each will see increases in population. By the mid-2030s, Iraq will exceed fifty million with a population density of over three hundred people per square mile. With only four out of ten people able to read and write, the sectarian violence there is perhaps a symptom of a larger conflict over basic survival needs and over which group has control of the country's limited and nonrenewable resources. Aside from the possibility of developing more efficient uses of its oil reserves and the introduction of new industries, the beleaguered desert land will be hard pressed to expand its carrying capacity. Iran will have about ninety million people by midcentury, and Syria will need to feed nearly forty million people by 2050. By midcentury, the Shia Crescent will serve as the home of approximately 180 million people. That means the desert culture area must support over two hundred people per square mile, which is twenty-eight more people per square mile than the current number of people living on the arable lands in industrial Michigan.

Despite the oil wealth in Iraq and Iran, per capita GDP is only $2,100 and $7,700 respectively. Syria is in the middle with $3,400 (see table 1). There is, of course, no way of knowing how well national wealth is distributed in Iraq, but given the squalor in places like Sadr City, which was built in 1959 to house some of the country's growing Shiite population, it's evident that wealth distribution favored Sunnis, who, as a minority group, face an uncertain future as democracy empowers the formerly oppressed Shia. Sectarian violence will likely continue and cause an increase in the number of Sunnis immigrating to American and European cities. As Sunnis are generally better educated and more affluent than their Shia neighbors, Iraq's beleaguered economy will decline even more as the country loses its cultural capital.

Other Middle Eastern countries like Bahrain, Brunei, Kuwait, Qatar, and the United Arab Emirates, the so-called super oil-rich nations, have per capita GDPs in the range of middle-income European countries like Greece, Slovenia, and Liechtenstein. However, in terms of literacy levels, they are substantially below their European counterparts. These European countries boast a literacy rate more than 10 percent higher than the super oil-rich nations of the Middle East. The data suggest that these Middle Eastern countries either do not value formalized education or there is an inefficient wealth distribution system in place. Regardless of the reason, there are clearly large segments of people living in these countries that do not share in their respective nation's bounty. These citizens, of course, provide base populations for potential puritan Muslims who will rely on simplistic interpretations of regional and world affairs. No doubt religion will play a role in their interpretations of reality. However, it must be stated that there are well-educated puritan or fundamentalist Muslims. Their high literacy levels, though, often enable them to become the leaders of their less-educated counterparts.

Non-oil-producing countries such as Bangladesh, Ethiopia, Nigeria, Senegal, Sudan, and Yemen are economically much worse off than the poorest oil-producing countries located in the Shia Crescent. Thanks in large measure to the diffusion of medical technology aimed at combating, for instance, childhood diseases, in those areas of the Muslim world, their current combined population of 418,759,729 will reach one billion before the decade of 2050 is over. Their current per capita GDP ranges between $800 and $2,000 per year. In comparison to those who live in Western countries, the average citizen of a typical Muslim country lives in exceedingly poor conditions.

Economics and the Pull of the Western World

Most of Europe is wealthy when compared to even oil rich countries such as Qatar, Kuwait, and the United Arab Emirates. Saudi Arabia barely surpasses beleaguered Russia in per capita GDP, which is just under $10,000. With an annual per capita GDP of $12,000, Poland, despite its communist past, matches Saudi Arabia's economic output.[44] Moving westward across Europe, countries with democratic and capitalist traditions are much more productive. French and German workers benefit from a $28,700 per capita GDP. Similarly, Italians earn $27,700, and at $32,200 per person, Danes produce an even higher income. The Danish per capita income is still some $1,600 per year lower than that of the Swiss. The per capita GDP in the United Kingdom is $29,600. It should not be surprising then that many Muslims are attracted to European cities. The same thing can be said of cities in the western hemisphere. In North America, for example, Canadians currently earn an average of just over $31,000 per year while citizens of the United States enjoy an average annual income of over $40,000.

These Western countries have enjoyed a relatively higher standard of living, which has been paid for by decreasing birth rates and empowering women. While empowered women enjoy better education and employment choices, which often benefit their husbands as well as themselves, the forgoing or opting out of having children has a cost that will be felt in the future. Such is not the case throughout most of the Islamic world, and it is certainly an alien concept among puritan Muslims. With fewer children being born to Western mothers, there will be fewer workers to generate services and tax revenue to support an increasingly elderly population.

Summary

With respect to immigrants from Islamic areas of the world, their arrival in America and Europe has been something of a trickle, but their numbers were large enough to establish ethnic enclaves within the host countries. In places like Dearborn and Hamtramck, Michigan, we see an increasingly large Muslim community that, to some observers, may seem culturally diverse because the settlers are from various countries across the Middle East. However, it must be recognized that these immigrants chose to settle among others from countries that are both Arab and Muslim. In Hamtramck, Muslim influence in local politics is already overshadowing voices coming from long-established Christian communities. Since 2004, the city has permitted calls to prayer to be broadcast via loudspeakers across public spaces five times per day. Tony Manolatos, a writer for the *Detroit News*, says that "some fear the community is losing its European roots, but others embrace it."[45] As this situation illustrates, there is a strong sense of community among members of Muslim American communities, and that shared sentiment protects their enclaves from the larger ethnic cultures that surround them. With social networks maintained between Muslim Americans and others living in Africa, Europe, and Asia, including the Middle East, we can expect to see the trickle become a river as population pressures in their home countries create more unstable conditions.

Meanwhile, Western governments concerned about the welfare of these immigrants will establish more programs to help them feel welcome. The greater opportunities found in urban areas and supportive government programs will send a message, using the established communication lines, that Allah has provided the believers with lush gardens and flowing rivers beneath their feet. With declining birth rates among middle-class Americans, Europeans, and Canadians, economic elites in these societies see the newcomers from places such as Mexico, Central America, and the Middle East as a cheap labor source, so they are not likely to oppose bringing in more immigrants. Rulers in Middle Eastern countries, like the governing body counterparts in Mexico and Central America, see little need to change the opportunity structures in their countries because they are able to rid themselves of excess people by allowing them to fill economic niches elsewhere. It is among these people—reservoirs of potential immigrants—that rulers and economic elites fear revolution and the loss of their power, as we have seen in countries with civil unrest including Egypt, Yemen, Libya, and Syria.

A large and looming problem with this situation is that few people will take action to bring about social change in their home countries to reduce the underlying problems of high fertility and few economic niches to accommodate large numbers of people. This provides the West with the proverbial catch twenty-two: If we take action to bring about social and economic change in highly fertile countries, we threaten the power structure in those societies. Men hold power in those places, and their religion supports the maintenance of the status quo. As is seen in the oppressive actions in Yemen and Syria during the 2011 so-called Arab Spring, which outsiders regard as a democratization movement, hundreds of protesters have been killed in police actions sanctioned by the government intended to control civil unrest. Also, Western societies, perhaps plagued by a sense of guilt for colonial ventures that arguably contributed to the unequal accumulation of wealth in Middle Eastern countries, have endeavored to create social climates that encourage multiculturalism, so they are not inclined to get involved in the internal affairs of other countries. In recent years, Westerners have been taught to see all cultures as equals, and many Westerners now see their own cultures as flawed and oppressive to people living in less fortunate places. Aside from the actions of the Bush and Obama administrations and their British ally, there are no political and social forces at work anywhere in the West or in Muslim countries that have the capacity to create positive change for the future.

As the trickle of Muslim immigrants is about to intensify, it is important for the inhabitants of the transatlantic world to ask some important questions about its newest members. While there is no way of knowing who among the immigrants will be puritan Muslims and thus willing to publicly defend and die for their religion, it is necessary for us to know what drives them. Since the power of unity among Arab and non-Arab Muslims is their religion, we must now turn our attention to the creation of puritan Islamic thought worlds to see how its followers shape their perceptions of self, others, space, and governance of people and places, for it is in these imagined worlds that potential conflict lies.

Chapter 2

Puritans' Views of Self and Community

Introduction

The secular self found in much of Asia, Europe, and North America, with its economic and social focus, is quite a contrast to the religious self of austere Muslims. The fundamentalists, like most followers of Wahhabism, Salafism, and other apologetic discourses that shape Islamism, rely on the Qur'an for guidance in the pursuit of the good life, including living peacefully in lands supplied with humanity's necessities. A fundamentalist understands that the Qur'anic path to eternal bliss is paved by a mixture of beliefs in divine election and merit-based redemption that could create a psychological imperative to demonstrate to her own satisfaction as well as to others that she is one of the true believers or members of the community (*umma*). Being regarded as a member of the umma is important because the concepts of self and community are tied to the social meaning of salvation. In contrast, failure to demonstrate behaviors that place her inside the community raises social red flags that she is an unbeliever. Muslims' interactions with unbelievers are quite different from those experienced with fellow members of the faith.

The contrast between secular communities and the umma were clearly on display in European cities between September 30, 2005, and October 1, 2006. During that twelve-month span, interactions between Muslims and secularists in European cities were tenuous. The troubles started when cartoons depicting Muhammad were published[1] and then when Pope Benedict XVI publicly mentioned acts of aggression in the name of Allah.[2] In each case, Muslim organizations carried out public protests and denunciations in a number of places, including in the Middle East. As one young Muslim man living in London stated to a television reporter during a protest against the pope, "We are Muslims. We don't turn the other cheek." This was a profound statement and one that the reporter failed to consider further. Whether one is a Christian or not, it is difficult to grow up in the predominantly Christian-influenced West and not believe that this comment is nothing more than a disgruntled man's angry reaction to a perceived slight. Nonetheless, it begs further exploration. What is the puritan Muslim's perception of the self, and why wouldn't he turn the other cheek? To answer those questions, it is necessary to delve into the puritan's imagination and see what shapes his thought worlds. Since "Islam" means submission to Allah, it is important to consider the self in relation to the divine and, of course, to other people and spaces. In this chapter, discussion is limited to the self and the Qur'an's concept of community.

The Self and the Crisis of Assurance

It is interesting that Muhammad moves between two voices in the Qur'an. At times, he speaks in the plural "we," meaning Allah or the angel Gabriel, and, in other places, he is clearly an individual, mortal being.[3] By switching back and forth, Muhammad can represent both the observations of the angel Gabriel in the presence of Allah, and himself as the Prophet Muhammad. The Qur'an speaks to readers as individuals and as members of larger social organizations such as towns and nations. In doing so, Muhammad addresses an individual's conduct and a society's conduct. Both individuals and societies are subject to Allah's wrath and his blessings.[4] In all things, both the individual and society must be in submission to Allah, for it is from him that both the good and the bad (as a form of punishment) flow.[5] There is little room to feel personal pride, knowing that success in life is the result of God's benevolence and not personal achievement.

Certainly, if a high level of self-esteem is a prerequisite for mental health in contemporary society, the Qur'an does not share that opinion. As recorded in Surah 16, "Your God is one God; so [as for] those who do not believe in the hereafter, their hearts are ignorant and they are proud. Truly Allah knows what they hide and what they manifest; surely He does not love the proud."[6] It is important to know that "whatever favor is [bestowed] on you it is from Allah; then when evil afflicts you, to Him do you cry for aid."[7] This conception of the self in relation to Allah is consistent with the Calvinist view of the self and God. Like the self as depicted by the sixteenth century Christian theologian John Calvin, the puritan Muslim's image of self is insignificant next to that of Allah.

When it comes to the larger question of the assurance of redemption, which, arguably, creates in some people a good bit of anxiety, Allah is sometimes shown as sovereign and directing, while at other times, he allows free will among would-be followers. Consider the puritan's mental state after reading the following two passages: "And if Allah please, He would certainly make you a single nation, but He causes to err whom He pleases and guides whom He pleases; and most certainly you will be questioned as to what you did."[8] While this passage from the Qur'an suggests that finding the straight path to righteousness is only possible with the help and guidance of Allah, the fundamentalist may become confused when he reads that "[t]he truth is from your Lord, so let him who please believe, and let him who please disbelieve; surely We have prepared for the iniquitous a fire, the curtains of which shall encompass them about; and if they cry for water, they shall be given water like molten brass which will scald their faces; evil the drink and ill the resting-place."[9] Knowing that he must demonstrate that he is guided by a divine hand, the individual fundamentalist may experience a psychological dilemma, or at least a need to assure both his own mind and others' minds that his face in eternity will escape the scalding effects of molten brass.

The belief that God guides those whom he pleases is similar to the predestination doctrine associated with Calvinism. Max Weber, the twentieth-century German sociologist who associated Calvinism with the rise of capitalism, argued that the doctrine of predestination creates a psychological crisis among believers because it causes them to ask the question: Am I of the elect?[10] Because Muslims have no real way of knowing if they are living in accordance with Allah's will, they seek assurance of their atonement, and in so doing, they create a situation in which they can demonstrate true faithfulness.[11]

As the Qur'an points out, the believer will most certainly be questioned about what he did in his lifetime. Here, Islam deviates from the Calvinist predestination model to a position that comes close to a free-will-and-works-based salvation plan. If it were a Christian theology, it would be labeled Pelagian, named for the ancient theologian Pelagius who argued that individuals could earn salvation through merit. This situation can hypothetically create an even greater psychological dilemma for the Islamic fundamentalist than that suffered by some Calvinists in sixteenth-century Scotland, where, during the Reformation, some Christians believed prosperity and other tangible signs of health and wellness revealed one's status in eternity. This is especially true when one recognizes that Scottish Calvinists were at least assured by the doctrine of perseverance of the saints, which regards salvation as a permanent condition.[12] The Muslim has no such assurance. As I will show, there are many other Qur'anic passages that support either a predestinarian view or free will view on the eternal redemption of the self. In all cases, however, the fate of the disbeliever is eternal chastisement featuring inextinguishable fire.

Underlying the notion of sovereign choice in matters of salvation or atonement is the all-powerful majesty of Allah. As written in Surah 3, "And whatever is in the heavens and whatever is in the earth is Allah's; He forgives whom He pleases and chastises whom He pleases; and Allah is Forgiving, Merciful."[13] Muhammad goes on to warn his readers and listeners to "guard . . . against the fire which has been prepared for the unbelievers."[14] This passage suggests that a Muslim may lose his salvation. Surah 16 indicates that salvation may not be a guaranteed condition. "He who disbelieves in Allah after his having believed, not he who is compelled while his heart is at rest on account of faith, but he who opens [his] breast to disbelief—on these is the wrath of Allah, and they shall have a grievous chastisement."[15] Muhammad continues, "Have not yet those who believe known that if Allah please He would certainly guide all people?"[16] Those who are not guided by Allah, including the erstwhile believers, face a future strewn with divine punishments. "They shall have chastisement in this world's life, and the chastisement of the hereafter is certainly more grievous, and they shall have no protector against Allah."[17] Surah 3 provides an even stronger statement that clearly tells us that salvation is not guaranteed. "Say: O Allah, Master of the Kingdom! Thou givest the kingdom to whomsoever thou pleasest and takest away the kingdom from whomsoever thou pleasest, and Thou exaltest whom Thou pleasest and abasest whom Thou pleasest; in Thine hand is the good; surely, Thou hast power over all things."[18] In the face of Allah's majesty, even believers have little power. Indeed even the length of their lives is held by the hands of Allah, as is their opportunity to share in the celebration of seeing the just punishments of the unbelievers:

> Allah makes to pass away and establishes what he pleases, and with Him is the basis of the Book [Qur'an]. And We will either let you see part of what We threaten them with or cause you to die, for only the delivery of the message is [incumbent] on you, while calling them to account is Our [business]. Do they not see that We are bringing destruction upon the land by curtailing it of its sides? And Allah pronounces a doom—there is no repeller of his decree, and He is swift to take account.[19]

These passages reveal a god whose will is sovereign and quite able to grant salvation to whomever it wills, while retaining the right to take it away. Here lies a predicament for the true believer. Puritan Islam, and even Sufism (a mystical interpretation of Islam in which the believer focuses his heart solely on God), requires a life of pious self-denial and the accumulation of works that gain Allah's favor. When people follow the teachings handed down to them from the Prophet through the Qur'an, they may find that their lives are out of step with secular institutions and ways of life found in European and North American cities. Here, the individual immigrant may well experience what Jean Piaget, a French pioneer in cognitive development and cognition, called disequilibrium.[20] In other words, the puritan's mental framework, charged as it is with firm teachings on austerity and salvation, can set the stage for a psychological crisis. What, if anything, must the puritan do to increase the likelihood that he will not lose favor with Allah? He may revert to the security of the holy book and a close-knit group of like-minded people to cope with the dissonance produced by trying to reconcile his understanding of Allah's world with the highly secular images he encounters in his new home.

As I mentioned briefly already, the individual must recognize that she has to earn the love and salvation offered to her by Allah. "Say: If you love Allah, then follow me [Muhammad], Allah will love you and forgive you your faults, and Allah is forgiving, Merciful. Say: Obey Allah and the Apostle; but if they turn back, then surely Allah does not love the unbelievers."[21] This notion is quite the opposite of Calvinism, which argues that salvation is an unconditional decision made by God.[22] Some Arminians, on the other hand, believe that God predetermined who he has chosen for eternal redemption, but his elections were made based on his foreknowledge of those who will choose him. In fact, sixteenth century Dutch reformer Jacobus Arminius, after whom the Arminians are named, argued that people can choose to reject God's offer of salvation.[23] Christians adhering to a more Pelagian view of redemption believe that God gave humans the capacity to earn their way into heaven by abiding by divine decrees.[24] These comparisons are relevant to our discussion on Islam because, as I will show shortly, it closely matches the latter interpretation. For Muslims must determine how to obtain Allah's love and eternal security in the hopes that their actions on earth will sway Allah to guide them through life. The choice of who obtains salvation in a puritan Muslim context may be made by God, but his choice is not set in concrete, so to speak. The individual has a role to play. The same can be said for political leaders of towns or geographic communities; the Qur'an warns: "[Consider] a town safe and secure to which its means of subsistence come in abundance from every quarter; but it became ungrateful to Allah's favors, therefore Allah made it to taste the utmost degree of hunger and fear because of what they wrought."[25]

In Surah 4, Muhammad spells out what must be done for salvation's sake. "O you who have been given the Book, believe that which We have revealed, verifying what you have, before We alter faces then turn them back on their backs, or curse them as we cursed the violators of the Sabbath, and the command of Allah shall be executed."[26] A Muslim had better believe what is commanded of him by the Prophet because submission requires visible actions as well as internal convictions, for the Qur'an warns would-be-believers: "[As for] those who disbelieve in Our communications, We shall make them enter fire; so oft as their skins are thoroughly burned, We shall change them for other skins, that they may taste the chastisement; surely Allah is mighty, Wise."[27]

The fundamentalist immigrant must now rest on the knowledge that he is to follow the teachings of the Prophet found in the Qur'an. To insure himself of Allah's love and favor, he must strive for personal purity. The only way to know how to achieve that lofty state of being is to be diligent in his quest to know the ways of Allah. He is reminded that if he is "careful of [his duty to] Allah, He will grant [him] a distinction and do away with [his] evils."[28] The Qur'an repeatedly admonishes the believer that it is his duty, indeed his responsibility, to take its contents seriously. Failure to do so will be painful. "Surely those who conceal any part of the Book that Allah has revealed and take for it a small price, they eat nothing but fire into their bellies, and Allah will not speak to them on the day of resurrection, nor will He purify them, and they shall have a painful chastisement."[29] In a softer tone, Muhammad explains that, in reference to the Qur'an, "this is a book We have revealed, blessed; therefore follow it and guard [against evil] that mercy may be shown to you."[30] In discussing corporate purity of worship, and the building and use of the mosque (*masjid*), Muhammad declares that "in it are men who love that they should be purified; and Allah loves those who purify themselves."[31] In Surah 2, Muhammad further claims that "surely Allah loves those who turn much [to him], and He loves those who purify themselves."[32]

Let us briefly look at how these doctrines on salvation compare to Christianity. As we have discussed previously, there are common ideas about the need for purity in worship, as well as personal and corporate living. This was especially true of dissenting Protestants living in seventeenth-century England, Scotland, Ireland, and North America.[33] Allah, like the Christian God, is liable to dispense His wrath on towns and nations, so there is a strong psychological and sociological imperative to purify conduct in both private and public spaces. It is interesting to note that the Christian doctrine of sanctification of the soul (divine help in achieving perfection) by the internal workings of the Holy Spirit separates these two Abrahamic religions.[34] There are two reasons for making this claim: First, the reader must recognize that Islam rejects the role of the Holy Spirit as an agent of divine sanctification. Second, the above passages show that it is the individual's and the town's responsibilities to seek purification. Again, if this were Christianity, it would be labeled semi-Pelagian because a person has the capacity to abide by God's laws on her own for a time, until God is swayed by the believer's merit and decides to offer her guidance. However, Muhammad claims that Allah guides those whom he pleases and rejects those whom he wills.[35] When one looks below the surface of this notion, which suggests a predestinarian-like doctrine, it does deviate somewhat from Calvinism because the Qur'an proclaims that Allah loves those who purify themselves, and redemption is given to those whom Allah loves. There is little doubt that the individual will experience a psychological need to earn his salvation. As with Puritan Christians in the seventeenth century, believers must call for purity in corporate worship, for the sins of the few invite divine wrath on the many, including the geographic community.

Puritan Christians and their Muslim counterparts do not agree on the doctrine of grace that teaches followers that salvation is a free gift, which does not require merit on the part of the believer. Even in the Christian realm, debates over this topic have raged throughout the centuries. For example, the famous dialogue between sixteenth-century church reformers Desiderius Erasmus and Martin Luther is a noteworthy example of diverging Protestant Christian views on the doctrine of salvation. According to Erasmus, free will was part of God's plan for humanity. By free will, Erasmus meant that a person could reject Christ's offer of salvation. However, Luther, author of *The Bondage of the Will*, claimed that salvation was initiated by God's sovereign will and that the individual's faith was given to him through the Holy Spirit without merit or request, hence Luther's belief in "the bondage of the will." At the heart of the Erasmusian and Lutheran debate was the issue of *sola* (Latin for solely or only) attached to grace (*gratia*), which is called, "monergism versus synergism in the initiation of human redemption."[36] Effectively, this means that salvation is either God's choice alone (monergism) or a combination of human and divine wills (synergism). When Islam is compared, there is yet another interpretation of grace. Grace, many Protestants have argued, literally means an unmerited free gift of salvation.[37] In a Muslim context, it means that Allah does not have to offer salvation to anyone, but he does so through an act of grace. However, the believer must win Allah's love and grace through his own human merit; thus, the burden of finding the right path to salvation is placed squarely on the shoulders of the believer; he must initiate the process. One finds the individual at this point potentially perplexed as he strives to find the path to righteousness. If he can find the correct route to salvation, he will gain the favor of Allah who may, or indeed may not, decide to guide him. Although the Qur'an provides examples of blessings from Allah, which mostly seem to involve rivers flowing beneath the recipients' feet,[38] the fact that those cooling waters could be replaced by the fires of eternal chastisement could create some anxiety or a psychological crisis in him. This is especially true as he finds himself living in a larger secular society that sees him and his community as just another piece of its multicultural mosaic.

Now that we have looked into the Qur'an's vision of the self, we can now turn our attention to its conception of the many. In other words, who makes up the true Muslim community?

Qur'anic Image of Community

Admittedly, the concept of community is not well defined in the Qur'an. However, it is possible to build an image of the concept of community by piecing together passages that address attributes of it. To some people, community is a spatial construct like a village or a town while others may view it as a psychological structure, as in the case of the Islamic umma. The umma stresses emotional or psychological connections among people, regardless of where they live and work. This is also the kind of community that is invoked, for instance, when considering identities such as the Muslim community, the Christian community, and the gay community. Clearly not everyone in these communities knows each other, but they understand concepts, beliefs, and issues that they have in common. This understanding and sharing is foundational to a psychological community, as opposed to a geographic community in which members live in close proximity to one another but do not necessarily understand each other or share with each other.

One could argue that when a town is mentioned in the Qur'an it can be assumed that there is a psychological and cultural connection shared among the residents. Also, just as an individual can invite divine punishment, a town or a community can receive Allah's wrath for the sins of even a few people living within it. When the Qur'an was written in the seventh century, towns like Mecca, Jerusalem, and Medina were small settlements. No doubt most people who were born and raised in them knew their fellow residents. In many respects, these towns were what sociologist Ferdinand Tönnies called *Gemeinschaft* worlds.[39] The German term roughly translates to "informal community," meaning a community tied together by nongovernment institutions and intimate psychological bonds.

Intimate and informal geographic communities such as those described by Tönnies are places where secrets are hard to keep—especially secrets of a sinful nature. Residents who fear God's wrath for the sinful behaviors of their neighbors often place a premium on enforcing laws that conform to divine laws. The mostly desert lands that encircled these settlements provided seasonal grazing cover for sheep and camels, and they served to keep social activities contained within the small confines of the settlement. The Qur'an is clear in showing that Allah dispenses judgment on both towns and entire nations. As it declares, "We will say: Enter into the fire among the nations that have passed away before you from among jinn [a supernatural spirit or genie] and men; whenever a nation shall enter, it shall curse its sister . . . the last of them shall say . . . Our Lord! These led us astray; therefore give them double chastisement of fire. He will say: Every one shall have double but you do not know."[40] The Qur'an continues, "And [as for] these towns, We destroyed them when they acted unjustly, and We have appointed a time for their destruction."[41] According to the Muslim holy book, towns and nations are well-defined, spatial constructs, but how does the Qur'an conceive psychological communities?

It is important to know how the Qur'an discusses community, for, next to family, community is the basic social organization that defines how the individual views and relates to other people. The Qur'an conceives Islam as a psychological community that extends beyond the spatial parameters of a town or a nation. As such, Islam is a highly corporate or social religion, so community is close to the heart of a believing and practicing Muslim. To be sure, "The reward of the prayer offered by a person in congregation is twenty-five times greater than that of the prayer offered in one's house or market."[42] This is quite a departure from the teachings of Jesus, who thought that prayers offered in private were more likely to be sincere.[43]

As mentioned in the introductory chapter, Islam, unlike Christianity, has a restricted range of interpretations. Because of this restriction, there are more universally understood words and objects than there are in Christianity, which includes numerous phrases, symbols, and practices. The commonalities among Muslims act as centripetal forces, drawing followers together toward the center, or the foundation, of Islam. Consider, for example, the differences in the symbolisms associated with the ritual of the Lord's Supper and the Holy Communion. Some people might think that the Lord's Supper is just a rustic way of expressing the Holy Communion. In fact, the two are very different. Whereas a Southern Baptist may take part in the Lord's Supper to remember Jesus' crucifixion and resurrection, Roman Catholics see the ritual as a means to obtain grace for salvation. Moreover, Roman Catholics believe in the doctrine of transubstantiation, which claims that the bread and wine have been *transformed* into the body and blood of Christ, whereas Protestants use the bread and wine to *symbolize* the body and blood of Christ. The Qur'an does not seem to have such a range in rituals and their symbolic meanings. There are differing juristic traditions and Qur'anic ambiguities, to be sure, but, with only one writer possessing a modest vocabulary, most of the Qur'an is remarkably precise and consistent. This fact alone helps ensure a sense of bonding in the Islamic community.[44]

Perhaps the most powerful and unifying concept in Islam's community is the doctrine of the Five Pillars of Islam or, as it is also known, the Five Fundamentals of Faith.[45] They include the creed (*shahda*), prayer (*salat*), almsgiving (*zakat*), Ramadan (*sawm* or fast), and pilgrimage to Mecca (hajj). As theology professors and Christian converts from Islam, Ergun Mehmet Caner and Emir Fethi Caner write, "The Pillars are non-negotiable. They are not to be questioned, but believed to the utmost. To criticize the five pillars is, in fact, paramount to treason, perceived as heresy and blasphemy, punishable in many Muslim countries by imprisonment or worse."[46] Although politics and governance of space is a topic we will discuss in more detail later, it is worth pointing out that government-imposed punishment for dishonoring the Five Pillars is not possible in a secular society. Such actions would require government officials to serve the will of Allah and his Prophet. This type of power arrangement is best described as a theocracy. Since Allah is liable to punish towns and nations for their sins, puritan Islam necessarily requires a theocracy to ensure adherence to the Qur'an and safety from Allah's wrath.

No matter where Muslims live out their lives, they are required to memorize and recite aloud the creed, one of the pillars, in Arabic: "Ilaha illa Allah. Muhammad rasul Allah" (There is no god but Allah. Muhammad is the messenger of Allah.) Christians and Jews would agree with the first part of the creed: there is no god but "the god" (Allah). However, they would have difficulties with the statement that Muhammad is his messenger.

In matters of community, the Qur'an categorizes people into groups identified as believers and unbelievers, including Jews and Christians, along with idolaters. Only a man or woman meeting the criteria as a believer can be part of the puritan's umma. As described in the Qur'an, "Believers are only those who believe in Allah and His Apostle then they doubt not and struggle hard with their wealth and their lives in the way of Allah; they are the truthful ones."[47] That passage establishes the criteria for the first pillar of Islam. Further, Muhammad admonishes his readers: "Let not the believers take the unbelievers for friends rather than believers; and whoever does this, he shall have nothing of [the guardianship of] Allah, but you should guard yourselves against them, guarding carefully; and Allah makes you cautious of [retribution from] Himself; and to Allah is the eventual coming."[48] The Qur'an goes on to declare: "We have created you of a male and female, and made you tribes and families that you may know each other; surely the most honorable of you with Allah is the one among you most careful [of his duty]; surely Allah is knowing, Aware."[49] As Muslims see it, it is certainly the will of Allah for Muslims to form a tight-knit community, a *Gemeinschaft* world.

The second pillar of Islam establishes the need for prayer, and corporate prayer is the most highly regarded form of prayer. In his revelation that mysteriously took him from Medina to Jerusalem and then to heaven itself, Muhammad was told both by God and Moses that prayer must be performed multiple times a day. Based on the advice of Moses (*Musa*), Muhammad settled on five periods of prayer scattered throughout a twenty-four-hour period. Each prayer is publicly called and heard beyond the private spaces of the home and family. It is intended to call together the community. You might be interested to know that prayer requires Muslims to make themselves ready for communication with the divine by cleansing themselves in the ablution (*wudu*) ritual. The call to prayer is actually a repetitious chant that reminds adherents of Allah's greatness and of Muhammad's role as his messenger. All prayers are to be uttered while facing toward Mecca. In recent years, on transatlantic flights, movie screens periodically show the direction to Mecca for any Muslim passengers who would need to know this in order to pray.

The third pillar requires Muslims to give alms (*zakat*) to those less fortunate. Almsgiving literally means "purification,"[50] and is gained by shedding some of one's excess wealth and earthly baggage in a deliberate effort to guard against greed and selfishness. One must recognize that giving to the poor is limited to members of the Muslim community.[51] Unlike the Red Cross, which may provide aid to all people regardless of religious affiliations, the Red Crescent, its Islamic counterpart, should not be so inclined. Efforts from the Red Crescent, the puritan would argue, should be limited to helping only Muslims in distress. As I will show, there are Qur'anic prohibitions against providing friendly assistance to unbelievers.

Ramadan is the fourth pillar and it honors the arrival of the Qur'an. During this month-long observance that runs roughly from the third week of September to the third week of October (the duration of the ninth month of the Muslim calendar), all Muslims are required to fast from sunup to sunset. Since abstaining from some social practices is required, umma-wide acceptance of Ramadan has to be far-reaching and pervasive. For example, members of the umma cannot engage in business luncheons or in intimate daytime rendezvous during Ramadan.

The Qur'an tells the believer and his community: "Fasting is prescribed to you as it was prescribed to those before you, that you may [learn] self-restraint."[52] Self-restraint, as reflected in public observance and support of the pillar throughout the community, runs counter to the message of secular society. No doubt this issue will create quite a stir in secular spaces as Muslims gain more political power in Western democracies.

The fifth pillar demands that all Muslims who are able participate in a pilgrimage (*hajj*) to Mecca, the holiest of Islamic sites.[53] It was this experience that did much to teach Malcolm X that Islam is not just a black man's religion. Born Malcolm Little in Omaha, Nebraska, Malcolm X embraced Islam as a way to cope with perceived racial discrimination in America. Islam is a religion in which all races are allowed; however, as the location of Mecca and Islam's emphasis on Arabic show, the faith does have an ethnocentric orientation that elevates Saudi Arabia and its culture to a higher plane.

Summary

From the discussions in this chapter, it is possible to see that Islam conceives the self as part of the larger Muslim community. In some respects, this idea is similar to Christianity and the doctrine of the universal church or the church catholic. Also, like Calvinist Christianity, the Islamic conception of Allah in relation to the self is one of complete sovereignty and omnipotence. The follower of Islam, like his Calvinist counterpart, is dependent on the will of the divine to grant eternal salvation. However, the God in Calvinism made his decision about who will be counted among the elect (those chosen to receive eternal bliss) before the foundation of the earth was laid.[54] In Muhammad's way of thinking, Allah's will is not set in stone, so to speak. To be sure, Allah may decide against a believer if her heart and lifestyle fail to maintain Allah's high standards. Theological doctrines like these arguably create a psychological crisis among true believers, perhaps even more so than among Puritan Christians, who at least had the doctrine of perseverance of the saints ("once saved, always saved") to soothe their anxieties. As we will discuss later, the basis for deciding who is elect and who is not has profound implications for human interactions and the governance of people. Also, because land and places have the capacity to take on sacred qualities, they, too, can be set apart from other, more profane places. While it may not be readily apparent, the identification of space can create a psychological dilemma for the true believer, for she must decide whether or not she will follow traditions of Islamic jurisprudence and recognize that some places are to be contested while others are not. This is even more troubling to her because, in the past, even so-called moderate Muslim jurists have disagreed over the precise boundaries of contested and noncontested spaces, the latter of which refers to places inhabited by unbelievers.

In the final analysis of the Muslim self and community in relation to the divine, a person's life is judged for eternity on its own merits, while his earthly actions may invoke Allah's wrath and may lead to the destruction of his town and nation. Beliefs like these among adherents to Islamism are taken seriously and form the basis of their vision of civil governance. Though it may not seem obvious, civil governance of space to ensure safety against divine wrath will impact the lives of secularists and other unbelievers and the uses of their spaces. Before looking into the Qur'an's view on governance, though, it is important to take a longer look at how the Qur'an views and treats unbelievers, for modern societies are made up of a wide range of religions.

Chapter 3

Puritans' Perception of Unbelievers

Introduction

In 2006, while delivering a lecture at Regensburg University, Pope Benedict XVI offended Muslims by publicly contrasting Christian and Muslim tactics of winning souls, or gaining converts, for their respective faiths. Later that year, he visited Turkey, apparently in an attempt to ameliorate any feelings of insult or outrage. While this initial offense was, in and of itself, a nonevent, he quoted Byzantine Emperor Manuel II Palaiologos, who, in a 1391 dialogue with a well-educated Persian, described the spread of Islam as militant and irrational. Also, the pope wanted to act ecumenically to help heal ecclesiastical rifts that began back in the eleventh century when the Eastern Orthodox Church broke away from Rome's domination.[1] In working to heal old wounds in the Christian world, the pope also wanted assurances from the Turkish government that minority religions would be allowed to practice their faiths without fear of repression.[2] Given that Turkey, a celebrated center of early Christianity, with churches at Galatia and Ephesus, is now nearly 100 percent Muslim, the pope established quite a goal for himself.

It could be argued that the pope, a former professor of theology named Joseph Ratzinger, wanted to use his trip to Turkey to publicly contrast Catholicism with Islam. He was a professor with a reputation for conservative ecclesiastical reform. Moreover, it is likely that, during this visit to Turkey, the pope wanted to show Muslims how they had deviated from Catholicism—what he and other Catholics see as the one true faith. As *Wall*

Street Journal columnist Peggy Noonan wrote in an article for *Time*, this pope has been called God's rottweiler.[3] Pope Benedict XVI wants to rid the earthly body of Christ, according to Noonan, of the "filth that had entered the church."[4] He was perhaps stirring the pot, so to speak, believing that his faith has a different worldview, especially as it relates to unbelievers. By going to Turkey, he was showing the world that old-school Muslims, who abide by the literal word of the Qur'an, hold unbelievers in great disdain, no matter how apologetic their petitions for friendship might appear. The pope likely knew that the Qur'an does not obligate Muslims to welcome unbelievers to their tables, symbolically or in reality. On the contrary, its perception of unbelievers is alien to some Christians who believe that it is moral to turn the other cheek when offended or to offer help to those less fortunate, regardless of their faith or tribal affiliation. To the puritan Muslim, any solicitude from unbelievers, short of full conversion, is meaningless. The Qur'an's depiction of unbelievers is important because it frames the puritans' mental images of those around them. It is likely that these imaginings encourage Muslims to contest spaces inhabited by unbelievers, believing that the spaces rightfully belong to those who follow the teachings of Muhammad.

Nevertheless, from some of the writings on Islam, it appears that a number of observers believe that old scars and festering wounds exacerbate the current tenuous situation between Western societies and Islamic followers. Perchance there is hope among these authors, and officials like President Barack Obama, that by admitting a sense of guilt for the West's past and especially present conduct toward the Muslim world, liberal Muslims will be compelled to engage in peaceful relationships with the West. In her lengthy book *The Battle for God: A History of Fundamentalism*, Karen Armstrong, a former nun, argues that the recently raging voices of fundamentalism among Jews, Muslims, and Christians coincided with the rise of the modern nation–state in Europe. She begins her history in 1492, in Spain at the battle of Granada, which ended the seven-hundred-year-long Reconquest (*Reconquista*) of Iberia by Spanish Christians. The *Reconquista* was designed to recapture the lands Spain lost to the Muslim Berbers from Morocco in the eighth century. Armstrong, however, ignores the events and years leading up to the battle of Granada in 1492. It seems to her, then, that the battle for

God began with the militant action of the allied Christian forces of Queen Isabella and King Ferdinand of Spain.[5] Before she ends her first paragraph, she tells her readers that the obviously close-minded Christian leaders of Spain forced the remaining Muslims to either convert or leave the country. Not content with this disclosure in the first paragraph, she next tells her readers about the signing of the Edict of Expulsion on March 31, 1499. This act, she proclaims, forced some eighty thousand Jews to migrate to Portugal and another fifty thousand to immigrate to the Muslim Ottoman Empire, "where," she declares, "they were given a warm welcome."[6] There is no denying that these events took place, nor is there any reason for claiming that these actions were morally correct. The issue here, like that of many writers, is that she is only telling part of the story. She begins her version of history in the middle, rather than at the beginning, of monotheism's long-standing battle for God.

Similarly, author and editor Kelly Knauer's 2006 publication *The Middle East: the History, the Cultures, the Conflicts, the Faiths* epitomizes the way in which some secular writers in the West express guilt over partially understood, highly contrastive theological undercurrents that have shaped the events that led to the current conflicts between the Christian West and the Islamic nations. Arguably, according to Knauer, the Christian West destroyed a highly advanced Muslim society, as Knauer's work explains in a section titled "A First Clash of Cultures":

> For centuries, while Europe languished in the Dark Ages, Muslim scholars, artists, astronomers and mathematicians flourished. But as Europeans emerged from their long stagnation, their renascent energies found direction across the Mediterranean. The liberation of the historic sites of Christianity from the Muslim hands was a sacred duty: "God Wills it!" A series of long, bloody, often inconclusive Crusades followed, and the scars of dishonor they left on the Islamic world have never faded away. Even today, al-Qaeda kingpin Osama bin Laden refers to U.S. and European leaders as "Crusaders."[7]

Former president Jimmy Carter has added his *Palestine: Peace Not Apartheid* to the growing list of books written by Westerners that includes authors such as Huston Smith, Karen Armstrong, and Khaled Abou El Fadl.[8] In a sense, Carter's goals are both controversial and admirable. His view is that we can avoid further regional and even global conflict by resuscitating his Camp David Accord and the road map to peace, which he initiated while in office. Carter acknowledges that there are extremists who do not want peace, but, as if he were negotiating peace between two equally motivated combatants, he takes the higher moral ground by arguing that these minority voices are on both sides of the Palestinian–Israeli divide.

President Carter, and no doubt many others, sincerely believe that ending the Palestinian–Israeli impasse "would remove one of the major causes of international terrorism and greatly ease the tensions that still have the potential to spark a regional or even global conflict."[9] However, in the realm of the other causes of this religious-spatial conflict, such as demographic transition and the appeal of fundamentalism (which offers a concise explanation of reality while prescribing a path to optimize one's earthly and eternal lives), the former president seems less informed. As he sees it, the new ideas he proposes are based on his understanding of the history of the conflict and not the conflict itself. Tellingly, Carter begins his review of the epic battle for God with the creation of the modern Israeli state in 1948.[10] It seems he limits his interpretations of the conflict to questions about Palestinian space and autonomy. However, to fundamentalists, there are deeper ethnic and theological issues at work here, and they have been at work for a much longer period of time.

There are a number of people in the American media who have well-meaning thoughts about the motives of Islamic fundamentalists, including those the West labels as terrorists. Their sentiments, however, reveal a rather limited understanding of the geotheological undercurrents that shape the fundamentalists' views of unbelievers. The American television personality Rosie O'Donnell, for instance, told her audience on the daytime talk show *The View* that we need not "fear terrorists: they're just moms and dads."[11] On September 12, 2006, she equated radical Christianity in America with radical Islam, arguing that one is just as frightening as the other.[12]

Islam itself, though not to the extent of Christianity, has been plagued by internal strife, even during a golden age (pre-Crusades) of Islam in the

Middle East, filled with expansion and conquest. Moreover, Islamic jurists who showed some level of tolerance toward Jews and Christians during those years held puritan Muslims in contempt.[13] "They [Puritans] were designated *muharibs* [literally, those who fight society] . . . Muslim jurists argued that any Muslim or non-Muslim territory sheltering such a group is hostile territory that may be attacked by mainstream Islamic forces."[14] According to the noted scholar of Islamic jurisprudence Khaled Abou El Fadl, the most noticeable characteristic of puritan movements within Islam has been the power of extremist theology and overt hostility toward non-Muslims and other Muslims belonging to different schools of thought. Those who remain neutral have not escaped the extremists' wrath either.[15] The Qur'an guides the fundamentalist in shaping his perception of the world. Because Islam is a highly social religion that can sometimes place pressure on adherents to categorize humans as believers or unbelievers, an in-grouping and out-grouping process continues to define social interactions of fundamentalist Muslims. This process causes one to view those like oneself as safe and trustworthy while others, who have a different set of beliefs and cultural practices, make up an amorphous body of people to be excluded from one's group of intimate acquaintances. Looking ahead to the middle of the twenty-first century, one must recognize that this feature of puritan Islam will produce a host of unsavory political and social consequences as America and Europe reconstruct their secular spaces to accommodate the arrival of millions of Muslims, and yet puritans will regard non-Muslims as unsafe and untrustworthy.

In the meantime, authors like former president Jimmy Carter and Karen Armstrong unwittingly provide ammunition to Islamists, who are unashamedly enemies of the West and its emerging secularist worldview. While secularism does not carry the symbolic attributes of Christianity that puritan Muslims dislike, it is nonetheless a mindset that classifies the unaffiliated individual as an unbeliever. Puritans, despite being disinterested in history per se, regard these kinds of historical interpretations and admissions of harsh dealings with them as evidence of their own persecution in the name of Allah. On the contrary, high-minded compromises and self-effacing admissions of guilt feelings do not appease fundamentalists. Many politicians and secular writers like those previously discussed are unable or unwilling to get inside the heads of modern Islamists to see how they truly regard unbelievers, which, to the dismay of these politicians and writers, includes them.

An examination of Qur'anic passages shows how unbelievers are perceived by puritan Muslims.[16] This is important because the Qur'an is quite clear about how it divides humanity. To puritans, there are believers, who compose their umma, and there are unbelievers, including those who are nominal or liberal Muslims, Jews, and Christians as well as polytheists. Of course, atheists and agnostics, too, are cast into the unbeliever's category. The true believer of Islam has little choice but to create space between himself and unbelievers; moreover, there is language in the Muslim holy book that could lead some devoted adherents to take actions that are much more severe than just creating space between the two camps.

The Source of Labels and Identity Nomenclature

It is important to have an objective eye to fully appreciate what the Qur'an has to say about labeling people as believers and unbelievers. We have already touched lightly on what the Qur'an has to say about itself and its perception of believers. Now, we will focus on how the Qur'an conceives unbelievers. These Qur'anic delineations are important to consider because, unlike the believers of the Christian Bible, which is held by the faithful to be inspired by God, puritan Muslims believe that the Qur'an is the word of the God, Allah. Muhammad left little room for ambiguity about the source, purpose, and meaning of the Qur'an. As he wrote, "this is a book We have revealed, blessed; therefore follow it and guard [against evil] that mercy be shown to you. . . . Who then is more unjust than he who rejects Allah's communications and turns away from them? We will reward those who turn away from Our communications with an evil chastisement because they turned away."[17] Those who reject the communications of Allah and his Prophet are considered to be evil. "Evil is the likeness of the people who reject Our communications and are unjust to their own souls."[18] Anyone who rejects the Qur'an's communications is rejecting Allah and is thus labeled an unbeliever.

There is no divine pressure on true believers to be concerned about the eternal state of those who have rejected Islam, including polytheists: "It is not fit that the Prophet and those who believe that they should ask forgiveness of the polytheists, even though they should be near relatives, after it has become clear to them they are inmates of the flaming fire."[19] The Qur'an encourages compassion for members of the umma, rather than compassion for those who reject its communications. As Muhammad wrote, he "is the Apostle of Allah, and those with him are firm of heart against the unbelievers, compassionate among themselves."[20] Giving to the poor, which is regarded as one of the five Pillars of Islam, does not include providing relief to unbelievers.

The Qur'an warns against watering down or diluting its message, which sets the stage for dissension among the ranks of Muslims, themselves, as they look down upon those who do not take the Qur'an at its word. "And when Our clear communications are recited to them, those who hope not for Our meeting say: Bring a Qur'an other than this or change it. Say: It does not beseem me that I should change it myself; I follow naught but what is revealed to me; surely I fear, if I disobey my Lord, the punishment of a mighty day."[21] Muhammad makes it clear that those who dread a meeting with Allah and his Prophet are overly focused on their present life, which is typical of the interests of people in secular societies. "Surely those who do not hope in Our meeting and are pleased with this world's life are content with it, and those who are heedless of Our communications: [As for] those, their abode is the fire because of what they earned."[22] Again, Muhammad reminded his followers that "this Qur'an is not such as could be forged by those beside Allah, but it is verification of that which is before it and a clear explanation of the book, there is no doubt in it, from the Lord of the worlds."[23] Now that we have seen that the Qur'an declares itself to be the word of God and empowered to grant to mere mortals a license to judge people as believers or unbelievers, we can move forward to see how the true believer is told to view and treat others outside his umma.

The Qur'an's Perception of Jews and Christians

When Islam was born in the seventh century, the arid Saudi peninsula was already occupied by "unbelievers" who coalesced into communities of Christians, Jews, and polytheists. There was no regional government to collectivize the highly dispersed masses into a single people with a common set of beliefs and ideologies. In the Qur'an, respect is shown for Old Testament leaders and prophets like Abraham (*Ibrahim*), Moses (*Musa*), David (*Dawood*), Saul (*Talut*), Isaac (*Yitzchak*), Noah (*Nuh*), Jacob (*Yaqoub*), and Jonah (*Yunus*). There is also respect given to the Gospel (*Injeel*) of Jesus (in Arabic, *Isa*), and Mary (*Marium*), Jesus' mother. On the surface, it is hard to know this and think that puritan Islam would have a negative view toward Jews and Christians. After all, as some might believe, "we are worshiping the same God."[24] These same people logically assume that the animosity expressed toward others who share a biological or theological link to Abraham must be a result of centuries of mistreatment at the hands of the Crusaders and Western countries while working for the maintenance of a Zionist state.[25] Within days of the formation of Israel in 1948, Arab armies from Jordan, Syria, Lebanon, Iraq, and Egypt assembled to invade the new Jewish state. If both Jews and Arabs descend from Abraham, why were Jews so resented? After all, as heirs of Abraham, this land was promised to them, too. While former president Carter and others believe that Palestinian resentment of Jews rests with the issue of space and the sovereign rule of Palestine, the Qur'an provides a geotheological explanation of Israel that is quite distinct from earthly political posturing, as we will discuss in depth in chapter 8.

Arguably, the largest faith communities in existence in the Middle East during Muhammad's time were composed of Jews and Christians. The Prophet declared that he knew the meaning of both the Torah (*Taurat*) and the gospels (*Injeel*). As a member of the family that controlled access to the ancient holy site in Mecca (*Kaaba*), he must have resented polytheists and half-hearted Christians and Jews who made offerings at that holy place. Being a believer in the monotheism that descended to him through Abraham and the prophets, Muhammad, like the patriarch of his faith, no doubt longed for a religious community (*Gemeinschaft*) tied together by psychological bonds and shared beliefs that would return his people to the true faith. His perception of the religious landscape around him must have been one of frustration, for the presence of polytheists and idolaters at the holiest site in his world spoke volumes of the ineffectiveness of both Jews and Christians in bringing about Allah's earthly kingdom. Paradoxically, Muhammad readily accepted the prophets of both communities, but he saw those who practiced Judaism or Christianity as having left the true faith by breaking covenants and reinterpreting the Gospel of Jesus (*Isa*). In speaking about the children of Israel, the Qur'an states: "The likeness of those who were charged with the Taurat [Torah], then they did not observe it, is as the likeness of the ass bearing books, evil is the likeness of the people who reject the communications of Allah; and Allah does not guide the unjust people. O you who are Jews, if you think that you are the favorites of Allah to the exclusion of other people, then invoke death if you are truthful."[26] Much earlier in the Qur'an, Muhammad explained why he felt that way about Jews. "But on account of their breaking their covenant We cursed them and made their hearts hard; they altered the words from their places and they neglected a portion of what they were reminded of; and shall always discover treachery in them excepting a few of them so pardon them and turn away; surely Allah loves those who do good."[27] Muhammad declared that Christians have been cursed to suffer in hell as well. As he explained, "And those who say we are Christians, We made a covenant, but they neglected a portion of what they were reminded of, therefore We excited among them enmity and hatred to the day of resurrection; and Allah will inform them of what they did."[28]

In contrast to Christianity, Islam rejects the deity of Jesus, although he is regarded as a messiah. For Christians, the Nicene Creed, written some three hundred years before Muhammad lived, speaks of a completely different being whose life, according to the New Testament, was dedicated to expiating the sins of the elect. Lay people and secularists who care little for theological discourse must at least recognize that the theological conception of *Isa* of Islam is not the same as the Jesus of Christianity.[29] According to the Qur'an, "The Messiah, son of Marium is but an apostle; apostles before him have indeed passed away. . . . Certainly they disbelieve who say: Surely Allah is the third [person] of the three [Trinity]; and there is no god but the one

God, and if they desist not from what they say, a painful chastisement shall befall those among them who disbelieve. Will they not then turn to Allah and ask His forgiveness? And Allah is forgiving, Merciful."[30] As that passage from the Qur'an suggests, Muhammad must have found Christians and Jews a perplexing lot. He writes, "And they say: None shall enter the garden [or paradise] except he who is a Jew or a Christian. . . . And the Jews say: The Christians do not follow anything [good] and the Christians say: The Jews do not follow anything [good] while they recite the [same] book."[31] As for the Jews, Muhammad believed that they had broken God's covenant with him, and, as a result, they lost their opportunity to live in lands under which flow rivers that give life to flourishing gardens.[32] The Christians, on the other hand, erroneously try to make three gods out of one.[33] According to Muhammad, both Christians and Jews have diluted the true religion, which is Islam, with false teachings.

In the West, it is not uncommon for evangelical Christians to go door–to–door, handing out invitations to attend religious meetings. Pamphlets and other materials are also frequently provided to invitees, regardless of whether they want to receive them or not. Islamists are not obliged to act similarly. In the following passage, one is led to assume that the believer is directed to leave unbelievers alone unless provoked, but, the earthly and eternal fates of unbelievers are dire. As written in Surah 109, "Say: O unbe-lievers! I do not serve that which you serve; nor do you serve Him Whom I serve: Nor am I going to serve that which you serve, nor are you going to serve Him Whom I serve: You shall have your religion and I shall have my religion."[34]

The Qur'an teaches that nonbelievers are not only to be left alone, they are to be shunned: "the Jews will not be pleased with you, nor the Christians until you follow their religion. Say: Surely Allah's guidance that is the [true] guidance. And if you follow their desires after the knowledge that has come to you, you shall have no guardian from Allah, nor any helper."[35] The Qur'an also warns that the follower is not to count Christians and Jews among his friends. "Do not take the Jews and Christians for friends; they are friends of each other; and whoever amongst you takes them for a friend, then surely he is one of them; surely Allah does not guide the unjust people."[36] This side of an honest conversion to Islam, no amount of guilt for colonial crimes stemming from the Christian Crusades will make the fundamentalist see Christians and Jews any differently because their views are shaped by deep theological imaginings. Failure to demonstrate anti-Jewish and anti-Christian behavior in public spaces, especially when there is any public affront to Islam or the Prophet, invites a backlash against them by those in the umma who take the Qur'an at its word.

Some other scholars argue that Islamic societies have historically tolerated the existence of Christian and Jewish communities within their midst. Although there is some regional truth in that notion, the Islamic world is made up of spatial areas in which varying juristic traditions have not made such allowances. That thought must also be tempered by the realization that belonging to a non-Muslim religious community costs the individual some political and social prestige. In other words, there is incentive to abide by the teachings of Islam in even the most tolerant Muslim society. As the data in table 2 show, countries with strong historic ties to Judaism and Christianity boast few Jews and Christians living in them today. If the percentage of Christians living in these countries is any indication, there is little political benefit in being one.

Table 2. Religions: Countries with Historic Christian & Jewish Ties (% of Population)[37]

Country	Muslims	Christians	Jews & Others
Israel	15	2	77
Lebanon	60	39	1
Egypt	94	6	0
Syria	90	10	0
Turkey	99.8	≤ 1	0
Iraq	98	≤ 2	0
Iran	99	≤ 1	0

While Lebanon and Syria, to some extent, have small Christian populations, other Muslim countries do not. Contact with Western countries has no doubt encouraged and perhaps even intimidated pragmatic leaders in Lebanon and Syria to respect the survival of their historic Christian communities; however, the policies of both countries favor protection for Islamic traditions and laws. Interestingly, and despite the Crusades, Israel has few Christian residents. It should be recognized that Christianity existed in the region for nearly six centuries before Islamic armies forced their way onto the political scene.

In the Syrian capital city of Damascus, the ancient Church of St. John the Baptist, which was established by Emperor Theodosius of Byzantium in 379, was seized in 715 by Al-Walid, the Umayyad Dynasty's head of state (*caliph*), who was in charge of enforcing Islamic (*sharia*) law. The three-and-a-half-century-old Church of St. John the Baptist was converted into the Umayyad Mosque shortly after Damascus fell into Muslim hands. Syracuse University history professor Hibba Abugideiri notes: "At the same time, Al-Walid saw to it that Christians could build four other churches in the city. Nevertheless, today the Umayyad Mosque, much expanded over the centuries and still in active use, is considered Islam's oldest monumental mosque."[38]

Except for Lebanon, there is already a higher percentage of Muslims (some thirteen million) living in the twenty-seven member European Union (EU) than there are Christians living in Middle Eastern countries, despite the holiest sites in Judaism and Christianity being situated in those lands. Meanwhile, the EU is trying to find ways to integrate Muslims into its society and its economy, which means the adoption of an American-style affirmative action scheme. To this end, the EU has created the European Monitoring Center on Racism and Xenophobia (EMCRX) to persuade employers and society into "bridging the gap" between themselves and Muslims.[39] The need for this agency suggests that there is little grassroots support among native Europeans for increasing the numbers of Islamic people in their midst. European leaders are, nevertheless, making room for Islamic expressions of faith in secular places because one of the goals of the EMCRX is to reassure Muslims, and indeed other immigrants, that they will not have to lose their culture to become citizens of the EU.

Is the EU being kind or is it just responding to demographic and cultural realities? Without restrictive immigration policies or radical shifts in the distribution of education, wealth, and power in Muslim countries, the EU is looking at an increasingly larger Muslim community. Undoubtedly, that community will have many members not willing to assimilate and shed their identities. Followers of puritan Islam will certainly not be swayed by policies designed to move them into the mainstream of secular society. At the same time, they are likely to see the economic wealth of Europe as a gift to them from Allah. The Qur'an is clear in stating that Allah owns and disperses the resources of this world.[40] European secularists, Jews, and Christians will likely pay higher taxes to provide for more public services for those immigrants falling into their governments' social nets. They will also experience increased competition for a limited number of jobs, especially those in the primary and secondary employment sectors. The Qur'an offers the natives of historically Christian, yet increasingly secular, European countries little solace: "And the Jews and the Christians say: We are sons of Allah and His beloved ones. Say: why does he then chastise you for your faults?"[41] The Qur'an also tells the believer: "Ask the Israelites [and their Christian friends] how many a clear sign have We given them; and whoever changes the favor of Allah after it has come to him, then surely Allah is severe in requiting [evil]."[42] Israeli and European leaders should not expect gratitude from Islamic fundamentalists, for Islamists who believe in the literal interpretation of the Qur'an regard all unbelievers as deserving of Allah's wrath in this life and in the hereafter.

As Allah is seen as omnipotent and judging, it follows that earthly authority must be similarly structured. Gaining control of what social theorist Karl Marx called the superstructure of society could bring about near universal submission, at least in public spaces. It is not surprising then that even among puritan Muslims there are disagreements over who should hold political power. Nevertheless, the type of political power required to bring any of their visions of society to fruition must be rooted in theocracy. While there may be elected officials who wield the sword of power, behind them will be an assortment of *mullahs*, *imams*, and *sheiks* who shape their policies.[43] In such a society there are seldom referendums on ballots. Policy, whether domestic or foreign, will be shaped by puritan theology. It is important to recall here that high natural increase rates coupled with closed economic niches in the puritans' home countries will offer them little choice but to resettle in the prosperous lands provided to them by Allah. As Muhammad wrote, "And [as for] the foremost of the migrants from Makkah [Mecca] and the people of Medina, and those who followed them in goodness, Allah is well pleased with them and they are well pleased with Him, and He has pre-pared for them gardens beneath which rivers flow, to abide in them forever; that is a mighty achievement."[44] Earlier, in Surah 4, Muslims are told that they "will find in the earth many a place of refuge and abundant resources."[45] The Prophet then tells them that "when you journey in the earth, there is no blame on you if you shorten the prayer, if you fear that those who disbelieve will cause you distress; surely the unbelievers are your open enemies."[46] It is important to see that while geographers and other scholars regard humans and human activities as parts of the landscape, puritan Islam does not. Indeed, unbelievers are distinct from the blessed land provided to good Mus-lims, regardless of whether or not those lands are in cold northern places and the rivers beneath their feet carry industrial goods to and from markets built by the labor of unbelievers.

The Qur'an's Perceptions of Atheists and Polytheists

Before considering the ways in which the Qur'an views atheists and poly-theists, it is necessary to establish some parameters and decide on nomencla-ture. When Muhammad wrote the Qur'an, few people, if any, declared an atheistic world view. There were lovers of the world to be sure, but, to see how Muhammad regarded these people, the reader must recognize that atheism was not an identifiable and alternative worldview. Rooted perhaps in varied aspects of cosmology and sustained by a theoretical process of per-petual random selection in nature, writers are left with few adjectives to fur-ther define the unbeliever living in the time of Muhammad other than atheist. The Qur'an describes the archetypical nonbeliever as those who do not "turn [to Allah], who serve [Him], who praise [Him], who fast, who bow down, who prostrate themselves, who enjoin what is good and forbid what is evil, and who keep the limits of Allah; and give good news to the believers."[47] In effect, the Qur'an provides a guide to identify those who believe and those who do not believe (i.e., atheists and agnostics).

Many people who grew up in the Christian-influenced cultures of Europe and Anglo-America often hear the refrain "judge not lest you be judged."[48] Islam departs from Christianity on this important aspect of social life. The Qur'an clearly tells Muslims not to be concerned about those who are inmates of the fire (hell), even before they die and suffer eternal torment. Muslims must be judgmental to determine whether or not a person, perhaps even a close relative, is destined to suffer such a fate. Once that determination is made, Muslims are to leave him alone and offer no prayers of forgiveness on the doomed person's behalf.[49] Muhammad wrote, "These [individuals] are they who buy the life of this world for the hereafter, so their chastisement shall not be lightened nor shall they be helped."[50]

Passages such as these certainly do not encourage the puritan to be concerned about the plight of those who are not part of her umma. Indeed, Muhammad assured the true believer that those who make light of their lives and beliefs will take a back seat on resurrection day. Even the means of survival in this earthly existence are at risk for such behavior because "[t]he life of this world is made to seem fair to those who disbelieve, and they mock those who believe, and those who guard [against evil] shall be above them on the day of resurrection; and Allah gives means of subsistence to whom He pleases without measure."[51]

Muslims are required to judge the actions and the hearts of others. Furthermore, the Qur'an instructs them to not make friends of unbelievers. Earlier, in Surah 8, the believer is told to fight disbelievers who are preparing for war against him. If he does not, "then he, indeed, becomes deserving of Allah's wrath, and his abode is hell."[52] However, at times, the Qur'an softens its rhetoric: "Allah only forbids you respecting those who made war upon you on account of [your] religion."[53] It could be argued that respect for an enemy and going to war against an enemy are two distinct ways of looking at one's nemesis. While those preparing for war for any number of secular reasons, it seems, could be respected and fought against, those who war against Islam are not worthy of any respect. "O you who believe! Do not take My enemies and your enemies for friends. . . . If they find you, they will be your enemies, and will stretch forth towards you their hands and their tongues with evil, and they already ardently desire that you may disbelieve."[54] Alas, the puritan is left to interpret and judge the intent of the efforts of others to create a meaningful dialogue between his community and secular leaders. His willingness to accept an olive branch of peace is tempered once again by these words: "[As for] those who do not believe in Allah's communications, surely Allah will not guide them, and they shall have a painful chastisement. Only they forge the lie who does not believe in Allah's communications, and these are the liars."[55] The Qur'an does not encourage friendly relations with unbelievers, although through a miracle or act of Allah, a friendship could be formed.[56] However, the believer is certainly not encouraged to seek friendships with unbelievers.

The Qur'an's Perception of Liberal Muslims

When Islamic schisms are examined, the underlying issue is often not differences in Qur'anic interpretation, although it is sometimes used as the pretext for claiming that others have left or denied the true faith. Nevertheless, all Muslims regard the Qur'an as the primary source of authority.[57] Instead, the real issue creating dissent in the puritan Muslim world is arguably power.[58] Because Muslims have varying levels of attachment to national, ethnic, and religious identities, as well as diverging views on who should serve as *caliph*, schisms may form. Such was the case among seventh-century Muslims after Muhammad died. Manu, or descendents of ancient Persians, tended to follow Ali, Muhammad's son-in-law. They became the Shia. Non-Persians tended to follow a *caliph* and companion to Muhammad named Umar. They became known as Sunnis.

While schisms involve large groups of people, individuals who depart from the perceived path of righteousness are another matter. The Qur'an states that "everyone has a direction to which he should turn, therefore [know that] . . . Allah will bring you all together; surely Allah has power over all things."[59] The Qur'an also points out: "Whatever is in the heavens and whatever is in the earth is Allah's; and whether you manifest what is in your minds or hide it; Allah will call you to account according to it; then he will forgive whom he pleases and chastise whom he pleases, and Allah has power over all things."[60] People with yearnings to please Allah must use their talents as leaders, if they are aware of them, to bring Allah's people together. Failure to do so invites divine wrath. Completely rejecting the true teachings of the Prophet also invites Allah's wrath and the public consternation of those who seek Allah's favor through abiding by a literal understanding of the Qur'an. The subject of divine wrath is discussed in chapter 4, focusing on geotheology—the relationship between people, lands, and governance and the worship of the divine.

In Islam, the acceptance of the idea of salvation through God's grace is up for rejection and abandonment. This attitude parallels the Arminian Christian doctrine of free will in the matter of salvation. (Arminian Christianity is named for Dutch theologian Jacob Arminius, a Protestant reformer in the sixteenth century who argued against the Calvinist doctrine of predestination.) It is important to see how those who claim submissive adherence to Allah and his Prophet regard those who turn their backs on the true faith, for these perceptions contribute to the formation of contested space. It is handy to refer to those formerly religious people who have since left the faith simply as backsliders. Though this is not necessarily a word found in the lexicon of Islam, there is no doubt that the concept is discussed in the Qur'an. More importantly, it is a well-understood concept used by contemporary Islamists to differentiate between friend and foe. The concept of backslider has clear political and social ramifications in the Muslim world. As America and Europe will witness a sustained migration of Muslims into their secular spaces throughout the foreseeable future, those who are too friendly with non-Muslim people and their ways of life run the risk of being seen by other Muslims as backsliders. I will develop this topic further in the next two chapters. But for now, let us return to an examination of how puritans perceive backsliders.

A large part of the Qur'an is devoted to unbelievers in general, but, when it does address backsliders, it is unequivocal in its declarations: "He who disbelieves in Allah after his having believed, not he who is compelled while his heart is at rest on account of faith, but he who opens [his] breast to disbelief—on these is the wrath of Allah, and they shall have a grievous chastisement. This is because they love this life more than the hereafter and because Allah does not guide the unbelieving people."[61] These people are especially worse off than others because "[t]hese are they on whose hearts and their hearing and their eyes Allah has set a seal, and these are the heedless ones."[62] In other words, these people have been divinely cut off from Allah and the truth of his ways. In the same chapter, Muhammad warned Muslims that they are not to take a small price for their faith, arguing that the blessings of Allah are clearly better for them.[63]

While observers often call Muslims who are willing to make political compromises moderates or liberals, puritan Muslims, like al Qaeda leader and Islamic theologian Ayman al-Zawahri, call them "secular traitors."[64] Al-Zawahri adds, "Those who sold Palestine, the secular traitors, cannot be your brothers. Do not recognize their legitimacy. . . . And don't sit with them."[65] His comments are a thought-for-thought rendering from the Qur'an, which indeed has much to say about the geoeschatological state of all unbelievers.

Geoeschatology of Unbelievers

Muhammad prophesied the future for believers, which projects a vivid geoeschatology, or the relationship between end times scenarios and people, lands, and governance, that features gardens with rivers flowing through them. He also painted a frightening geoeschatology for the fate that lies ahead for unbelievers, which we will discover in chapter 4.[66] In using that kind of imagery, the Qur'an employs a theology of deterrence that is similar to "hellfire and brimstone" sermons associated with fundamentalism in Christianity.[67] As if it were looking ahead to the days when Muslims would migrate over or around the Mediterranean Sea and eventually across the Atlantic Ocean, the Qur'an tells believers: "We have sent you among a nation before which other nations have passed away, that you might recite to them what We have revealed to you and [still] they deny the Beneficent God. Say: He is my Lord, there is no god but He; on Him do I rely and to Him is my return."[68] The Muslim holy book also points out that the unbelievers they will encounter in their new nation may present themselves as fair-minded and understanding of the ways of Allah, but Muslims must be aware that unbelievers' "plans are made to appear fair-seeming to those who disbelieve, and they are kept back from the path; and whom Allah makes err, he shall have no guide. They shall have chastisement in this world's life, and the chastisement of the hereafter is certainly more grievous, and they shall have no protector against Allah."[69] Also, according to the Qur'an, believers are to know that "[b]y Allah, most certainly We sent [apostles] to nations before you, but the Shaitan [Satan-like figure] made their deeds fair-seeming to them, so he is their guardian today, and they shall have a painful punishment."[70] If a believer were to be seduced into moral and even political compromise with people of other faiths, he, in the minds of puritans, invites the wrath of Allah. Considering his Qur'anic instructions, a believer may well distrust Americans and Europeans, including fair-seeming agencies like the EU's European Monitoring Center on Racism and Xenophobia. The Qur'an offers little to support an attitude of tolerance toward unbelievers who are destined for chastisement.

In pointing out what will befall unbelievers, the Qur'an employs a number of metaphors, many of which were likely drawn from the gospels (*Injeel*) and the teachings of Jesus: "Surely [as for] those who reject Our communications and turn away from them haughtily, the doors of heaven shall not be open for them, nor shall they enter the garden until the camel pass through the eye of the needle;[71] and thus do We reward the guilty."[72] Unbelievers will be made inmates of the fire, and, as they experience their punishment, they "shall call out to the dwellers of the garden, saying: Pour on us some water or of that which Allah has given you. They shall say: Surely Allah has prohibited them both to the unbelievers."[73] People who articulate another conflicting message of faith are seen as forging a lie against Allah and his Prophet; they too will meet a terrible fate:

> And who is more unjust than he who forges a lie against Allah, or says: It has been revealed to me: while nothing has been revealed to him, and he who says: I can reveal the like of what Allah has revealed? And if you had seen when the unjust shall be in the agonies of death and the angels shall spread forth their hands: Give up your souls; today shall you be recompensed with an ignominious chastisement because you spoke against Allah other than the truth and because you showed pride against His communications.[74]

Angels, as the Qur'an envisions, will make certain that these false teachers will have their just rewards: "[As for] those who disbelieve, surely neither their wealth nor their children shall avail them in the least against Allah, and these it is who are the fuel for the fire."[75] Later in Surah 3, a hellish final destination is again described: "[we] will cast terror into the hearts of those who disbelieve, because they set up with Allah that for which He has sent down no authority and their abode is the fire; and evil is the abode of the unjust."[76]

The geoeschatology of the unbeliever features fire, isolation, and certainly pain. The puritan also believes that the Qur'an warns him against developing compromising relationships with unbelievers, lest he invite the wrath of God on himself, his town, and his nation. That is a topic discussed further in chapter 4 regarding the sanctity of Allah's World.

Summary

The possession and exercise of power are arguably the most important dividing factors among Muslims. This situation is made even worse by the emergence of a plethora of juristic traditions across the Muslim world. In the mind of the puritan, the preeminence of the Qur'an in shaping attitudes and behaviors toward unbelievers nevertheless trumps all forms of jurisprudence. Beyond the issue of disputes over power among Muslims themselves, there are theological imaginings in the Qur'an that contribute to the formation of contested spaces with those judged to be unbelievers. A number of Qur'anic imaginings grant license to puritans to categorize others as unbelievers. Power sharing with unbelievers, including liberal Muslims, is less likely.

Atheists and people of other faiths are not to be respected by puritan Muslims, unless it is miraculously facilitated by Allah. As with most social situations in Islam, the burden of judging the morality of others as well as choosing the appropriate action to take toward them rests with the believer and his understanding of the true religion. The burden is no less heavy when judging others who claim to be Muslims. This is seen quite clearly in the way Sunnis and Shia viewed the execution of the former Iraqi dictator Saddam Hussein. If the media coverage of his execution, which occurred on

December 30, 2006, was any indication of how he was regarded, Sunnis tended to see him as a fallen martyr while the Shia, more often than not, cheered his demise.

Chapter 4

The Sanctity of Allah's World

Introduction

From the tormenting fires of hell to the images of blissful lives spent amid lush gardens with life-giving waters flowing through them, the world of Muhammad is alive with vivid depictions of spaces, all of them the products of an omnipresent, omniscient Allah. As we discussed earlier, the Qur'an was shown to encourage believers to move to other places that would offer more of Allah's bounty. Just as Muslims, along with the ancestors of all non-African peoples, have relocated to places outside the Near East (the heart of the Middle East), and will continue to do so in the future, new spaces will become sacralized. Previously in our discussion, these ideas were mentioned in a cursory manner in the context of how the Qur'an views the Islamic community and those who are judged to be believers or unbelievers. Here, we take a deeper look at the Qur'an's imagery of natural and human-altered landscapes to understand how the believer is to apply a sense of devotion and sacredness to space, regardless of its location.

Islamic Cosmology and Eschatology

Most religions feature a set of beliefs that explains the origins or cosmology of the earth and its occupants. Many, especially Abrahamic religions, also delve into the imagined parameters of eschatology, which involves the end of temporal life, or existence, and heaven and hell. One might ask why these aspects of the Qur'an are important. Since the recognition of sacred space is intimately tied to the divine, there is no better place to start an exploration of the beginning of sacred history or cosmology than at the original condition of created space, for it is in that state that the closest connection to the creator is found. More importantly, such an image provides the basis for the construction of sacred space. Any alterations in that image of space are the result of punishments or rewards given to humanity or segments of humanity. As the highest form of creation, Abrahamic religions see humanity as inextricably tied to the scenario of benefit-reward versus punishment-payment, geotheomisthosis and geotheokolasis, respectively. All other creatures are unable to elicit God's wrath or reward for moral or immoral thoughts and public behaviors. Therefore, any alterations from the pristine condition of original creation are the result of Allah's judgments of wayward people, including individuals, towns, and nations. Judgments regarding eternity do not often involve the larger community; they are placed on the individual (although a passage in Surah 7 declares that nations will be punished in eternity for their actions as a whole).[1] In effect, the Qur'an insists on both personal and community adherence and submission to Allah's will.

Omniscient, omnipresent, and omnipotent are words associated with the God of Judaism, Christianity, and Islam. Like Christianity, Islam looks forward to a day in which human residents of the world will be judged according to each individual's works. Both the Christian Bible and the Qur'an refer to that event as Judgment Day; thus, humanity's earthly existence has a beginning and an end. The Qur'an provides a clear description of the joining together of those two distinct end points in earthly time. "And He it is Who has created the heavens and the earth with truth; and on the day He says: Be, it is. His word is the truth, and His is the kingdom on the day when the trumpet shall be blown [Judgment Day]; the knower of the unseen and the seen; and He is the Wise, the Aware."[2]

According to the Qur'an, humans and their ecumene were created by Allah from natural elements: "All praise is due to Allah, Who created the heavens and the earth and made the darkness and the light . . . He it is Who created you from clay, then He decreed a term; and there is a term named with Him; still you doubt. And He is Allah in the heavens and in the earth;

He knows your secret [thoughts] and your open [words], and He knows what you earn."[3] Not only does Allah know everyone's secret thoughts, he owns what humankind earns, possesses, and occupies, so the means of life itself are controlled by Allah. "And to Him [Allah] belongs whatever dwells in the night and the day; and He is Hearing, the Knowing."[4]

Muslims believe that all secular objects and events are governed by the sovereign Lord of the universe. "Allah's is the kingdom of the heavens and the earth and what is in them; and He has power over all things."[5] In Surah 16, Muhammad tells the reader that Allah is responsible for men's enjoyment of nature's bounty. "He it is Who sends down the water from the cloud for you; it gives drink, and by it [grow] the trees upon which you pasture. He causes to grow thereby herbage, and the olives and the palm trees, and the grapes, and of all the fruits; most surely there is a sign in this for a people who reflect."[6] Also, every living thing in the heavens and the earth makes obeisance to Allah alone, including the angels.[7] The Qur'an warns Muslims that they must "guard . . . against a day in which you shall be returned to Allah; then every soul shall be paid back in full what it has earned, and they shall not be dealt with unjustly."[8]

In many respects, the geoeschatology, or relationship between end-times scenarios and people, lands, and governance, of Islam reads a lot like that which is imagined in Christian circles. Whereas eternal life in paradise is the reward for those who believe and submit to the will of Allah, fire is the punishment for those who disbelieve.[9] It is perhaps an understatement to say that the Qur'an has more references to hell than to heaven. The Qur'an employs a theology of deterrence, so it uses images of hell to create a sense of dread and, thus, repentance: "Is he, therefore, better who lays his foundation on fear of Allah and [Allah's] good pleasure, or he who lays his foundation on the edge of a cracking hollowed bank, so it broke down with him into the fires of hell; and Allah does not guide the unjust people."[11] Muhammad further described hell by writing: "We [have] created ... hell [for] many of the jinn [genies] and the men; they have hearts with which they do not understand, and they have eyes with which they do not see, and they have ears with which they do not hear; they are as cattle, nay, they are in worse errors; these are the heedless ones."[10] Apparently, like the sermons of circuit-riding preachers in the colonial American backcountry, Qur'anic images of hell are intended to instill fear in the hearts of those who believe, galvanizing them to a life bent on service to the creator and owner of all things.

The Qur'an goes beyond telling about the fires of hell in describing the final destination of unbelievers. As it warns, "And surely Hell is the promised place of them all [who disbelieve]; It has seven gates; for every gate there shall be a separate party of them. Surely those who guard [against evil] shall be in the midst of gardens and fountains; enter them in peace and secure."[12] It is clear that the hereafter presents two distinct spaces for humanity. Unbelievers will be cast into hell where none will be spared and no sin will be overlooked, for the fire scorches the mortal.[13]

On the other hand, much is said in the Muslim holy book about gardens of paradise. When there is mention of these lush places, though, the Qur'an often quickly moves back to a more frightful geoeschatology laid out for unbelievers and Muslims who might be led astray.[14] Only Allah, through his grace, decides who can enter the garden of paradise. As the Qur'an points out, "And wherefore did you not say when you entered your garden: it is as Allah has pleased, there is no power, save in Allah?"[15]

What about the spaces of those living in the present life? Are they to be divided among the living? According to Islamic jurisprudence scholar Khaled Abou El Fadl, Muslim jurists have divided the world into three spheres of imagined spaces: the space of Islam, the contested space, and the space of peace or nonbelligerence.[16] He contends that Muslim jurists have long disagreed over the exact location of these spaces as well as the legal cause of fighting non-Muslims. As with most disputes over the precise locations of boundaries, conflict has often been the result. As the Islamic world spreads through relocation diffusion, these spaces will necessarily have to be adjusted in their size and scope, whereupon the secular world may well experience political tension and social strife as more spaces become contested by immigrants inspired by the perceived need to sanctify Allah's entire world.

Puritans' Geopiety and Their Identification of Sacred Places

The Qur'an depicts the entire world as belonging to its creator, but it does state that certain places, especially in the Middle East, are sacred or set above the rest. Not only is the world Allah's creation, it is his to rule. The rise of nationalism has also added to the geopious sentiment that some spaces are sacred while others are not so blessed. Although the Qur'an regards the whole world as the domain of Allah, many traditional Muslims regard the Middle East as the heart of the Islamic world. Centuries of struggles against a multitude of internal and external forces bent on injuring, if not destroying, Islam in the Middle East have galvanized its place in the hearts of Muslims. This is seen clearly in a letter written on July 9, 2005, by al Qaeda leader Ayman al-Zawahiri to Abu Musab al-Zarqawi, his compatriot in Iraq.[17] As al-Zawahiri wrote, "I want to be the first to congratulate you for what God has blessed you with in terms of fighting battles in the heart of the Islamic world, which was formerly the field for major battles in Islam's history, and what is now the place for the greatest battle of Islam in this era, and what will happen, according to what appeared in the Hadiths of the Messenger of God about the epic battles between Islam and atheism."[18]

Outside of the Middle East, Islam nevertheless has identified and established centers of worship that are regarded as sacred. One of the primary actions of Muhammad was to establish mosques (*masjid*) in diverse places across conquered lands, while retaining special reverence for the *Kaaba* (the most sacred spot on Earth) in Mecca and the Quba Mosque in Medina—the city of the Prophet.[19] Muhammad called these places "sacred" and "exalted."[20] Still, the sacredness of the Middle East arises more from the sentiments attached to its lands by the followers of Islam. Muhammad, as I will argue, held that the entire world is the handiwork of Allah and that the Lord of the heavens and the earth is willing to bless or curse any part of it as the merits of its human occupants warrant. It is not difficult to see that a basic goal driving puritanism is a desire to divert Allah's wrath away from home and nation. This is similar to the beliefs of Christian Puritans, who argued that by making the church and society pure, they would receive more blessings and fewer punishments through forces of nature.

The notion that the Middle East is favored by Allah is further height-ened because of the language chosen by the angel Gabriel to communicate the Qur'an to Muhammad. Arabic became sacred, so, by extension, the lands occupied by Arabic speakers became especially sacred to Muslims. According to al-Zawahiri, the Islamic world, therefore, centers on the Middle East with particular focus on Egypt and the neighboring states of the nearby Saudi Peninsula and Iraq.[21] Places like Chechnya, Afghanistan, Kashmir, and Bosnia Herzegovina are regarded by al-Zawahiri as being among the "far-flung" regions of the Islamic world, which presumably means they are less sacred.[22] There is little doubt that as Islam diffuses throughout the world, the Middle East, will continue to be held as sacred and governments around the world will be pressed to involve themselves in Middle Eastern affairs with the scale of favorable relations tipping in favor of Muslim-controlled states and away from Israel. I will address this topic further in chapters 8 and 9. Nonetheless, to the puritan who takes direction from the Qur'an, Allah does have an interest in other lands. However, those other lands are the homes of unbelievers, and so, these spaces are subject to Allah's wrath or his sanctioned takeover by a more deserving people.[23] If Allah blesses the unbe-lievers' lands with his bounty, puritans may well see this situation as provi-dentially provided to them by Allah. Newly arriving Muslims who hold puritan beliefs would regard such bounty as a reward. As Muhammad wrote, "Glory be to Him Who made His servant go on a night from the Sacred Mosque to the remote mosque of which We have blessed the precincts, so that We may show to him some of Our signs; surely He is Hearing, the Seeing."[24] The sacred mosque referred to in that passage is in Mecca. As Muhammad conceived Allah's world, nature not only provides special places to be venerated, it also provides the means to punish or reward people.

Qur'anic Images of Geotheomisthosis and Geotheokolasis

In Surah 2, Muhammad recounts the creation of Adam. In his original state, Adam was healthy and obedient to Allah. His pristine garden provided all of his needs, but in verses 35 to 36, Allah is seen giving Adam directions on what and what not to eat. These directions were clearly not followed, for the Qur'an swiftly declares that Adam and his unnamed kin were immediately banished from the bounty of Allah's garden.[25] The Qur'an's retelling of the Genesis account of creation and Adam's original sin is rather brief. Humanity's flawed condition, which results from selfish choices and actions, has plagued humankind ever since, and it established the beliefs in geotheokolasis and geotheomisthosis, the rewards–punishment plan used by Allah. In Islam, there is no way to be freed from the consequences of sin except through Allah's good pleasure and his free will, which depends heavily on earning his favor. To say that the Qur'an uses fire and water as the basis for punishment (*kolasis*) and reward or payment (*misthosis*) is not an understatement. Perhaps nowhere in the Muslim holy book is this more evident than in Surah 9: "Allah has promised to the believing men and believing women gardens, beneath which rivers flow, to abide in them, and goodly dwellings in gardens of perpetual abode; and best of all is Allah's goodly pleasure—that is the grand achievement."[26] Not content with resting on the blessed promise, Surah 9 tempers the blissful image of a future paradise for those deserving of Allah's good will and grace by issuing a command to Muslim leaders: "O Prophet! Strive hard against the unbelievers and the hypocrites and be unyielding to them; and their abode is hell, and evil is the destination."[27] This chapter in the Qur'an also suggests that true believers are not to worry about the plight of unrepentant souls.[28] When calamities like hurricanes strike the non-Muslim world, puritans will not likely be inclined to provide relief to recipients of Allah's geotheokolasis. To the puritan Muslim, there cannot be an innocent victim of nature; in the puritan mind, natural disasters are just one of the forms of punishment Allah uses against non-Muslims and unbelievers.

For a dweller of a desert land, as Muhammad clearly was, lush gardens and flowing water must have been seen as the basis for the good life. However, Muhammad believed in the importance of the Mosaic laws and was not alone in seeing decrees of divine justice in the natural world. For many years in the United States, some Christians have believed that storms and other destructive events in nature are to be regarded as "acts of God." In fact, the phrase has become part of the legal lexicon of American jurisprudence.[29] It may be one of the few existing concepts associated with secular life in America that the puritan Islamic community will recognize and support.

Nevertheless, to the puritan and his *umma*, there can be little doubt that both the good and the bad that come by way of nature are known and approved by an omnipotent Allah. "And with Him are the keys of the unseen treasures—none knows them but He; and He knows what is in the land and the sea; and there falls not a leaf but He knows it, nor a grain in the darkness of the earth, nor anything green nor dry but [it is all] in a clear book."[30] In writing to his followers, Muhammad warned them, "Do you not see that Allah created the heavens and the earth with truth? If He please He will take you off and bring a new creation, and this is not difficult for Allah."[31] Allah is able and willing to change his mind about dispensing blessings to his believers in their earthly existence. Muhammad even reminded himself: "Maybe my Lord will give me what is better than your garden, and send on it a thunderbolt from heaven so that it shall become even ground without plant. Or its waters should sink down into the ground so that you are unable to find it."[32]

Qur'anic images of geotheomisthosis and geotheokolasis often bring to mind gardens, fires, and even the impenetrable dark of night. Each is used to contrast the fates of the good and the evil. "For those who do good is good [reward] and more [than this]; and blackness or ignominy shall not cover their faces; these are the dwellers of the garden; in it they shall abide. And [as for] those who have earned evil, the punishment of an evil is the like of it, and abasement shall come upon them—they shall have none to protect them from Allah—as if their faces had been covered with slices of dense darkness of night; these are the inmates of the fire; in it they shall abide."[33]

While those depictions are vivid illustrations of geotheomisthosis and geotheokolasis, there are perhaps few better examples of divine punishment on a sinful people by natural means than the story of the great flood. In some of these images, one can see strong implications for theocratic control of society. Noah (Nuh), as told in both the Bible and the Qur'an, built an ark to save himself and his family from a watery death. According to the Qur'an, Noah warned his fellow men, but they refused to listen to him and submit themselves to Allah. "But they rejected him," writes Muhammad, "so We delivered him and those with him in the ark, and we made them rulers and drowned those who rejected Our communications; see then what was the end of the [people] warned."[34] Muhammad believed that others outside of the ark survived the flood event and became the people ruled by Noah and his family. Apparently, survivors were not given Noah's warning to submit to Allah, since they did not suffer the consequences of failing to surrender to Allah. As I will later describe, the geotheomisthosis scenario portrayed in the flood event portends a political vision of the future, for those who have submitted to Allah are to be the rulers over others. For now, however, let us take a closer look at divine wrath and blessings administrated through natural forces.

As a product of a dweller in a desert environment, the Qur'an uses water in images of geotheomisthosis. Images project life-giving water coming from clouds and flowing through gardens. "Who made the earth a resting place for you and the heaven a canopy and [Who] sends down rain from the cloud, then brings forth with it subsistence for you of the fruits; therefore do not set up rivals to Allah while you know."[35] Muhammad clearly saw flowing rivers and gardens rising on their shores as rewards for carrying out the duty of a Muslim. "But as to those who are careful of [their duty to] their Lord, they shall have gardens beneath which rivers flow, abiding in them; an entertainment from their Lord, and that which is with Allah is best for the righteous."[36]

Not only was Muhammad convinced that water from the sky is a blessing from Allah, he believed that other celestial bodies were designed for human use, although most assuredly under the auspices of Allah. "And He has made subservient for you the night and the day and the sun and the moon, and the stars are made subservient by His command; most surely there are signs in this for a people who wonder."[37] Muhammad also recognized the role played by stars in helping ships to cleave the sea.[38] The seas are made to provide believers with "fresh flesh" and ornaments, such as pearls and shells, from the depths.[39] The Qur'an further points out that Allah's world is created with various hues, so it is a pleasure for the eye to behold.[40] In all of the bounty found in Allah's world, Muhammad insisted that the creator's divine hand can be seen. This insight, however, is only available to those who are mindful, who ponder, and who do not show pride. Furthermore, Muhammad promised, in effect, that there is a sign from Allah in the hydrologic cycle for those who listen. In the desert, water is the most precious commodity; water gives life to the earth and to civilizations and with Allah's blessings, the desert-dwellers' needs will be met.[41]

Whereas the water cycle is used by Allah as a means to bring forth life where there was none, he uses the forces of violent storms to decimate life where humans displease him. "When Allah intends evil to a people, there is no averting it, and besides Him they have no protector. He it is Who shows you the lightning causing fear and hope and [Who] brings up the heavy cloud. And the thunder declares His glory with His praise, and the angels too for awe of Him; and He sends the thunderbolts and smites with them whom He pleases, yet they dispute concerning Allah, and He is mighty in prowess."[42] In a message that is reminiscent of the refrain heard in some Christian circles, "the Lord giveth and the Lord taketh away," the Qur'an tells of a man who did not spend his wealth in a way pleasing to Allah. Though the man's life was spent for the most part in lush environs, the fruits of his life's work were minimal and fell short of Allah's expectations. "Does one of you like that he should have a garden of palms and vines with streams flowing beneath it; he has in it all kinds of fruits; and old age has overtaken him and he has weak offspring, when, [lo!] a whirlwind with fire in it smites it so it becomes blasted; thus Allah makes the communication clear to you that you may reflect."[43] Muhammad described Allah as ready, willing, and able to take away that which he has given. There is certainly a psychological imperative in these passages that does not permit a believer to become over-confident in her position relative to Allah. On the contrary, the fear of having violent storms descend upon one's house could well produce a persistent level of anxiety in the devoted follower of the Prophet.

Muhammad's Use of Nature in the Lessons of Life

In addition to direct examples of natural events and conditions used by Allah to reward or punish people, the Qur'an employs metaphors to teach lessons about life and humanity's dependence on Allah for survival. This is not unlike certain Christian writers, especially those texts written by Puritans that reference the sea.[44] Surah 10 illustrates this point by revealing that Allah makes people travel by sea and that all is well while the ship is under the power of a pleasant breeze. However, when the ship becomes tossed about by a contrary, violent wind, the passengers offer prayers of petition to

Allah to convince him to still the dangers confronting them. They plead with Allah: "If thou dost deliver us from this, we will most certainly be the grateful ones. But when He delivers them, lo! They are unjustly rebellious in the earth. O men! Your rebellion is against your own souls—provision [only] of this world's life—then to Us shall be your return, so We will inform you of what you did."[45] From this passage, it is not much of a stretch to argue that believers should not become too secure about their place in Allah's world. Indeed, when Allah does still the waters of life, the believer must remain diligent and not fall back on sinful ways. In Surah 69, Muhammad used a seafaring metaphor to remind his followers of their dependence on Allah's good will: "And they disobeyed the Apostle of their Lord, so He punished them with a vehement punishment. Surely We bore you up in a ship when the water rose high, so that we make it a reminder to you, and that the retaining ear might retain it."[46]

After telling about a man's loss of his home to the will of Allah through the forces of nature, Muhammad went on to write: "And his wealth was destroyed, so he began to wring his hands for what he had spent on it, while it lay, having fallen down upon its roofs, and he said: Ah me! . . . And he had no host to help him besides Allah nor could he defend himself. Here is protection only Allah's, the True One; He is best in [the giving of] reward and best in requiting."[47] Muhammad's message in using these nature-based metaphors is clear: Allah gives and Allah takes away, so the believer must always be diligent in learning and following Allah's teachings.

Muhammad believed that earthquakes and tremors are used by Allah to teach wayward people to see the truth. Even building of houses out of rock cannot prevail against Allah: "And the dwellers of the rock certainly rejected the messengers: and We gave them Our communications, but they turned aside from them; and they hewed houses in the mountains in security. So the rumbling overtook them in the morning. And what they earned did not avail them."[48] In telling the story of the exodus from Egypt, the Qur'an describes how Allah used an earthquake to kill seventy people, as chosen by Moses (*Musa*), as payment for their reversion to paganism. This aspect of the exodus from Egypt is actually a significant departure from the Jewish Torah and the Christian Bible.[49] Muhammad described the events that followed the worshiping of a golden calf: "And Moses chose out of his people seventy men for Our appointment; so when the earthquake overtook them, he said: My Lord! If thou hadst pleased, thou hadst destroyed them before and myself [too]; wilt thou destroy us for what the fools among us have done? It is naught but Thy trial, Thou makest err with it whom thou pleasest and guidest whom Thou pleasest: Thou are our guardian, therefore forgive us and have mercy on us, and Thou art the best of the forgivers."[50] Here, the Qur'an used nature to reinforce the belief that the individual's salvation is strictly earned at the discretion of Allah.

Summary

The concept of geotheology, including geopiety, geotheomisthosis, and geotheokolasis, provides a fuller understanding of Islam and its relationship to space. It is important to remember that puritan Muslims do not simply want to prove a theological point to encourage others to follow in their footsteps. They are compelled to serve a bigger vision of the world, both in earthly time and in the hereafter. They have imagined geographies of how life should be lived both in the present time and in the afterlife; the source of their imagined world is the Qur'an coupled with Muhammad's imagination. As Muhammad's use of the exodus story illustrates, Muslim leaders have a role to play in deciding who is punished for a nation's sins. Chapter 5 takes a closer look at the ways in which Allah's wrath and rewards are dispensed and awarded to towns and nations. A puritan follower of Muhammad wants to avoid Allah's wrath on his lands and people, so he may well risk it all to make sure that everyone in his community and nation submits to the will of Allah. This is an example of just one significant geotheological reason for the expansion of contested spaces in the West.

Chapter 5

Toward a Theocratic Nation

Introduction

In the wake of the events of 9/11, the Bush administration and its coalition allies seemed determined to take the fight against terrorism directly to radical Muslims. Although invading Iraq was publicly argued to be based on Iraqi president Saddam Hussein's possession of weapons of mass destruction (WMDs), the Bush administration's actions suggested other motives. In fact, the administration's actions suggested it knew that certain puritan Muslims were engaged in terrorist activities, and these puritans would divert their human and financial resources to defend the Muslim heartland against foreign invaders. Supposedly, this would lead to fewer terrorist attacks in Europe and the United States because, as with most religions, the idea that certain places are holy and, indeed, holier than others, is important. As I discussed in chapter 4, puritan Muslims regard the Middle East as the hearth of Islam and well worth protecting.

Such a regard for space, including the governance of human settlements and social organizations like towns, cities, and nations, is not unique to Islam. Clearly, Jews, Puritan Christians, and Shintoists, for instance, have perceived certain lands as sacred. Many religions are classified by geographers as ethnic religions because of their identification with specific cultural groups. In the case of universalizing religions that seek converts of every race and ethnicity, such as Christianity and Islam, ethnic interpretations have certainly played roles in creating schisms and in sacralizing and desacralizing places.[1] Landscapes and seascapes are often associated with the formation of an ethnic group's identity (for example, by making them a farming community or a fishing village), so they are more often than not tied to the group's political and religious identities. Spatial connections such as these, therefore, have clear implications for framing the worldviews of the group's members. Even universalizing religions such as Islam and Christianity, which seek a global following, have various ethnicities outside of the Middle East that believe certain places and nations, including their own, have been chosen by God for his purposes. Even some Americans, including past and present political leaders, believe that the United States has a divine mission—to serve as a beacon of democratic hope for the world.[2] This idea is rooted in colonial Puritanism and is a continuance of manifest destiny. It is, therefore, a mistake to think that Islamic recognition of sacred and defensible spaces is fixed and limited to traditional Arab lands. As more spaces, towns, and nations are added to the expanding world of Islam, there will be a corresponding spreading out of militants who are compelled to protect holy places from disbelievers. There are theological motives for puritans to want to create a spatially expansive Islamic nation that can protect Muslims from the consequences of geotheokolasis. Given that these motives will give rise to more contested spaces within existing sovereign states, it is worth exploring Qur'anic imagery that inspires puritan Muslims to press forward with theocratic visions of governance.

Puritans' View of Islamic Governance

There are currently forty-six countries worldwide that have Muslim majorities, and a number of other countries have sizable minority Muslim populations, including Ghana, Guinea-Bissau, and Malawi. Although not a plurality, India's Muslim population, which, as a percentage of the entire country's population, grew by 2 percent between 1995 and 2006, is now over 140 million citizens.[3] Muslim populations already represent a significant portion of the body politic of the United Nations (UN). Of the planet's 196 independent countries (which is a debated number), 192 are members of the UN.[4] Although affected by regional juristic traditions, this means that nearly one-quarter of the UN is already influenced to some extent by various incarnations of Islamic social and political views. Beyond the United Nations, the world's second largest intergovernmental organization is the Organization of Islamic Conference (OIC) with fifty-seven member nations.[5]

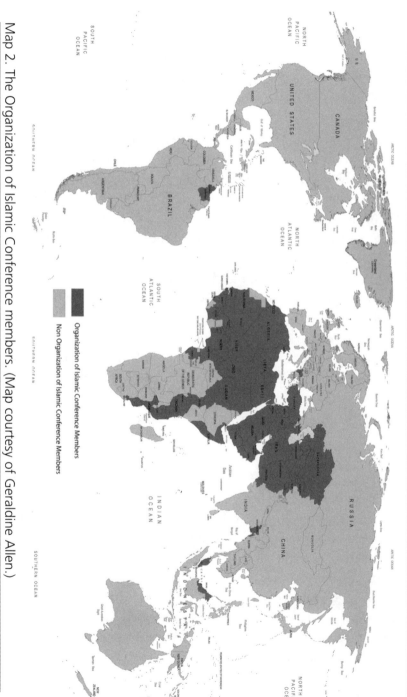

Map 2. The Organization of Islamic Conference members. (Map courtesy of Geraldine Allen.)

Large enclaves are forming in the United States and in Europe; there are also sizable Muslim communities growing in Latin America. For example, the South American country of Guyana is now the home of some 76,000 Muslims, representing a 15 percent increase since 1995.[6]

With the possible exception of Turkey, nearly all of the countries with Muslim majorities are at least tolerant of legislation inspired by *sharia* law, which are the laws regulating Islamic society. With other countries boasting significant Muslim minority populations expressing a worldview taken from Qur'anic imagery, Islamic influence in global politics will likely increase. In the case of those who subscribe to puritan Islam, there is an insistence on the purity of lifestyles among the residents of a town or nation, for fear of inviting geotheokolasis. Moreover, they believe that they have multiple divine, evangelical, and punitive missions to fulfill. As puritan Muslims spread throughout the world, they believe they are fulfilling a geoteleological vision or prophesy, much like manifest destiny. Muhammad was clear about this future vision of an expanding Muslim world: "And on the day when We will raise up a witness out of every nation, then shall no permission be given to those who disbelieve, nor shall they be made to solicit favor."[7] To the puritan Muslim, the establishment of mosques in Western cities signifies that it is time to deliver Allah's warning to those nations, lest they should experience Allah's wrath for not converting to the one true faith.

The Qur'an offers no mercy for people and nations that disbelieve and reject the words of their appointed apostle. Consider this passage: "And when those who are unjust shall see the chastisement, it shall not be lightened for them, nor shall they be respited."[8] Further on in the Qur'an, reference is made to cities that had been previously warned about the consequences of disbelief. "The overthrown cities did He overthrow, so there covered them that which covered . . . this is a warner of the warners of old. The near event draws nigh."[9] This passage emphasizes the belief that punishment awaits residents of cities, including some followers of Islam, if Allah views the city as sinful. Puritans are, therefore, certainly inclined to discourage others from public displays of unbelief. When a puritan thinks that the city in which she is living has, indeed, rejected the teachings of her faith, she may turn to the Qur'an for a deeper understanding of the situation. She will find that Allah has always punished disbelieving cities, but he will deliver his wrath on his schedule. "And [as for] these towns, We destroyed them when they acted unjustly, and We have appointed a time for their destruction."[10] In the minds of some residents of Muslim nations and enclaves, there is a psychological imperative and a sociological need to enforce Allah's laws on the entire nation. Because the self and the small group can provoke Allah's wrath on towns and nations, so, among puritans, there are strong social and psychological pressures on them to use the political apparatus of the state to police both private and public behaviors. As related in the Qur'an: "We did destroy generations before you when they were unjust, and their apostles had come to them with clear arguments, and they would not believe; thus do We recompense the guilty people."[11]

Figure 5. OIC Flags over the American Heartland. (Photo courtesy of the author.)

With specific respect to towns, the Qur'an declares that followers should "[consider] a town safe and secure to which its means of subsistence come in abundance from every quarter; but it became ungrateful to Allah's favors, therefore Allah made it taste the utmost degree of hunger and fear because of what they wrought."[12] The text further declares: "When we wish to destroy a town, We send Our commandment to the people of it who lead easy lives, but they transgress there in; thus the word proves true against it, so We destroy it with utter destruction."[13] It is possible, therefore, to see that any and all generations and towns, including those made up of believers, are subject to the Qur'an's image of societal chastisement at the hands of Allah. Again, the Qur'an warns even the believer: "Do you not see that Allah created the heavens and the earth with truth? If He please He will take you off and bring a new creation."[14] On the other hand, those who abide by the Qur'an's vision of social order will be permitted to enter gardens under which flow life-giving rivers.[15]

In earlier chapters, I explained how a fear of eternal damnation could create a psychological crisis in some believers. This condition, which was well described by the turn of the century sociologist Max Weber in his seminal work on Calvinism and capitalism, can logically be applied to Islam. Indeed this mental crisis is made worse by the fear of Allah's wrath being leveled on one's town or nation. The Qur'an explains the root cause of this geo-theological crisis: "They hope for His mercy and fear His chastisement; surely the chastisement of your Lord is a thing to be cautious of. And there is not a town but We will destroy it before the day of resurrection or chastise it with a severe chastisement; this is written in the Divine ordinance."[16] To some puritan Muslims, these passages have the capacity to create deepening psychological dilemmas over a concern for the ways in which their neighbors, Muslim or non-Muslim, conduct their lives. Together with the psychological burden of understanding one's own behavior in light of Allah's will, the social aspects of divine retribution make the thoughts of the puritan Muslim perplexing to consider and difficult to understand for the secular mind.

Imagery of a Puritan Islamic Nation

Puritan Islam sees all human life in its original, created form as one undivided nation that is defined here as a group of people who share a common heritage and a mutual desire to control space. In the Qur'an, the multiplicity of nations and states is the result of sin. The pristine Qur'anic image of one global nation under Allah provides puritan Muslims with a strong motive to return to that idealized *Gemeinschaft*, or, roughly, "informal community," existence. Hence, there is a desire among fundamentalists to adopt and enforce laws that demand godly lifestyles and cultures. That is the intent of *sharia* law. To describe this geotheological vision, it is necessary to frame Qur'anic passages as concepts that readers in the twenty-first century can appreciate and understand.

In the United States, Islam projects a varied complexion. While there are enclaves of Shia and Sunni Muslims living in the United States, the Nation of Islam (NOI), which was founded and operated by African Americans, and other similar organizations, create significant diversity in the growing American population of Muslims. Indeed, as I will show in the next chapter, the NOI, under the leadership of minister Louis Farrakhan, signifies the formation of a distinct community, based in large measure on an ethnic and a racial interpretation of Islam that is regarded by many traditional Muslims as heresy.[17] The primary reason for traditionalists seeing the NOI as heretical is because of its recognition of modern-day prophets, including the ongoing belief that Wallace Fard Muhammad, founder of the NOI, was God himself.

Minister Wallace Fard Muhammad lived and preached in Detroit, Michigan, during the 1930s. He claimed that he was the *mahdi* (or divinely guided one), the second coming of Christ, Jehovah, and various other names that suggested a divinely appointed mission to share truths with a restricted segment of Allah's people.[18] (It is interesting that he would allow himself to be called Christ because Sunnis and Shia would not have used this title, as it is associated with Christianity. It does, however, reveal the influence of Christianity among African American converts to Islam.) When Wallace Fard Muhammad died in 1934, Elijah Muhammad, a devoted follower originally named Elijah Poole, carried on Fard's mission. While historic Islam seeks converts from all races, NOI is an ethnic, racially-centered interpretation of a universalizing religion. Its mission is to "teach the downtrodden and defenseless Black people a thorough Knowledge of God and of themselves, and to put them on the road to Self-Independence with a superior culture and higher civilization than they had previously experienced."[19] Nonetheless, the NOI's conception of "nation," absent its focus on race, is consistent with the use of the term found in the Qur'an. Its emphasis on sovereignty places it at odds with the larger, secular society because the organization has historically wanted to govern its own country, carved away from the United States.

The goal of self-independence, based on a shared cultural heritage, is what defines a nation. Hence, it is important to illuminate the critical geopolitical distinctions between ethnic and national groups. In thinking about the emerging world of Muhammad, it is necessary to consider its materialization in light of those distinctions. In the Qur'an, the words "nation" and "town" occur rather frequently, while the more precisely bordered political unit called a state, in any of its various guises, is virtually nonexistent. Furthermore, ethnicity is a relatively recent sociological categorization, so the Qur'an does not use it. Nonetheless, when reading the Qur'an, we can infer that an ethnic group is similar to a nation. Both are made up of people who share common beliefs and cultural characteristics, but, there is a crucial difference: Attachment to land or a specific place and a desire to govern it seems to differentiate a nation from an ethnic group. This, unfortunately, has the capacity to lead to conflict over the governance of space.

Whereas a community, as discussed in chapter 2, may be defined in geographical or psychological terms, nations and towns are tied to specific spaces. As people move away from one country and settle in emerging ethnic enclaves in foreign places, immigrants may adopt new national identities and community memberships. When these new identities and memberships get mixed up with geotheological imaginings inspired by the Qur'an, it is possible that conflicts between charter residents and puritan immigrants may develop, especially if the settlers believe that the lifestyles of the charter citizens and moderate Muslims invite the wrath of Allah on the immigrants' new towns and nations.

Now that we have established some concepts to frame Qur'anic images of towns and nations, it is possible to see how modern followers of Islamism are liable to view everyone's behavior in public spaces. This undertaking also enables us to appreciate why theocracy is the preferred polity of fundamentalist Muslims. Islamism's view of theocratic governance is taken from the Qur'an, so, as a movement, it is dedicated to the re-creation of a super Islamic nation, which knows no boundaries. Since the Qur'an's conceptions of towns and nations, as well as their political implications, are vastly different from Western and highly secular understandings, conflict is likely to happen.

The Need for Theocracy

The southern border of Saudi Arabia is not a clearly demarked boundary; on a map, it appears as hash lines. These lines represent the separation of the country from its neighbors, Yemen, Oman, and the United Arab Emirates, but these hash lines tell a deeper story about the regional culture. When Muhammad wrote the Qur'an, nomadic life in the desert was even more pronounced than it is today. In nomadic societies, where residents practice transhumance, or the seasonal moving of sheep and other livestock between grazing lands, there are few permanent housing structures, outside of cities, that enable populations to be generally fixed in place. The map's hash lines indicate frontiers rather than definite boundaries. The border between Saudi Arabia and its southern neighbors is more of a transition zone between sovereign states. Even today, nomads move back and forth across the shifting sands of the southern portion of the Saudi Peninsula in search of forage for their animals and, with that, the means for the nomads' own livelihoods. In this case, it made better political sense to establish frontiers rather than boundaries. Imagine the difficulties associated with accounting for residents of Yemen, for example, when perhaps a sizable portion of its population is absent half the year. In cases like this, personal identity as reflected in nationality is extremely important, given that nations, in this sense, refer more to ethnic groups that want to govern themselves than to formal countries or states. To Muhammad, it seemed that nationality took on that sort of meaning; it did not have clearly demarked boundaries.

In the Abrahamic tradition, it can be argued that all social organizations, like ethnic groups and nationalities, have divine purposes. In cosmology, humans were members of one *Gemeinschaft*-like nation made up of intimate groups: "We have created you of a male and female, and made you tribes and families that you may know each other."[20] The concept of multiple nations, as Muhammad imagined it, was a product of groups of people rejecting Allah's communications. As mentioned previously, absent the focus on race, the Qur'an's model of the nation is similar to the nation conceptualized by the Nation of Islam. Such an impression of humanity has global geopolitical implications because the adoption of national identities is often the product of myths concocted by states to create a sense of unity among their people. It is arguably easier to rule over people who believe it is natural to submit to the rules of one's own people rather than to another group's notions of proper social behavior. As Muhammad explained, "[All] people are a single nation; so Allah raised prophets as bearers of good news and as warners, and He revealed with them the Book with truth, that it might judge between people in that which they differed; and none but the very people who were given it differed about it after clear arguments had come to them, revolting among themselves; so Allah has guided by His will those who believe to the truth about which they differed; and Allah guides whom He pleases to the right path."[21] Divisions within humanity are, therefore, the result of sin, but Allah continues to guide those people, including nations, that he finds worthy. In their original, natural state of being, all people lived in harmony with each other and with Allah. There was no need for secular government to control the wayward behaviors of disbelievers.[22] This is the essence of *Gemeinschaft*— living among others who share a psychological bond as well as an attachment to a certain place or geography.

With humanity divided by sin, Allah administers two kinds of chastisements on towns and nations. One kind is expected on Judgment Day—its results are absolute and final. The other is both corrective and punitive; it is administered on earth while there is still time to submit to the will of Allah and his Prophet. Earthly punishments can be placed on individuals, towns, or nations. Obviously punishments leveled on towns and nations will impact individuals, so, as mentioned earlier, there is a psychological dilemma for those concerned about how the behaviors of those around them can impact themselves and their families. To ease concerns about how humans should govern space, the Qur'an declares that of all towns, Mecca is to be set apart to guide all nations: "Most surely the first house appointed for men is the one at Mecca, blessed and a guide for all nations."[23] To the puritan, it seems then that whoever controls the spaces of Mecca will be at the center of the global Islamic nation, the emerging world of Muhammad.

Seeking Allah's guidance in national affairs and governance of people and spaces is supported in the Qur'an. It tells us that Abraham (*Ibrahim*) and Ishmael beseeched Allah to guide their descendants. In Surah 2, Muhammad recalled their prayer of petition: "Make us submissive to Thee and [raise] from our offspring a nation submitting to Thee, and show us our ways of devotion and turn to us [mercifully] . . . and raise up in them an apostle from among them who shall recite to them Thy communications and teach them the Book and the wisdom, and purify them."[24] On the other hand, failure to be guided invites a certain punishment, and that chastisement will occur in earthly time. As Muhammad warned, "certainly We raised in every nation an apostle saying: Serve Allah and shun the Shaitan [Satan]. So there were some of them whom Allah guided and there were others against whom error was due; therefore travel in the land, then see what was then the end of the rejecters."[25] It is worth pointing out that whatever punishment is inflicted on rejecters, puritan Muslims believe that the consequences of Allah's punishments can be seen on the physical landscape.

Earnest followers of another religion or another prophet are likewise due to receive Allah's wrath. Muhammad warned: "If you desire for their guidance [leaders of other religions], yet Allah does not guide them who leads astray, nor shall they have any helpers"; even a nation can be doomed.[26] As mentioned above, earthly punishments are corrective in nature, "so that He might make manifest to them that about which they differ, and that those who disbelieve might know that they are liars."[27] In other places, Muhammad pleaded with people to be aware of the consequences on collective groups of people who fail to abide by Allah's will. In Surah 11, he wrote: "We send not messengers but as announcers of good news and givers of warning; then whoever believes and acts aright, they shall have no fear, nor shall they grieve. And [as for] those who reject our communications, chastisement shall afflict them because they transgressed."[28]

Eternal punishments are given out on Judgment Day to those who fail to submit to Allah. Though nations, as political and sociological concepts, and individuals can both be eternally punished, nations cannot, however, exist in eternity's blessed lands flowing with life-giving rivers, as individuals can. On the surface that may seem odd, but, when one considers that towns and nations are products of Allah's will for this world and for the benefit of his people, it makes sense. As Muhammad described a wayward nation's plight, "Enter into the fire among the nations that have passed away before you from among jinn [genies] and men; whenever a nation shall enter, it shall curse its sister, until when they have all come up with one another into it; the last of them shall say with regard to the foremost of them: Our Lord! These led us astray, therefore give them double chastisement of fire. He will say: Every one shall have double but you do not know."[29] Muhammad most likely knew of the past's failed nations; the Roman Empire and the empire under Alexander the Great were certainly vague memories. No doubt, puritan Muslims of today believe the same fate befell the Union of the Soviet Socialist Republics. To the devoted followers of Islamism, the same can be said for the future of France, the United Kingdom of Great Britain and Northern Ireland, and the United States of America—their days are numbered. In the puritan way of thinking, only a true Islamic nation will be left unscathed by divine wrath.

Muhammad saw nations, and by extension ethnic groups, as short-lived organizations. He wrote that "for every nation there is a doom, so when their doom is come they shall not remain behind the least while, nor shall they go before."[30] Muhammad further declared that Allah is the source of both the good and the bad things that befall individuals, towns, and nations, but he insisted that nations would not last, regardless of their morality: "And every nation had an apostle; so when their apostle came, the matter was decided between them with justice and they shall not be dealt with unjustly. . . . I do not control for myself any harm, or any benefit except what Allah pleases; every nation has a term; when their term comes, they shall not then remain behind for one hour, nor can they go before [their time]."[31] Muhammad assured his followers that those nations punished by the hand of Allah deserve their ultimate and final chastisement: "By Allah, most certainly We sent [apostles] to nations before you, but the Shaitan made their deeds fair-seeming to them, so he is their guardian today, and they shall have a painful punishment."[32] Towns, too, have a fixed term. "Never did We destroy a town but which it had a term made known."[33] Alas, "No people can hasten their doom nor can they postpone [it]."[34] With respect to the fate of towns and nations, there is divine justice at work in ending their existence, and in every case, each town and nation is warned of its impending doom. It is anyone's guess as to what reaction a puritan Muslim settling in a Western enclave will have if his new government offers him bridge-building policies and programs. Will he see Allah at work in guiding his new country or will he see such efforts as the work of Shaitan, designed to mislead Allah's people by seeming to be fair to them?

Non-Islamic nations and towns can be blotted off the landscape by divine retribution for disbelief or because their times have simply expired. Muhammad again and again reminded his readers that Allah sends apostles to warn nations of impending destruction if they refuse to submit to the will of Allah: "And We certainly did destroy generations before you when they were unjust, and their apostles had come to them with clear arguments, and they would not believe; thus do We recompense the guilty people."[35] These pronouncements, which are examples of the puritan's theology of deterrence, are supported by multiple examples, featuring conquering armies waging war in the name of Allah. Successors to the prophet or *caliphs*, such as Abu Bakr, Uthman, and Ali from the seventh century, used Muhammad's examples to win converts and gain territories to satisfy their vision of a world in submission to Allah, and, of course, to themselves. As geographer Chris Park writes, "Within less than a hundred years [of Muhammad's death in 632], Arab Muslims had conquered lands over a vast area—stretching from the Atlantic Ocean in Western Europe to the borders of India, Central Asia, and including Spain, North Africa, Egypt, Syria, Mesopotamia and Persia."[36] Park also wrote that most of the populations subjugated in this expansion were Christian, so, he reasoned, they required political control because they were not guided by Islamic law or *sharia*.[37]

The Qur'an certainly discusses the subjugation of Christian nations. It is important to note that in the preceding and following passages there is scant evidence suggesting that Islam, in its purest form, is a religion of peace when challenged by social forces emerging from people with opposing geotheological views. As Muhammad wrote about the conquest of Christian lands and people, "They say: Allah has taken a son [to himself]! Glory be to Him; He is Self-sufficient; His is what is in the heavens and what is in the earth; you have no authority for this; do you say against Allah what you don't know? Those who forge a lie against Allah shall not be successful. [It is only] a provision in this world, then to Us shall be their return; then We shall make them taste severe punishment because they disbelieved."[38] In that passage, Muhammad was not waiting until the hereafter to deliver divine wrath on Christians. He ordered his followers to remind Christians about the troubles that befell the people of Noah's (*Nuh's*) time. Clearly, their punishment was delivered in earthly time. "Recite to them the story of Nuh when he said to his people: O my people! If my stay and my reminding [you] by the communications of Allah is hard on you, then have it executed against me and give me no respite."[39] The Qur'an goes on to declare that "they rejected him, so We delivered him [Nuh] and those with him in the ark, and We made them rulers and drowned those who rejected Our communications."[40] It is important to note that the wrath of Allah was delivered on Noah's generation because of its lack of belief.

To the puritan Muslim, there is no Qur'anic basis for accepting the presence of large secular institutions in their midst. Unbelieving political authorities are certainly not endorsed in the Qur'an either, for Allah punishes nations that do not believe in him or fail to follow the communications of his Prophet and apostles. Puritan Muslims are reminded by Muhammad that their nations are in jeopardy if Allah perceives their societies in a state of disbelief. As Muhammad warned his followers, "If He please, He can make you pass away, O people! And bring others; and Allah has the power to do this."[41] This passage should cast some light on a simple, yet often misunderstood, aspect of political reality among adherents to Islamism. To followers of Islamism, secularists and moderate Muslims are disbelievers whose presence among the fundamentalists can invite Allah's wrath on their entire nation.

Those who claim to be Muslims while making political and cultural compromises with obvious disbelievers are seen as hypocrites and traitors. In the geotheological imagination of puritans, their plight is now also severe, for Muhammad wrote that his followers are to "[a]nnounce to the hypocrites that they shall have a painful chastisement."[42]

On the other hand, accepting the communications of Allah, whether delivered by him or through one of each nation's appointed apostles, would produce positive results for the puritans and their lands. In Surah 3, Muhammad reminded his followers that "whatever is in the earth is Allah's; and to Allah all things return."[43] He further declared that "those who fly for Allah's sake after they are oppressed, We will most certainly give them a good abode in the world, and the reward of the hereafter is certainly much greater."[44] There is no indication that Allah's blessings on the lands are limited to traditional scared or holy places occupied by Arabs. As Muslims migrate out of those traditional lands, in efforts to escape sectarian violence and oppression, they will find a much better life in North America and Europe, even if they arrive at the bottom of the social ladder. To them, they cannot help but believe that Allah has fulfilled his promise to them. Some immigrants may feel compelled to encourage others around them to submit to Allah, for if Allah can deliver blessings, He will most certainly deliver His wrath upon an undeserving nation. By spreading Islam in their new nations, immigrants are looking to spare their new homes from Allah's punishments.

Summary

A nation in submission to Allah rejects the wrongs of perceived disbelief associated with secular society, does what is right in Allah's eyes, and enjoys the benefits of Allah's benevolence, his geotheomisthosis. In a geoteleological manner, envisioning the re-creation of a single Muslim nation, Muhammad admonished his followers to "hold fast by the covenant of Allah all together and be not disunited, and remember the favor of Allah on you when you were enemies, then He united your hearts so by His favor you became brethren; and you were on the brink of a pit of fire, then He saved you from it; thus does Allah make clear to you His communications that you may follow the right way."[45] Those nations that do not dutifully follow the teachings of Muhammad are cast into the fires of hell.

In the puritan's almost monochrome imagined world, he sees social order in only a few shades of gray. To hope for a return to the Qur'an's image of a pristine Muslim nation, there is no room for debate on most issues concerning an individual's life as it relates to the governance of lands and society. Public displays of disbelief invite the condemnation, ridicule, and perhaps even violent response of puritan Muslims. In their minds, the very deeds of the individual or small group invite the wrath or blessings of Allah. They believe that those towns and countries rejecting a literal relationship with Islam are doomed to an eternal fiery fate. Puritan Muslims' demand for a theocratic government is rooted in the fear that their towns and nations may be punished for disbelief in earthly time.

Chapter 6 takes an in-depth look at some of the organizations operating in the United States that are helping to expand the influence of Islam. Many of these organizations have liaisons with European and American agencies and entities that hope to bring about truly multicultural social environments. These environments, they believe, will ensure peace by creating a sense of shared space, not contested space. I will contrast the stated missions of those organizations with the Qur'anic geotheological imagery we discussed in this and previous chapters.

Chapter 6

American Islam's Two Communities

Introduction

On behalf of an African American community, a young Jordanian American man named Rami Nashashibi, executive director of a Chicago-based Muslim organization called the Inner City Action Network (IMAN), spoke before a gathering of middle-aged, well-dressed immigrant Muslims. The purpose of his speech was to ignite their passions and sympathies for underprivileged, inner-city folk against the economic power structure of the United States that, he believes, discriminates against the African American community. Nashashibi lectured his audience, informing them of their responsibilities to fellow Muslims in the inner city: "You want to build a mosque at the crossroads of the American dream, but you can't afford to ignore the problems of society. . . . I don't want, and you shouldn't want the American dream that is built on complacency. We must be engaged with the issues of America, the marginalized and oppressed; we must engage to transform society."[1] He never provided his audience with a clear depiction of what he meant by transforming society, but one thing is for certain, he wanted them to know that his adopted community needed their sympathy and, by extension, their economic and political support. His speech to immigrant Muslims on behalf of African American Muslim converts living mostly in the inner city suggests that there are two distinct Muslim communities in the United States. One community is filled with Muslim immigrants who have managed to flourish in their new country, and the other is still waiting to enjoy prosperity in the land in which they were born and raised.

121

While there are theological issues that clearly separate members of the American organization called the Nation of Islam (NOI) from other Shia and Sunnis living in America, a major factor separating Sunni converts, who are likely to be African American, from the immigrant community is assimilation.[2] Aminah McCloud, a member of the NOI and professor at DePaul University, echoes Nashashibi's central concern. At the same time, McCloud argues that the separation of American Muslims into either immigrant or American-convert communities has occurred because immigrants are too consumed with pursuing the American dream to be concerned about the plight of fellow Muslims living in urban areas.[3] "[I]n their pursuit of the American dream and whiteness," she argues, "the new arrivals have largely ignored African American Muslims and have assumed that immigrant Muslims can impose their understanding of Islam on African Americans."[4] With respect to economic dissimilarities between immigrants and African American converts, she is correct. For the time being, at least, the numbers of immigrant Muslims achieving middle-class status far outpaces that of their African American counterparts.[5]

Figure 6. No trespassing at this affluent mosque. (Photo courtesy of the author.)

The growth in the number of middle-class Muslim immigrants living in the United States has occurred while Islamic groups like IMAN lobby government officials to build bridges with Muslim Americans and, by extension, the entire Islamic world. As the example above revealed, many of these groups are influenced by politically savvy people drawn primarily from the African American population. Organizations like the American Muslim Alliance (AMA), Council on American–Islamic Relations (CAIR), Islamic Circle of North America (ICNA), and the Islamic Society of North America (ISNA) share association with a larger African American group called the Muslim Alliance in North America (MANA). This list of associations is rather lengthy, which is quite a feat considering that the majority of Muslims living in the United States were born in other countries and are less likely to identify with these causes, which are motivated by civil rights era issues. In the name of religion, these organizations carry out their missions as activist entities that could further separate them from Christian and even secular spheres of mainstream American life.

The trappings and social bonds of religion, outside the purview of Christian organizations, gives the members of these African-American-led organizations a higher level of uniqueness and a sense of connectedness to foreign people who have no real basis for understanding the African American experience and worldview. The connection with potential Muslim immigrants from diverse countries is of a political nature due to the fact that convert-led organizations exist for political reasons. In other words, their work, supposedly on behalf of Islam, connects these organizations to foreigners who they really do not know. Clearly the immigrant community does not know much about the African American experience either. They are two distinct communities linked by little more than the converts' false assumption that Islam is the black man's religion.

Many of MANA's leaders are employed as professors in American universities and some of them serve on boards of directors and advisory councils for think tanks whose aims are to benefit African Americans by associating their organizations with the political force of Islam. However meaningful those goals are for helping to create a sense of belonging and self-worth among the descendants of West African slaves, these groups ironically seek to align themselves with foreigners whose ancestors actively took part in the slave trade and whose racial identities are most often different from their own.[6]

Figure 7. Middle-class and mostly mainstream certainly describes this Muslim neighborhood near Cincinnati, Ohio. (Photo courtesy of the author.)

Figure 8. Route to the Mosque of Greater Cincinnati. (Photo courtesy of the author.)

Beyond a few religious words and personal names, African American converts probably know very little about Afghan, Arab, Berber, or Iranian cultures, let alone the Indonesian and Pakistani experiences, which are the world's largest Muslim-dominated countries. Despite the lack of shared histories and backgrounds, the work of these organizations' members, as politically active Muslims, is helping to pave the way for future groups of Muslim people, who carry with them cultures that are alien to all Americans of colonial descent, regardless of their racial and religious identities. As I will show shortly, the evolving social and political situation suggests that converts and immigrants are, at their cores, philosophically located at different extremes of the political spectrum. It appears to be a situation best described as: "the enemy of my enemy is my friend."

Already there are significant differences among American and immigrant Muslims in regard to certain attitudes. African American Muslims are the least likely segment of Islamic America to condemn al Quaeda,[7] due to a deep-seated distrust of the government that has oppressed blacks for centuries. This is especially important, considering that, all together, only 40 percent of Muslims in America believe that Arabs carried out the attacks of September 11, 2001; in fact, it is easy for them to believe that the Bush administration orchestrated the attacks in order to justify a war against Islam.[8] Further evidence of the separation of Muslim communities into two major camps is revealed by the fact that only 13 percent of African American Muslims have a favorable view of national conditions, compared to 29 percent for other native-born Muslims and 45 percent for Muslim immigrants.[9] African American Muslims and other converts born in the United States, according to the Pew report, are more likely to feel "singled out" by police and suffer harassment or other types of institutionalized racism and bigotry than those who have immigrated.[10]

Many politically active Muslim groups in the United States also have a mission to address traditional African American causes like affirmative action, universal healthcare, and urban renewal. From the discussion that follows, it appears that Muslim converts are interested in building bridges with Muslim immigrants to gain support for their causes and to create a larger block of voters; however, there are a number of issues that separate the two communities.

African American Islam

Despite its geographically expansive name, the World Community of Al-Islam in the West, which is better known as the Nation of Islam (NOI), is a phenomenon of the United States. As we discussed briefly in the previous chapter, it was founded in Detroit, Michigan, in 1930 by Wallace Dodd Fard. In keeping with public displays of submission to Allah, Fard changed his name to Wallace Fard Muhammad. Fard apparently received an epiphany while working with Timothy (Noble Drew) Ali, the founder of the Moorish Holy Temple of Science Organization, which would eventually grow to become the NOI. Ali taught Fard that African Americans were actually of Moorish or Arab descent, though this is, in actuality, false.[11] While the Moors and Berbers of Algeria, Morocco, and Tunisia are something of a Mediterranean people and are more likely to display white European physical traits rather than black African features, the ancestors of African Americans lived originally much further south on the west coast of Africa in Cameroon, Nigeria, Liberia, Togo, and the Ivory Coast.[12] These places are over a thousand miles away from the homelands of the Moors and Berbers.

More importantly, though, Wallace Fard Muhammad taught his followers that African Americans were originally Muslims and that the devil, in the form of the white man, had forced Christianity upon African Americans. The Qur'an provided Fard and his successor, Elijah Muhammad, with some tantalizing statements that seemed to confirm these ethnocentric and even racist ideas. The Muslim holy book confirmed that Abraham (*Ibrahim*) was indeed a Muslim, not a Jew or Christian.[13] Furthermore, it showed that the seed of Abraham and Imran, an ancient people of southern Jordan, Canaan, and northern Saudi Arabia, were the true chosen people. Apparently, the founders of NOI assumed that these places, despite being located on the other side of the continent of Africa and in southwestern Asia, were their ancestral homes. Nonetheless, as the Qur'an states, the famous patriarchs of Christianity and Judaism were Muslims. "And who forsakes the religion of Ibrahim [Abraham] but he who makes himself a fool, and most certainly We chose him in this world, and in the hereafter he is most surely among the righteous. When his Lord said to him, Be a Muslim, he said: I submit myself to the Lord of the worlds. And the same did Ibrahim enjoin on his sons and [so did] Yaqoub [Jacob]. O my sons! Surely Allah has chosen for you [this] faith, therefore die not unless you are Muslims."[14]

This message would have resonated well among a people in need of a positive identity. Indeed, in the 1920s and 1930s, African Americans, who most often had little formal education, and whose parents had experienced untold misery as slaves and subsequently as second-class citizens in the so-called land of the free, should not be blamed for finding salve for their tortured identity in Islam's distorted message. To some of them, the lessons taught in the Qur'an must have had great appeal. Imagine that you are poor, disadvantaged, and segregated, and the education provided to you in public schools is of meager quality. To you, the world, literally, is black and white; therefore, any place outside of white Europe must be the home of the black man. Once you have accepted the notion that Christianity and Judaism appear to be dominated by white men, and that, according to the Qur'an, father Abraham was neither a Jew nor a Christian, but a submissive Muslim, you might begin to see Muhammad's teachings as good news. "Surely Allah chose Adam and Nuh [Noah] and the descendants of Ibrahim and the descendants of Imran above the nations."[15] Muhammad assured his followers that they are chosen, asking, "Do they envy the people for what Allah has given them of His grace? But indeed We have given to Ibrahim's children the Book and the wisdom, and We have given them a grand kingdom."[16]

To an oppressed and poorly educated people, geography was as obscure and abstract as the strict methodology used in the discipline of history. To African Americans, there were only three historic eras: a golden age that existed before slavery; slavery; and post-slavery days that brought only hard work, if it could be found, and little security. The idea that the Qur'an was written five or six centuries after the gospels and the epistles of Paul made little difference to them. For those who knew that there was a significant expanse of time between the writing of the Christian gospels and the days of Muhammad, it meant little to discount the message of the Qur'an because, after all, it was the angel Gabriel who revealed the truth to Muhammad, and he was told, as Muslims believe, that the earlier spiritualists were in error.

Revealed by the biography of Malcolm X, a twentieth-century African American rights activist, newly acquired literacy skills and travel to Mecca opened his eyes to racial diversity within global Islam. Malcolm X, who was originally named Malcolm Little, was assassinated by black nationalist Muslims in 1965 after his pilgrimage to Mecca (*hajj*) and subsequent conversion to Sunni Islam. The motive behind his murder rested with his path toward building a multiracial Islamic community in the United States.

The idea of a multiracial Muslim American community did not die with Malcolm X. Warith Deen Mohammad, born in 1933 as the succeeding son of the black separatist Elijah Muhammad from the Nation of Islam, also sought to leave behind notions of black separatism. Going against his father's teachings, he tried to move the NOI, which went through several name changes, toward a more mainstream position on Islamic matters and perspectives, principally those of Sunni Islam. In 1981, Louis Farrakhan, who did not like the idea of allowing non-blacks into his community, started his own movement, handily renamed the Nation of Islam. His views were a continuation of Elijah Muhammad's teachings. Despite this splinter, American Islam, under the leadership of Warith Deen Mohammad, moved into a new era of reaching out to all Americans.

In the 1990s, Warith Deen Mohammad became the first Muslim to deliver an invocation before the United States Senate, and in 1993 he became the first Muslim to deliver an Islamic prayer at the inaugural Interfaith Prayer Service held by then-president Bill Clinton. He had the same honor in 1997. One of Warith Deen Mohammad's goals was to make connections with the broader Islamic world, especially the Sunnis in the Middle East. However, by 2003, his efforts to build a bridge between native-born Muslim converts and immigrants produced few success stories.[17]

The Nation of Islam, in its formative years (1930s to 1975), sought separate spaces for black Muslims. Meanwhile, black Christian leaders like Martin Luther King Jr., Ralph Abernathy, and many others, believed that lasting change and black improvement were best achieved within the existing infrastructure of the American political and educational systems. These leaders saw themselves as Americans and as Christian brothers to white Baptists, Catholics, and others, so they demanded to be treated thusly. An unknown number of whites supported their efforts to achieve equality before the law.

The political empowerment methods popularized by Martin Luther

King Jr. have, to some extent, been embraced by Muslim Americans who have found that the existing political infrastructure provides an effective means for achieving their goals. Many Americans no doubt believe Islam belongs not to American converts but to those whose origins lay in the Middle East. However, Islam is now seen by nearly one million African Americans as a means to achieve a sense of community and identity. Despite religious rhetoric and notions of social bridge-building, especially that which comes from organizations like the American Society of Muslims and the North American Muslim Alliance, the goal of these organizations is still rooted in issues that appeal to the liberal leftist segment of the African American community. However, the African American community is now diversifying itself over religion, economics, and, to a lesser extent, politics. According to the missions of organizations associated with the African American Islamic community, it seems that these groups make a number of assumptions about Muslim immigrants suggesting political linkages with them are expected and advantageous to both segments of American Islam (meaning Muslim immigrants and American converts). It is important to take a longer look at Muslim organizations operating in the United States and compare them to what is known about Qur'anic geotheology.

In the Name of Religion

A number of relatively new domestic organizations have dedicated themselves to advancing traditional black issues, but they are doing so in the name of Islam. Among the leaders of this new movement is a University of Kentucky associate professor of Islamic Studies named Ihsan Bagby. He was identified by Jewish social commentator David Horowitz as one of America's most dangerous academics—a charge he vehemently refutes.[18] Nevertheless, Bagby is a politically active professor working on behalf of issues that appeal to the black community. As an African American convert to Islam, he has developed a liberal view of Muhammad's faith. He holds a PhD in Near Eastern Studies (received in 1986) from the University of Michigan and, according to the University of Kentucky, he teaches an Arabic language course, along with courses such as Women in Islam, Islamic Civilization, and

Fundamentalism and Reform in Islam.[19] Bagby's specialty is Islamic law, so he has spent the past ten years conducting research on Muslims in America, apparently in the hope of using law to improve his community's prospects.

In an interview, he argued that "the ground rules have to be accepted—America is not going to be an Islamic state and Muslims do not want to impose Islam on anybody. . . . Most Muslims have a strong love for the things Americans value—freedom of speech, respect for individualism and hard work."[20] However, it is not clear how Muslims' political actions would be affected by their beliefs if they were to achieve power. For, if Muslims' political organizations are based on religion, it is likely that their governing policies would be shaped by Islamic perspectives. As we discussed in previous chapters, the Qur'an does not invite secular governments to rule over Muslims. As more active Muslim voices enter the political arena, a shift to the conservative Muslim right in noneconomic areas should be expected, for where on the planet can one find a truly leftist Muslim country? Nevertheless, the African American Muslim community embraces policies situated on the left side of the political spectrum.

Voting behaviors are quite distinct between America's two Muslim communities. According to an Associated Press (AP) story written by Rachel Zoll on August 30, 2003, immigrant Muslims, who are better off financially and live in more suburban areas than African American converts, supported George W. Bush in 2000. In Dearborn, Michigan, a suburb west of Detroit with a large Muslim population, some 52 percent of the ballots were cast for Bush.[21] On the other hand, African American Muslims living in Detroit followed the usual pattern of voting for the Democratic ticket.[22] The predominantly African American population of Detroit, whether Christian or Muslim, has never supported a Republican presidential candidate. Indeed, the weight of Detroit's large African American population offset the votes cast for Bush in Dearborn and the rest of suburban Wayne County. Bush received only 29.6 percent of the total ballots in the county.[23]

The policy positions of African American Muslims are similar to those of the Democratic Party; therefore, it is unlikely that a community that sees these issues as important would ever vote for a conservative Republican presidential candidate. According to a study conducted in 2004 by Ihsan Bagby, Muslim Americans in the Detroit area are not extremists:

They are virtually unanimous in supporting community and political involvement, and most mosque participants demonstrate their engagement in civic matters by being registered to vote. Because of these moderate views, mosque participants cannot be described as isolationists, rejecters of American society, or extremists. A significant number of mosque participants are unhappy with the moral climate in America, viewing certain aspects of American society as immoral. Mosque participants strongly support universal health care, affirmative action, tougher environmental laws, and cutting the income tax. An overwhelming number (85%) of mosque participants disapprove of President Bush's job performance.[24]

Do the views of African American Muslims living in Detroit really reflect the views of all Muslims, including the majority who were born outside the country? Bagby insists that Muslim Americans living in the Detroit area are an accurate microcosm of the overall Muslim community in the United States; however, the voting patterns in and around Detroit suggest the existence of two vastly different Muslim communities.

A closer look at the data raises more questions about Bagby's interpretations, especially on matters of social behaviors. The Pew report did not gather data on attitudes toward abortions, but other social values and perceptions were measured. There are marked differences between African American Muslims and their immigrant counterparts. On the subject of gay marriage, 61 percent of all Muslims think that gay marriage should be discouraged, but 75 percent of African American Muslims hold that view.[25] On the matter of feeling singled out by police or civilians for being Muslim, African Americans are twice as likely to believe that they have been victimized.[26] According to the Pew report, "Notably, more Muslim immigrants see themselves as well-off financially."[27] In terms of believing that hard work leads to success, only 56 percent of African Americans hold this view, but 75 percent of native-born, non-African-American Muslims and 74 percent of immigrant Muslims are convinced that their labors will produce success.[28] The number of Muslims in the United States who believe that suicide bombing is often, or at least sometimes, favorable is high. Whereas the Pew report provides percentages of people who hold this view, which may make the data seem small, they are, in fact, large when seen as actual numbers of people living in America. For example, there are already some 42,300 Muslims of foreign birth in America who feel suicide bombings are at least sometimes favorable.[29] With a total population only one-third of the size of their immigrant counterparts, 28,200 members of the African American Muslim community agree with them.[30]

These data gleaned from the Pew report show significant differences between African American Muslim and immigrant Muslim communities. Conclusively, it is quite a stretch to agree with Bagby's assertion that African American Muslims in Detroit are a microcosm of the entire Muslim community living in the United States. There is little evidence suggesting that American Islam is one community.

In previous chapters, I illustrated the nature of the first waves of Muslim immigrants into North America. Those immigrants are better off financially than those they left behind in their native countries. We looked at how they used European locations as their points of departure in coming to the United States and Canada. It is not surprising, then, that in comparison to Muslim communities in Western Europe, which are marked by high unemployment rates, America's Muslim immigrants are much better off financially.[31] Future immigrants to America will likely have ties to these European enclaves facilitated by international organizations and through family ties. These future immigrants to America will not be as well off financially, nor will they be as well educated as the pioneering immigrants. Furthermore, future immigrants' ability to assimilate themselves will not be great, so they will follow the settlement and socialization patterns found in the European enclaves. Left on the fringes of society, they will be hard pressed to disbelieve Qur'anic images of community, disbelievers, and the governance of space and people. There are already a number of organizations that are working to ensure Islam's place in the West.

American Islamic Organizations

It is ironic and even paradoxical that American Muslims have embraced an economic and socially liberal political agenda because Islam, when viewed through the pages of history and the Qur'an, is quite conservative. Although giving to the poor (provided the recipient is Muslim) is one of the Five Pillars of Islam, it is an individual act made on a voluntary basis, not through taxes and government redistribution. Elijah Muhammad certainly intended the Nation of Islam to act as a conservative group centered on his own community. Islamic organizations that dutifully follow the teachings of the Prophet Muhammad will eventually have to insist that the laws of the land match the laws of Islam as reflected in the Qur'an. Nonetheless, those who have political and economic interests that can best be described as "liberal" in national politics are paving the way for more fundamental and, hence, more conservative and intolerant immigrants. As the Muslim population grows through immigration, these activist groups are making it possible for proponents of *sharia* law to have a voice in American politics.

African American Muslims assume that immigrants will be persecuted by white and Jewish America. They also assume that these immigrants will accept the African American converts' lead in making life better for all Muslims through economic and political empowerment. As African American convert and Muslim activist Mahdi Bray revealed, "People in the immigrant community just discovered racial profiling . . . [but] for African Americans, we've known it for quite a while."[32] Warith Deen Mohammad claims that "[o]ur people are still remembering and feeling the pain of social disrespect, and they have experienced that with immigrant Muslims."[33] However, as the Pew report shows, African American Muslims are twice as likely to feel singled out by non-Muslims than their immigrant counterparts. Aside from political posturing, there is little evidence to support a claim of shared persecution.

A leading advocate for civic empowerment of Muslims is the Institute for Social Policy and Understanding (ISPU). It is a think tank with an egalitarian-sounding mission:

> The Institute for Social Policy and Understanding is an independent non-profit research organization committed to studying US domestic and foreign policy. ISPU's research aims to increase understanding of key policy issues and how they impact various communities within America. The Institute was established on the premise that every community must address, debate, and contribute to the pressing issues that face our nation. It is our hope that this effort will give voice to the diversity of our country

and provide alternative perspectives to the current policy-making echelons
of the political, academic and public-relations arenas of the United States.
Based on this approach, ISPU produces scholarly publications that build on
the ideas of various communities in the United States.[34]

On the surface, this organization seems equally interested in the economic
plight of white Missionary Baptist communities in Southern Appalachia as
it is with any other interest group, including Muslim converts in Detroit.
However, the group projects a bias in favor of Muslim interests. In 2007, the
seven board members directing the ISPU did not have any obvious connections to Southern Appalachia, the Deep South, or anywhere outside of large
cities for that matter. However, Detroit, Chicago, and Kansas City are well
represented. The Institute's executive director is Iltefat Harnzavi, a medical
doctor who serves on the faculty at Detroit's Wayne State University. He also
holds a degree in sociology from the University of Michigan. He is joined by
a physician named Muzammil Ahmed. He, too, holds a sociology degree
from the University of Michigan. The University of Michigan has also produced another member, Zareema Grewal, who, in 2007, was finishing a
PhD. Mazen Asbahi is a lawyer in Chicago, where he also serves as the president of the Muslim Bar Association of Chicago. Fakhia Rashid, a 2007
graduate student at the University of Chicago, is another Chicago-area board
member. Afser Shariff holds a medical doctorate from Kansas City Medical
School. Shariff is the ISPU's director of communications and media relations.
Farid Senzai lives on the West Coast, where he works as an adjunct professor
of political science at California State University.

In the area of research, the ISPU seems to support issues impacting foreign Muslims more than it supports projects aimed at urban renewal, educating the young, building physical infrastructure to support economic
growth, and inspiring others to harness the forces of positive cultural and
social change that can create self-sustaining communities. Instead, this
organization, which claims to seek understanding and share its findings with
all parties interested in its work, appears more interested in building bridges
with foreign Muslim communities. The ISPU has supported studies like
"Zarqawi: The Man, Message, and Video Star"; "Give Iran Positive Incen-

tives to Halt Its Nuclear Program"; and "Don't We Have Enough Enemies Already?" To show a concern for democracy with a sarcastic tone, the ISPU has also published an article titled "To Save Democracy, Bush's War Will Target Shias Too" (Iran and Iraq have Shia majority populations).[35] These studies clearly show a focus on Muslim communities abroad, possibly as an effort to attract immigrant Muslims, including puritan Muslims, to support the ISPU in return. However, the influence of immigrants, if they choose to involve themselves in the organization, will likely instill more conservative values in it.

These organizations are useful to puritan Muslims who strive for a global caliphate, or global Muslim nation. In his thought-provoking book *Jihad vs. McWorld*, Benjamin R. Barber uses the Islamic concept of *jihad* as a metaphor for anti-Western, antisecularist struggles everywhere. To develop his thesis, he discusses Islam and governance. He points out that Islam conceives situations "in which the Muslim religion and the Islamic state are co-created and inseparable, and some observers argue that it has less room for secularism than any other major religion."[36] Few historical figures have coveted political power more than Adolf Hitler, and, interestingly, the German dictator admired Islam's capacity to dismiss practices of liberal governance in favor of right-wing fascism. In speaking about Germany's unfortunate legacy as a Christian country, Hitler argued that "it's been our misfortune to have the wrong religion. Why didn't we have the religion of the Japanese, who regard sacrifice for the Fatherland as the highest good? The Mohammedan religion [Islam] too would have been more compatible to us than Christianity. Why did it have to be Christianity with its meekness and flabbiness?"[37] A society that promotes and celebrates issues such as religious tolerance, gender equity, gay marriage, and separation of mosque and state is alien to historic Islam (although Turkey is a possible, albeit experimental, exception). The ISPU's vision of a liberal democracy, as depicted in its mission statement, is certainly a leftist, African American interpretation of Islam.

The Muslim American Freedom Foundation (MAFF) likewise sees itself as an advocacy group for the rise of Islam in the name of liberalism. According to information made available by the MAFF, it has serious concerns about the plight of its own Islamic community and, indeed, all Americans:

Despite Islam's growth in America, there are certain groups in and outside
of America that have long used bigoted distortions of Islam; portraying
Muslims in America as seditious, dangerous, and totally incompatible with
American life. Since the Sept. 11th tragedy, these same forces have inten-
sified this vile propaganda with reckless abandonment. It is important that
Muslims in America not be viewed as a "fifth column." Muslims must continue to build a grassroots movement that supports an all-encompassing
approach of total integration into American Society for the express purpose
of fulfilling the mandate of Allah (SWT) "to enjoin that which is good and
forbid that which is bad," in a quest to make a better America for ourselves,
our children, and all Americans.[38]

To show its connection to a truly African American experience, namely
the civil rights movement and the methods employed by Martin Luther King
Jr., the MAFF mission statement touches on familiar themes: "To build an
integrated empowerment process for the American Muslim community
through civic education, participation, community outreach, and coalition
building; to forge positive relationships with other institutions outside of our
community, that will ensure and facilitate the protection of civil rights and
liberties for American Muslims and all Americans."[39] The groups MAFF
identified as collaborators in its mission include voter registration and education organizations; local civic groups; municipal and state officials; members
of Congress; civil rights and progressive political groups such as NAACP,
ACLU, ANSWER (a Los Angeles-based organization that wants to legalize
illegal aliens); the Southern Christian Leadership Conference (SCLC); organ-
ized labor; members of the Media; college campuses; immigrant groups;
black, Hispanic, and Asian churches; and other non-Muslim religious institutions.[40] However, despite their religious affiliations and unlike many Hispanic and Asian folk, 64 percent of American Muslims of Arab descent identify with the white race.[41] Furthermore, concepts such as civic empowerment
and community outreach have special meanings for African Americans, but it
is unclear how these concepts will be understood by various immigrant
groups, especially Muslims with non-Western values and identities.

The MAFF and the ISPU are not alone in their defense of Islam. The
Muslim Alliance in North America (MANA) is made up of member groups

drawn from the African American Muslim community. Like the other organizations discussed above, MANA has a stated mission:

> MANA is a national network of masjids [mosques], Muslim organizations and individuals committed to work together to address certain urgent needs within the Muslim community. These needs include the great social and economic problems that are challenging Muslim communities especially the inner city; the need for the involvement of masjids and Muslims in community service projects which are aimed at improving society as a whole; the need for systematic and effective dawah programs to help bring more non-Muslims into Islam; the need for new Muslim [education] programs that will help them grow in Islam. MANA is therefore an open organization that is agenda driven.[42]

It is difficult to find fault with any of the organization's basic empowerment ideas. However, MANA's mission statement is based on perceived oppression that would require larger cultural and social changes to remedy its concerns. Those changes would be based on appealing to a sense of guilt among all members of the middle and upper classes for allowing negative views of Islam. Increasing the social and political focus on conservative Muslim worldviews through *dawah* (meaning a call toward Allah, or spreading the message of Islam) and education programs runs counter to American liberalism, which is, for example, more receptive to openly gay relationships and women's empowerment. This would, in turn, lead to contesting public and perhaps even private spaces.

Like the organizations described above, MANA has a board of directors. Siraj Wahhaj is among its eight leaders. He was originally named Jeffrey Kearse and had once served as a Christian Sunday school teacher. He was also a character witness for Omar Abdel-Rahman, the "blind sheik" associated with the first World Trade Center bombing. Another board member is Amir Al-Islam, a professor at Medgar Evers College of the City University of New York. Al-Islam is dedicated to studying African diasporas and to celebrating contributions their descendants have made in shaping the modern world.[43] Also on the board is Ihsan Bagby, the University of Kentucky professor discussed above. He serves as the general secretary of MANA. The leadership of this organization is made up of committed African Americans who sincerely believe they are paving the way for the true religion. That religion, of course, assumes that all Muslims, including those immigrants from Iran, Bosnia Herzegovina, and Indonesia, share their interpretation of Islam and American society.

MANA and the other organizations we have discussed believe that they are empowering people who have little voice in the larger affairs that impact their lives. But, will their political activism someday result in demands for laws based on *sharia* law? The logic that inspires that question is based on the following deduction: Religion is the basis of these Muslim organizations, and they want to grow in power and influence. Given the population projections shown in chapter 1, these organizations' work, along with a rise in Muslim immigrants with conservative views, will likely make it easier for municipalities and other levels of government in the United States to adopt laws based on *sharia* law.

Figure 9. The Islamic Council of America in Dearborn, Michigan. (Photo courtesy of the author.)

It is necessary to take a longer look at what the Qur'an teaches about some of the issues popular among members of the secular left. As suggested by issues advocated by Muslim advocacy groups in the United States, it is assumed that immigrant Muslims' expectations for living a holy life are compatible with secular liberalism. Is that an accurate assumption, considering that in the imagined worlds of the Qur'an there is no separation of mosque and state? Is there compatibility among Qur'anic images of society, governance, and a liberal, secularized society? I will answer those questions in chapter 7.

Chapter 7

The Incommensurability of
Liberalism and Puritan Islam

Introduction

G iven the rate of growth in Muslim countries and their already
stretched economic conditions and limited carrying capacities,
geographer Wilbur Zelinsky's mobility transition model suggests that the
projected number of 300 million Muslim Americans by midcentury is theoretically possible.[1] The American political and social landscapes in the
decade of 2050 will likely witness significant change, resulting from the
incommensurability of liberalism and puritan Islam. As demographers
know, however, there are many events that could take place between now and
the year 2050 capable of changing the global Muslim population and migration patterns, so that number may not be reached. Depending on the nature
of these events, the Muslim American population could even be higher than
the projected 300 million. While moderate Muslims may tolerate life in
Western countries that feature liberal social behaviors and political policies,
puritans believe it is necessary to change these policies. Failure to do so, with
respect to geotheokolasis, invites the wrath of Allah on the puritans and their
new country.

As I will show, the Qur'an, which provides puritans with images of community, nation, and governance as they relate to proper conduct in public
spaces, offers critical guidance on some of the liberties that residents of
Western democracies take for granted. To safeguard civil liberties, the notion
of separation of church and state needs to be morphed into a more inclusive

doctrine of separation of religion and state. This change is needed because puritan Islam maintains different views of women, people with disabilities, and people who openly live homosexual lifestyles. Muslim groups, who are using minority status as a vehicle to escape public scrutiny, can increase their influence on the policies that shape the social and political landscapes of the United States. Domestic Islamic organizations, whose aims are to monitor and, indeed, influence American foreign and domestic policies, are already at work, preparing for others to come who will see social liberalism as a pretext for geotheokolasis.

The Separation of Religion and State

As discussed in the introductory chapter, many writers and members of the media see evangelical Christianity as a threat to liberal democracy, although some Christian writers disagree with that contention and regard Islam as a greater threat to liberalism. Sociologist Anthony Giddens of the United Kingdom believes that the Christian Right forms a new political thrust in the United States that seeks to create nothing short of a theocracy. As he writes, members of the so-called New Christian Right "have founded a number of universities to produce a new generation of 'counter elite' schooled in funda-mentalist Christian beliefs and able to take up prominent positions in the media, academia, politics and the arts. Liberty University, Oral Roberts University, Bob Jones University and others confer degrees in standard academic disciplines, taught within the framework of biblical infallibility."[2] What he fails to realize is that Christian and church affiliated colleges and universities have been functioning in America since its founding as an English colony. Institutions like Tusculum College and Blount College were established west of the Blue Ridge Mountains in the 1790s.[3] They are part of the American cultural landscape and their existence has coincided with the historic trends and social movements within the United States. On the other hand, the values as projected by Muslim political action committees appear, at least on the surface, to be consistent with the ethics that underpin the ideals of separation of religion and state. However, there are subtle hints of an evolving orientation toward influencing the policies of the federal government. Consider the fact that the Muslim American Freedom Foundation (MAFF) hopes to use a mandate from Allah to transform American society into one in which Islamic laws forbid behaviors that Islam views as immoral.[4] Whose value system will be used to identify and separate the good from the bad? How will the forbidding of the bad be enforced? Will there be tolerance for other religionists and agnostics in public spaces? Given that the organization is guided by the will of Allah, the Qur'an will be used as the source of all knowledge about Allah's views on what constitutes good and bad behaviors. As more Muslims arrive on American shores who do not see Islam as a leftist political tool to improve the lot of urban communities, it is important to turn to the Qur'an to see how puritan Muslims view liberal social behaviors and government policies. There is a good deal of evidence in the Muslim holy book to suggest that civil libertarians will not like following many of the mandates of Allah.

With ideas such as those of the MAFF, it would seem that civil action groups, including the American Civil Liberties Union (ACLU), would be concerned about a new form of religion and state. However, with respect to those groups, there are few public demands for the separation of mosque and state. As we saw in the previous chapter, the ACLU actually collaborates with the MAFF in helping to achieve its mission. To some on the Christian Right, the country needs to recommit to its Christian roots in order to save the nation for what lies ahead. Should there be a call for a more encompassing separation of religion and state?

To answer that question, it is important to know that the Qur'an makes many assumptions about government that separate Islam's view from that of the Christian values that, regardless of whether one is a Christian, still influence political values and behaviors in America. For instance, in the first century, Jesus described the geotheological image of two spheres or kingdoms of human existence: "Render therefore unto Caesar the things which are Caesar's; and unto God the things that are God's."[5] Unlike Christianity, the Qur'an does not imagine two coexisting yet distinct realms of earthly and spiritual power, although unbelievers occupying distant micro-spaces are to be left alone to fend for themselves. Like the blessing of water to replenish the earth, so, too, are law and order given from Allah, and they are to be interpreted by his apostles (*imams*). Of course, to the puritan all laws must be in harmony with the Qur'an, for it, they believe, reveals the mind of Allah.

Disagreements over who has the correct view of Allah's will have contributed greatly to puritans' dissatisfaction with mainstream Islam, as well as with Christianity and the secular West. The Qur'an describes times in which some political leaders, who claim to be Muslims, will make excuses for failing to abide by the Qur'anic teachings. It further issues warnings to other Muslim leaders who might be led astray: "Or lest you should say: If the Book had been revealed to us, we would certainly have been better guided than they; so indeed there has come to you clear proof from your Lord, and guidance and mercy. Who is more unjust than he who rejects Allah's communications and turns away from them? We will reward those who turn away from Our communications with an evil chastisement because they turned away."[6]

As we previously discussed, the "Qur'anic guidance" actually infers orders or dictates, especially when one considers the consequences for disobedience. Geotheokolasis can be delivered now, in earthly time, or on Judgment Day and can afflict towns and nations, including their leadership. In that case, punishments can be delivered through natural means, such as an earthquake, or by military conquest. As the Qur'an warns, "Do you not see that Allah created the heavens and the earth with truth? If He please He will take you off and bring a new creation, and this is not difficult for Allah."[7] The Qur'an provides even more geotheological imaginings that do not suggest two spheres of existence and militate against the doctrine of separation of religion and state.

The Qur'an employs a theology of deterrence as a means to inspire people to willingly submit to the will of Allah. "We will cast terror into the hearts of those who disbelieve, because they set up with Allah that for which He has sent down no authority, and their abode is the fire; and evil is the abode of the unjust."[8] These punishments are not assigned to the vagaries of the hereafter. "I will cast terror into the hearts of those who disbelieve. Therefore strike off their heads and strike off every finger print of them."[9] Some might argue that these passages—arguably a theology of deterrence—are mere metaphors for some deeper theological and perhaps even psychological meaning. For example, we should let those who offend us walk away without us suffering any undue stress worrying about who does or, indeed, who does not, like us; therefore, we should not interpret this passage literally. While that is perhaps good advice from a psychological perspective, it is not what the Qur'an means, nor is it the interpretation of many Muslims already living in American and European cities. The puritan inspired by a literal reading of the Qur'an sees no disconnect between mosque and state. As products of an omniscient and omnipotent Allah, they are, indeed, one and the same. While the following statement may seem harsh to Western Christians who hold a two-kingdom geotheological image of existence and governance (i.e., separation of church and state), it necessarily delineates nations in conflict, not individuals against individuals: "The punishment of those who wage war against Allah and His apostle and strive to make mischief on the land is only this, that they should be murdered or crucified or their hands and their feet should be cut off on opposite side or they should be imprisoned; this shall be as a disgrace for them in this world, and in the hereafter, they shall have a grievous chastisement."[10] Surah 8 provides more imagining that suggests a synthesis between religion and state: "O Prophet! Urge the believers to war; if there are twenty patient ones of you they shall overcome two hundred, and if there are a hundred of you they shall overcome a thousand of those who don't believe, because they are a people who do not understand."[11] To some Westerners, these acts, when carried out by Islamic organizations, are seen as deviant and discrete acts of terrorism; but to those who carry them out, they are acts of war in fulfillment of geotheological imaginings. To puritans, these Qur'anic passages communicate a mandate from Allah because, according to Khaled Abou El Fadl, a scholar in Islamic jurisprudence, puritans are "uninterested in critical historical inquiry and [have] responded to the challenge of modernity by escaping to the secure haven of the text . . . [where] they came to consider intellectualism and rational moral insight to be inaccessible and, thus, corruptions of the purity of the Islamic message."[12]

The Qur'an tells the puritan that he is a soldier, an instrument in the hand of Allah: "[Y]ou did not slay them, but it was Allah who slew them, and you did not smite when you smote [the enemy], but it was Allah who smote, and that He might confer upon the believers a good gift from Himself; surely Allah is Hearing, Knowing."[13] To achieve a military situation like this, political infrastructure must be dedicated to the service of Allah and the management of his world. It is, hence, difficult to find Qur'anic passages that suggest a separation of mosque and state.

Islamic Public Expressions as American Civil Liberties

In the United States, there is interest among some groups to initiate hate speech legislation to protect Muslims from non-Muslim Americans.[14] With heightened sensitivity toward Muslims and other religious and nonreligious communities, many Americans support the removal of nativity scenes from public spaces. The word "Christmas" is already used less frequently in commercials, while less offensive terms like "winter holidays" or "happy holidays" are gaining currency. Easter celebrations in public spaces are likewise being curtailed.[15] The ACLU and the Leadership Conference on Civil Rights (LCCR) support these changes. The ACLU has been at work for years to remove religious symbols from public spaces. It must be noted, however, that the ACLU only supports those Muslim groups that champion liberal causes focusing on pollution, climate change, and programs designed to ameliorate conditions associated with poverty and the overall economic inequalities that continue to plague American society.

If Wade Henderson, president and CEO of the LCCR, succeeds, politically active groups whose existence is based mostly on race, ethnicity, sexual orientation, gender, disability status, national origin, or religion can fight their political opponents by invoking claims that opposing views are expressions of hate speech.[16] In a similar fashion, the Council on American-Islamic Relations (CAIR) has issued a number of "incitement watches" designed to intimidate anyone who speaks out against the policies or actions of domestic and international Islamic groups.[17] Depending on the political climate and makeup of the Supreme Court, these laws could actually be used against Islamic leaders who criticize policies not framed by Qur'anic doctrines. It is important to recognize that the precedents of civil and even Islamic jurisprudence in establishing governing policies that allow for religious pluralism are not respected by puritan Muslims. As the Qur'an explains, "They have taken their doctors of law and their monks for lords besides Allah. . . . O you who believe! Most surely many of the doctors of law and the monks eat away at the property of men falsely, and turn [them] away from Allah's way; and [as for] those who hoard up gold and silver and do not spend it in Allah's way, announce to them a painful chastisement."[18] Hate speech legislation could also be used by puritans to silence moderate Muslims who challenge their hard-line positions. If a religious-political organization is able to hush its opponents, what freedoms are left to any group that holds contrary views?

Achieving a position of social dominance in the West obviously requires Islam to increase its number of adherents. This can happen through fertility and through winning souls to Islam. As described in chapter 1, the growth in Muslim communities in the United States is produced more by immigrants than it is by winning converts to the faith. Most of those who choose to become Muslims belong to racial minorities, primarily African Americans, who have been disadvantaged and are thus receptive to geotheological imagery that elevates their community within the spaces of religion and religiously inspired politics. This was certainly the case with the appeal of Christian Puritanism in Britain during the seventeenth century.[19] Given that the African American population today is made up of people with equally diverse motives, aspirations, and values, the pool of potential converts is limited. Those who do convert see Islam as a vehicle for achieving a unique identity apart from the dominant Anglo-based culture. It stands to reason, then, that further growth in Western Islam depends on the fertility of Muslim women. Puritan Muslims, like most religious fundamentalists, resist changing the cultural formula that maintains high levels of fertility. Women are, therefore, the critical factor in the rise of Islam. Having Muslim societies with well-educated, self-directing women in search of meaningful careers outside the family and role of wife is not compatible with the geotheological image of puritan Islam.

Qur'anic Images of Women

As Islamic values increasingly influence political thinking in Europe and the United States, feminist groups will likely forfeit some of the gains they have made because the Qur'an has much to say about women and their role in society. Since there is a functional need to maintain high fertility rates, the disempowerment of women in Western society is critical to the rise of Islam. It follows then that empowering Muslim women through education and workplace opportunities in Muslim-dominated societies will be resisted by the power structures in those countries.

Although Turkey and Egypt are exceptions, women in most Islamic societies are quite limited in what they can and cannot do outside of the family. Puritans certainly argue that the Qur'an provides ample justification for maintaining traditional roles for women. There are, however, moderate Muslims who hold an opposing view of the faith. Some scholars actually regard Islam as a liberator of women. According to Dr. Nahid Angha:

> One cannot emphasize enough the influence of the teachings of the Prophet (swa) and the verses of the Qur'an upon the advancement of civilization. In the history of humankind, none worked so much to protect human rights, especially women's, with such integrity, strength, strategic genius, beauty and divinity, or to honor humanity, by freeing it from the chains of prejudice, manipulations, personal and social injustice. His [Muhammad's] teachings regarding education, social and political rights, property rights, and ultimately human rights, are among the most valuable chapter in the book of civilization.[20]

Other Islamic scholars agree with Angha and argue that Muslim society reached a golden age before the Middle East was decimated by the Crusades. Still, the question needs to be asked: Was there a time in which Muslim women enjoyed the same level of literacy and personal empowerment as the males in their society? Angha insists that such was the case during the golden age of Islam. As she explains:

> Such positions, rights and equality among all were the result of the support and the teachings of the Prophet (swa). Women could take part in social, political, and military affairs. The result of his teachings was not only promoted human rights but also encouraging individuals to stand for their own rights. Fatima, daughter of the Prophet (swa), was well educated and highly respected. It is said that whenever Fatima entered the room, the Prophet would stand and give his seat to her. Her sacrifices to protect and support human rights were among the most praiseworthy acts.[21]

Does the Qur'an project an image of equality among the genders? One, source of Western criticism of Islam with respect to women, which is supported by the Qur'an, is polygyny, or having more than one wife at the same time. Islam for Today, a Muslim organization dedicated to recruiting Westerners to Islam, used an example of a Mormon plural spouse to show the value of polygyny and its compatibility with Islam. According to the organization, some feminists see polygyny as a better lifestyle than a monogamous marriage or living alone. In a speech before the Utah chapter of the National Organization for Women (NOW), a Mormon journalist named Elizabeth Joseph provided the feminist listeners with a justification for accepting polygyny:

> As a journalist, I work many unpredictable hours in a fast-paced environment. The news determines my schedule. But am I calling home, asking my husband to please pick up the kids and pop something in the microwave and get them to bed on time just in case I'm really late? Because of my plural marriage arrangement, I don't have to worry. I know that when I have to work late my daughter will be at home surrounded by loving adults with whom she is comfortable and who know her schedule without my telling them. My eight-year-old has never seen the inside of a day-care center, and my husband has never eaten a TV dinner. And I know that when I get home from work, if I'm dog-tired and stressed-out, I can be alone and guilt-free. It's a rare day when all eight of my husband's wives are tired and stressed at the same time.[22]

It is interesting that Joseph acknowledges that her husband's other wives provide her daughter with love and that her husband has never eaten a TV dinner. Her comments suggest that he is fully dependent on his wives for childcare and meals. Joseph is a wage earner and has a daughter, yet her co-wives cook meals. What does her husband do to deserve help inside and outside the home? Apparently the answer lies in his prowess as a lover. Joseph told her audience that, for over two decades, she has "observed how Alex's marriage to Margaret, Bo, Joanna, Diana, Leslie, Dawn, and Delinda has enhanced his marriage to me. The guy has hundreds of years of marital experience; as a result, he is a very skilled husband."[23] Joseph's logic falls outside the domain of basic feminism. While there are a number of variations in feminist social theory, one idea is common among them: "They all share in common the desire to explain gender inequalities in society and to work to overcome them."[24] In its truest form, then, feminism seeks to eliminate all forms of inequality, including a hypothetically reversed situation that could have Elizabeth Joseph coming home to spouses named Steve, Bill, Ahmed, Rufus, and Leo. Her reasoning behind polygamy does not provide a feminist perspective on her role as a spouse and a wage earner. As she discussed, "It's helpful to think of polygamy [or having more than one spouse at the same time] in terms of a free-market approach to marriage. Why shouldn't you or your daughters have the opportunity to marry the best man available, regardless of his marital status?"[25] In following that line of thought, why doesn't she ask, "Why shouldn't I marry the best men available?" In a truly equitable situation, women would be granted the same option of having more than one spouse at the same time. Regardless of how that question is answered, it provides a rationalization for women to accept an unequal place in Mormonism. Since her views were published by an organization called Islam for Today, the microspaces of the home could become contested if the Muslim wife chooses an alternative lifestyle.[26]

The contention that Islam improved the lives of poor Arab women is not limited to Muslims per se. In Kelly Knauer's *The Middle East: History, Cultures, Conflicts, Faiths*, a section on women in Islam is introduced as follows: "When Islam swept across the Middle East in the 7th century, it profoundly changed the place of women in Arab society—for the better."[27] However, Knauer admits that today a woman's testimony in most Muslim courts is worth only half that of a man; moreover, women have difficulty obtaining a divorce while husbands are granted one virtually on demand. Knauer also confesses that in countries that rule through *sharia*, or Islamic law, a male is allowed to have up to four wives. Muhammad, however, had twelve wives.[28]

While admitting that Islamic countries are characterized by inequalities for women, Knauer explains that these conditions are the result of Western expansion in the eighteenth and nineteenth centuries. "Fearing cultural erosion," according to Knauer, "emerging conservative sects championed values that set Islam apart, including the repression of women."[29] Once again, Knauer, like some other scholars, exaggerates the impact of Western countries on the rest of the world, especially the Middle East. However, in a logic framed by Knauer's ideas, we would expect that puritan Islam, which seeks a theological return to a literal reading of the Qur'an, would elevate women to an equal footing with men. As Knauer writes, "Muhammad even decreed that sexual satisfaction was a woman's entitlement."[30] In Hadith 1.268, Anas, an early Muslim leader, wrote that "the Prophet used to visit all his wives in an hour round, during the day and night and they were eleven in number . . . the prophet was given the strength of thirty men."[31]

In contrast to Knauer's argument, let us now focus on Qur'anic endorsements of polygyny and gender inequality. According to the Qur'an, "Allah enjoins you concerning your children: The male shall have the equal of the portion of two females."[32] In the following passage from the Qur'an, a basic view of the dependent nature of women and wives is revealed: "Men are the maintainers of women because Allah has made some of them to excel others and because they spend out of their property; the good women are therefore obedient, guarding the unseen as Allah has guarded; and [to] those on whose part you fear desertion, admonish them, and leave them alone in the sleeping places and beat them; then if they obey you, do not seek a way against them; surely Allah is High, Great."[33] Muhammad must have seen women as sexually motivated, for, as the above passage shows, part of their punishment is sexual deprivation. Knauer admits that, in most Muslim societies, honor killings of disobedient wives by male relatives or husbands often go unpunished, or, if the perpetrators are convicted, their punishments are light.[34]

The Qur'an refers to wives as arable land ready for planting: "[W]ives are as a tilth [a field ready for plowing] unto you, so approach your tilth when and how you will."[35] There are no references in the Qur'an explicitly allowing women to say no to sex with their husbands if the mood strikes them. In the Hadith, male followers are told that their "[w]ives are playthings, so take your pick."[36] She may say no, but it is up to the man to honor her request or not. If he thinks that her refusal to have sex is evidence that she is about to leave him, he can beat her.[37]

In puritan Islam, preteen girls are eligible for marriage. The youngest of Muhammad's wives was Aishah. She was nine years old and he was in his mid-fifties when they consummated their marriage.[38] A Qur'anic solution for reducing the number of female orphans is to marry them. "And if you fear that you cannot act equitably towards orphans, then marry such women as seem good to you, two and three and four."[39] Muhammad gave his cherished daughter Fatima in marriage to his cousin Ali bin Abu Taleb. She was twelve when she married Ali. Today, however, most Muslim countries only allow young girls in their teens to marry. A special exemption issued from an Islamic court, however, allows preteen girls to get married.[40] Iran currently has the lowest age requirement (thirteen years old) for girls to marry.[41] According to American theologians and Christian converts Caner and Caner, however, it is not unusual to see arranged marriages for girls as young as twelve.[42]

Figure 10. Despite an urban, American location, this mosque features separate entryways for men and ladies. (Photo courtesy of the author.)

In terms of life opportunities outside the roles of mother, wife, and concubine, most women in Muslim-dominated societies have few choices. Education is critical for personal empowerment, especially as modern societies move away from labor-intensive jobs. Although Dr. Nahid Angha argues that the education of women is a high priority for Muslims,[43] the data simply do not support her contention. It should not come as a surprise to learn that in secular countries (oftentimes these are more developed countries) men and women share similar high rates of literacy, which are above 95 percent.[44] There are distinct patterns of gender-based inequalities in Muslim countries, even in Turkey, whose official domestic policy is to be neutral in religious matters. At between 0.1 and 4.9 percent, the difference between men's and women's literacy rates is, indeed, measurable in Turkey.[45] In Iran, the gender-based differences in literacy rates range between 5 and 19.9 percent; in more traditional countries, like the Sudan and Pakistan, the range in the literacy gap is over 20 percent.[46] According to James Rubenstein, a noted American cultural geographer, "Women in the Middle East and South Asia have especially low literacy rates compared to men. . . . Low female literacy rates are an obstacle to development throughout the less developed world but especially in the Middle East and South Asia."[47] With the exception of the lingering restrictive impact of the caste system associated with Hinduism, the only other religion in South Asia followed by a significant segment of the population is Islam. In the current situation, Muslim women will remain highly fertile.

Physically Challenged and Gay People

In puritan Islam, people with hearing and speaking impediments have less status than women. "The vilest of animals, in Allah's sight, are the deaf, the dumb, who do not understand."[48] To Muhammad, who believed in the absolute, sovereign power of Allah, this made sense because "if Allah had known any good in them He would have made them hear, and if He makes them hear they would turn back while they withdrew."[49]

The Qur'an also presents an unequal assessment of gay people. Surah 4:19–35 lays out guidelines for sex through marriage. Muhammad tells his followers that they are not to fornicate.[50] Marriage is the license for having sex, and it is to take place within the context of the bonds of matrimony between a man and up to four women. He made no provisions for having a same-sex relationship. Indeed, the Qur'an has no words for gay or lesbian. Despite the condemnation of homosexuality among Islamic leaders, though, it is surprisingly hard to find explicit guidelines for how to treat gay people and how to address homosexuality, although the Qur'an uses numerous references to the divine wrath leveled on Sodom and Gomorrah.[51] For instance, the Qur'an asks, "What! Do you come to males from among the creatures, and leave what your Lord has created for you of your wives? Nay, you are a people exceeding limits."[52] "Exceeding limits" is another way of identifying a behavior as sinful. Few, if any, Muslim societies encourage gay relationships, and gay marriages are certainly out of the question. Homosexuality, like all premarital and extramarital sexual encounters, is a sin in Islam. Like all sin, according to the Qur'an, such behavior will be punished by Allah and those dedicated to protecting the Islamic community, town, and nation from geotheokolasis.

Although no Muslim country recognizes same-sex marriages, there are Muslim organizations operating in secular Western countries that seek spaces in the public sphere for homosexual couples to get married. In 1998, a group calling itself Al-Fatiha Foundation was established in the United States as a nonprofit, nongovernment organization.[53] Its mission is "dedicated to Muslims who are lesbian, gay, bisexual, transgender, intersex, questioning, those exploring their sexual orientation or gender identity, and their allies, families and friends. Al-Fatiha promotes the progressive Islamic notions of peace, equality and justice. We envision a world that is free from prejudice, injustice and discrimination, where all people are fully embraced and accepted into their faith, their families and their communities."[54] Despite its egalitarian goals, a *fatwa* was issued against Al-Fatiha in 2001 by "al-Muhajiroun, an international organization that seeks the establishment of an Islamic caliphate."[55]

Nevertheless, members of Al-Fatiha helped establish a branch of their organization in London, which was named *Imaan* (Arabic for faith). The British organization has about three hundred members. Their commitment to Islam varies considerably from person to person, but they are, nonetheless, sufficiently committed to identify with the faith as well as being gay, lesbian, or transgendered. According to MSNBC reporter Jennifer Carlile, most of the members have not informed their families of their lifestyle.[56] Even the secretary of Imaan, a man known as Ubaid, does not publically reveal his last name for fear of reprisals from members of the larger Muslim community. According to Ubaid, the Muslim world regards homosexuality as a "Western disease."[57]

Along that line of thought, anthropologist Tom Boellstorff argues that Muslim leaders, especially those whom he has studied in Indonesia, seldom mention male homosexuality, but when they do mention it, "it is typically in terms of absolute rejection."[58] Boellstorff adds that these leaders see the gay lifestyle as a social illness and a reflection of a morally evil trend that must be eliminated. The practice of the gay lifestyle is not a human right, as claimed by Western gays. He points out that "Male homosexuality does not bifurcate into the meritorious and sinful: It is incomprehensible as a form of sexual selfhood, and this incommensurability is a fundamental difference between how gay Muslim Indonesians and heterosexually identified Muslim Indonesian men experience their sexualities."[59] Like in other countries, religion in Indonesia is more than just a function of personal belief; it is also a public expression that geotheologically connects the individual and community to the nation itself. Herein lay a potentially significant problem for practicing gays, for the gay lifestyle not only threatens their place in their religious community but also that roles in the public and civic spaces of their lives. Indonesian gays are often plagued by a sense of guilt and live a portion of their lives in obscurity.

Summary

While a number of scholars and civic organizations champion acceptance of Islamic ways of life in Western countries, including the United States, a number of their views are inconsistent with the social and geotheological imaginings delineated in the Qur'an. There are nevertheless Qur'anic passages that clearly portray women as different from men, and those differences are used as a justification for inequalities based on gender. One key example shown in this chapter is the practice of polygyny. Beyond the issue of gender inequalities supported in the Qur'an, justifications are also found for the unequal social positions of people with disabilities. Furthermore, homosexual men and women also face reprisals in the Islamic world for public displays of their lifestyles. Homosexuality is viewed as a sin, and complete submission to Allah and his prophet, regardless of personal desire, is not an option for gays, according to puritan Muslims. Underlying these contested issues are puritan Muslims' fears stemming from geotheological images associated with the sins of individuals and communities. As stated in the Qur'an, "Serve Allah and shun the Shaitan. So there were some of them whom Allah guided and there were others against whom error was due; therefore travel in the land, then see what was the end of the rejecters."[60] The wrath of Allah for sinful behavior—the lack of submission to all of the creator's guidance—is visibly evident on the landscape; hence, the incommensurability of liberalism and puritan Islam.

Chapter 8

Puritans' Perception of the State of Israel

Introduction

Most observers of the Middle Eastern peace process know that the failure of Muslim countries to recognize Israel's right to exist is a major obstacle to achieving regional, perhaps even global, stability. As a country established in 1948 to give persecuted Jews a homeland, Israel does not share its Arab neighbors' place in the world of Islam. Still, some 16 percent of the Israeli population is Muslim. There are also concentrations of Muslims living in the Gaza Strip, a densely populated, narrow coastal area about half the size of a typical county in Tennessee or Indiana.[1] Located along the Mediterranean Sea, Gaza is the ancient homeland of the Philistines, whom the Romans called Palestinians. It was also the native soil of Goliath, who, according to I Samuel in the Bible, was slain by a Hebrew boy named David (*Dawood*). The battle for God and control of his purported holy land has certainly lasted for millennia.

To some Western politicians and a number of authors, including a former American president, the most popular solutions to achieving peace in the ancient conflict have included the land for peace doctrine. This doctrine provides economic incentives to Israel's neighbors to encourage their recognition of the Jewish state's right to exist and aid to help Israel build and maintain a strong military as a hawkish deterrent to Arab and Iranian aggression. Since the rebirth of Israel in 1948, all of these approaches to peace have been attempted and well documented. As well-intentioned as these actions might be to achieving peace, they fail to address the fundamental issue plaguing the process: the conflicting geotheological images presented in the Qur'an, the Jewish Torah, and the Christian gospels, as well as a humanistic perspective of people, lands, and governance. As long as the thought worlds produced by those texts exist in close proximity to each other in an area of the world seen by each religion as sacred space, there will be conflicts. Israel is the ultimate contested space. Nevertheless, virtually all peace proposals that recognize Israel's right to exist have assumed that secular and even humanistic motives for achieving peace would supplant opposing religious impulses and objectives. Is it possible for humanism to grow in this region characterized by people with religiously inspired visions of life and politics? Or, will the slowly growing Jewish population in Israel be drowned by the rising human tide of Islam?

Answers to those questions are: yes and maybe, respectively. Since regional thought worlds belong to people who also see religion as an expression of their heritage, the challenges for secularizing the region are great. The situation is made even worse by the structure of the various religious communities. Each community has a hierarchy with self-protecting mechanisms in place. Beyond this simple comparison, however, we can fairly say that the leaders of puritan Islam, by virtue of their theocratic orientation and geotheological imaginings, have more to lose to secularism than the Jewish leaders of Israel, which is a surprisingly diverse country that is already characterized by secular and humanistic lifestyles. Also, Islam is built on a theology of deterrence featuring a strong internal justification for rejecting both secularism and strict humanism. These theological traits, together with regional demographic and economic conditions, present real challenges to achieving peace in the Middle East. Israel sits in a precarious geographic position.

Israel's Geopolitical Predicament

In the West, Switzerland provides, arguably, the best example of a small country surrounded by larger nations that, though they have warred with each other, have left the Swiss alone. Thus, the tiny, land-locked country has little need for border fences. However, what if Switzerland had not been so fortunate in its situation? What challenges would it have faced if it had been half of its current size of nearly sixteen thousand square miles and the neighboring countries of Austria, France, Germany, and Italy had invaded it three times over the last sixty years? One might conclude that poor Switzerland would be facing some major defense issues. That is precisely the situation that Israel has faced. Within weeks of its reestablishment in 1948, which had taken over fifty years and the Holocaust to accomplish, Egypt, Jordan, Syria, Lebanon, Iraq, and Saudi Arabia invaded the fledgling country. Not only was Israel able to defend itself, it actually acquired lands from Egypt and Jordan. In 1949, each country signed an armistice. Jordan occupied the West Bank of the Jordan River and Egypt gained control of the Gaza Strip. The 1949 agreements established Israel's boundaries, but the nation failed to obtain official recognition of its sovereignty. It is an ironic twist of international politics that, while Jordan and Egypt controlled the West Bank and the Gaza Strip, respectively, they made no offer of these lands to Palestinians, which would have given them a homeland. Nevertheless, that issue has resurfaced again and again among Arab nations and Iran as a point of contention against Israel. Despite decades of having the land and resources to grant Palestinians a homeland, Arab aggression against the Jewish state continued and Palestinians were left to wait. The Arabs' goal was the destruction of Israel through conventional military means.

As a result of another failed multinational invasion of Israel in 1967, Arabs again lost their opportunity to create a Palestinian state, a situation they had undeniably controlled since 1949. Also, Arab countries lost huge pieces of territory to Israel. This conflict—better known as the Six Day War—ended with Israel seizing the Sinai Peninsula from Egypt, the Golan Heights from Syria, and the West Bank from Jordan. To the embarrassment of Muslims everywhere, Israel also occupied East Jerusalem and the Dome of the Rock, the third holiest site in Islam after Mecca and Medina. Despite the success of the Israelis, the country's military troubles were not over.

On Yom Kippur (October 6, 1973), one of Judaism's most solemn holidays, Egypt and Syria yet again went on the offensive against their tiny, sandwiched neighbor. This time Israel repelled Syria and actually crossed the

Suez Canal in Egypt, where it remained until January 1974. This conflict, like the earlier wars, was halted by assertive actions taken by the United Nations (UN). The Yom Kippur War ended with a cease-fire agreement brokered by the UN on October 24, 1973. The Sinai Peninsula, however, was not returned to Egypt until 1979, when Egypt and Israel signed a formal peace agreement called the Camp David Accords (1978).

Despite peace with Egypt, Israel is still surrounded by large countries with questionable attitudes toward it. Israel's high population density makes suicide bombings and other terrorist acts effective and less destructive to its enemy's homelands than all-out war. While writers, including this author, cannot prove any direct state involvement in ordering terrorist acts against Israel, its neighbors do not publicly protest terrorist assaults against innocent Israelis. Since most of Israel's retaliations are against Palestinians associated with Hamas (the militant political arm of the Muslim Brotherhood operating in Palestine), and with an occasional thrust against Hezbollah insurgents in Lebanon, perhaps there is no evidence that links terrorist acts in Israel to foreign states. However, Hamas is connected to powerful and politically active foreign organizations, including Iranian charities. Even as far back as the 1980s, President Ronald Reagan was concerned about linkages between the Lebanese Hezbollah and the government of Iran.[2] Currently, Hamas operates with a $70 million annual budget, and almost half of it comes from Iran.[3]

In addition to an apparent money trail between Gaza and Tehran, statements made by current Iranian President Mahmoud Ahmadinejad suggest that terrorism and internal political actions designed to weaken Jewish resolve to defend its sovereignty have replaced conventional warfare. He regards Israel as a puppet nation established by the United States and the United Kingdom. Therefore, Israel has no legitimate reason to exist. As he proclaims:

> The first solution is that just in the same way as you mounted this regime in the past, you can remove it yourself. You know well that the Holocaust has nothing to do with the Palestinian people. That was just a pretext to create this regime. And it was not a good excuse. Just cease to support it. Don't use your people's money to assist this violent regime. This is the best

solution. If they do not accept the first solution, then they should allow the nation of Palestine to make their decision about its own fate. Anyone who is a Palestinian citizen, whether they are Christian, Jewish or Muslim, should decide together in a very free referendum. There is no need for war. There is no need for threats or an atom bomb either. All that is needed is logic and reason and the humanitarian basis adopted by the United Nations. And we should consider the right to self determination for the Palestinians too, and then the issue will be solved.[4]

Ahmadinejad wants the United States and Great Britain to turn their backs on Israel, call the land Palestine, and recognize a new government chosen freely by the people, regardless of their religious affiliations. Because of Israel's geopolitical predicament, Ahmadinejad has a good reason to feel confident about the way things would unfold in Palestine.

Ahmadinejad's call for a referendum to decide Israel's fate is reminiscent of a situation that contributed to the American Civil War (1861–1865). It is worth briefly reassessing that American situation to help make clearer Israel's future predicament. In the 1850s, the expansion of slavery became a matter of national unity. One solution was to allow residents to decide if their territories would be admitted to the Union as a free state or a slave state. The recruitment of proslavery and opposing free soil residents into Kansas led to violent outbreaks that gave the newly acquired state the nickname of "Bleeding Kansas." Imagine what would happen if a referendum were to determine the future existence of Israel. A brief look at the geography, demographic trends, and economic patterns in the region shows that there is real concern that Ahmadinejad's proposal for "peace" could create a "bleeding Israel."

At 8,019 square miles, Israel is about nine-tenths the size of New Jersey. Of US States, only Connecticut, Delaware, and Rhode Island are smaller in land area. However, its 6.2 million people make it a very dense place to live. In 2006, it was roughly equal to the combined total residents of Delaware, Montana, North Dakota, South Dakota, Vermont, Wyoming, Rhode Island, and the city of Akron, Ohio.[5] With so many people living in such a small place, suicide bombers and other terrorists have little trouble finding soft targets. The two largest urban areas, Tel Aviv and Haifa, are located only twelve and thirty-six miles, respectively, from Jordan, and Jerusalem is situated within sight of the occupied West Bank. In the north of Israel, the West Bank, which was taken from Jordan to stop shelling from its strategically important hill tops, is actually an upland area extending west of the Jordan River for about forty miles. Despite Jewish settlements built there since 1967, the region is home to mostly Palestinians who want the right to determine their own future. Nevertheless, many Jews regard the hills and small mountains as part of biblical Samaria and Judea, so there is strong resistance within Israel to relinquishing its control of the West Bank.[6]

While open to the Mediterranean Sea in the west, Israel borders countries dominated by Muslims, who, with the exception of Lebanon, are growing at a much faster pace. Israel will have about twelve million people by 2067, but in that same year, there will be over 110 million Saudis, more than 160 million Egyptians, and nearly 70 million Syrians.[7] This is similar to the population of Canada and the United States compared to the population of Pennsylvania crammed into a space smaller than New Jersey.

With Israel being a geographically small country with an aging Jewish population and a vanishing Christian community, president Ahmadinejad can no doubt see the proverbial writing on the wall. If the government of Israel were to allow its future to be determined in a public referendum that permitted Palestinians to vote, as suggested by the Iranian president, there would be unprecedented growth in the Palestinian population in the country resulting from Arab immigration to Israel. If Israel were to limit voting in the referendum only to citizens, it would provoke strong reactions among Palestinians and those across the globe who are sympathetic to their cause. Restrictions on nonpermanent border crossings would also be seen as discriminatory against Palestinians (who have benefited from jobs offered through Israel's diversified economic structure). Ahmadinejad is a smart man; he can see and read the demographic trends in the Middle East. Perhaps he is making more than idle observation about how to achieve regional peace.

Regional stability and, indeed, Israel's future are threatened by more than just a simple change in Middle Eastern population growth rates. Israel's economic strength creates quite a contrast to the standard of living offered in neighboring countries. This dissimilarity ensures that Israel will attract and employ Palestinians who come and go on a daily or short-term basis as well as those who come and decide to stay. Just as the economy of the United States exploits the labor of illegal immigrants, the low-wage employment sector of Israel does the same. In comparison to its neighbors, Israel is a wealthy, well-watered land. Its per capita gross domestic product (GDP) is over $20,000 while in Jordan, Syria, and Lebanon it ranges between $3,400 and $5,000. At only $12,000 per person, even the production of oil-rich Saudi Arabia pales in comparison to Israel's economic vitality. With Israel's secular population opting out of having children, the country depends heavily on immigrant labor, and with a ready and willing Arab population living on its doorstep, more and more Muslims, both legal and illegal, are going to seek Allah's economic blessings inside the Israeli border. With so much riding on a continual flow of Muslims into Israel, it is easy to see that Ahmadinejad's goal that the fate of Palestine be determined in a referendum indeed places the Jewish state in a quandary. If Israel severely restricts Muslim movement into and out of the country, especially if physical barriers are built, such actions will serve as political fodder for Israel's opponents. The increasingly powerful Muslim voices of opposition to building security fences will likely reach the chambers of the United Nations. This topic will be increasingly used by Muslim organizations everywhere to build resentment against Israel. However, if Israel does nothing, it will be inundated with millions of Arab immigrants. Given the mounting lobby power of Muslims in the United States and European countries, support for Israel to protect itself is likely to be short-lived anyway. With an increasing need for Middle Eastern oil, Western capitalists will see no reason to support Israel's right to protect itself from unfettered demographic transition. These situations further emphasize that Israel is in a precarious geopolitical position.

Even with the unfolding demographic scenario confronting Israel, the country continues to cope with committed political opponents; and it is facing a perfect storm swelling up from the combined forces of population, politics, and religion. What is not particularly clear to many observers of regional political and social movements and other events affecting Middle Eastern peace, is how puritan Muslims, inspired by the geotheological imagery of the Qur'an, view Jews, Israel, and its nonreligious people. Now, let us take a look at the Qur'an to see how it views Israel, and, perhaps more importantly, how it regards the treatment of Israel.

The Qur'an's View of Israel

Taking a look at Qur'anic images of Israel may seem like an unnecessary diversion from a discussion on the political problems facing the Middle East, but, since the Qur'an provides the geotheological framework for puritan Islam and Islamism, delineating those images is necessary in order to understand how leaders like Ahmadinejad see Israel. In the case of the children of Israel, the Qur'an is quite clear in describing their heretofore decimated condition. Perhaps more importantly, its pages show puritans how they are to regard the descendants of the former exalted nation.

When Muhammad was alive, Israel was already a vanquished nation. Indeed, Muhammad seldom refers to Israel as an intact nation, and, when its name is used in a political-state sense, it is often in reference to its original condition. The Qur'an most often employs "the children of Israel" in lieu of "Israel," which would suggest the recognition of governing structure.[8] The Qur'an does not envision a geoschatology featuring the re-creation of Israel.

It is historically accurate to note that political Israel was destroyed in the first century, and many of its Jewish residents were forced by the Romans from their homes in Palestine to outposts in places as far away as the modern-day states of Germany, Spain, and Great Britain. The Jewish Diaspora in 70 CE left Palestine a devastated place with quiet communities of Christians and Jews living among polytheists. To Muhammad, Israel's fate was the result of failing to follow the truths of the Torah (*Taurat*) and the gospels (*Injeel*). From a geoteleological perspective, the Qur'an uses the example of the children of Israel to show what can happen to a nation when it rejects Allah's faith. As described in Surah 3, "He has revealed to you the Book with truth. Verifying that which is before it, and He revealed the Torah and the Gospel aforetime, a guidance for the people, and He sent the Qur'an. Surely they who disbelieve in the communications of Allah—they shall have a severe chastisement."[9] It is not surprising then that in the Qur'an, Muhammad refers to the children of Israel in positive terms. However, after the children failed to abide by Allah's teachings, the Prophet shifts his tone to one of national condemnation.

As followers of Islam believe, the Qur'an is the final word from God. However, it was not the first. Neither was Muhammad nor his Meccan tribe the original recipients of Allah's revelations. That responsibility, according to the Qur'an, fell on Moses (*Musa*) and the children of Israel. Muhammad wrote, "And We certainly gave the Book to Musa, so be not in doubt concerning the receiving of it, and We made it a guide for the children of Israel."[10] Here the "Book" refers to the Torah, the five books of Moses (Genesis, Exodus, Leviticus, Numbers, and Deuteronomy).

Still, one must ask, what are specific Qur'anic images of the children of Israel? By describing its perception of them, it is possible to see how puritan Muslims view modern Israel. More importantly it allows an opportunity to get a clearer picture of some of the more serious political challenges facing the Middle East because there are those like Iranian president Ahmadinejad who do not give re-created Israel any biblical or, indeed, Qur'anic basis for existing. It seems that most of the puritan followers of Islam have a similar view of this modern incarnation of Israel. To many of them, its creation is not a re-creation. It is a construction of Western powers and not the result of the hand of Allah. Nevertheless, these and other Muslims generate their image of Jews (the children of Israel) from the Qur'an, so for our purposes, we will focus on Qur'anic images that lend themselves to the perpetuation of contested space in the Middle East.

Muhammad believed that, in its original state, Israel was an exalted people. In that condition, Allah was quick to grant Israel its requests through prayers of petition. "We revealed to Musa when his people asked him for water: Strike the rock with your staff, so outflowed from it twelve springs."[11] This text shows how Allah continued to shower Israel with blessings. To further illustrate this point, the Qur'an tells us: "We made the clouds to give shade over them and We sent to them manna and quails: Eat of the good things We have given you."[12] Some thirteen Surahs later, Muhammad, showing the consistency of his message, returns to this promise: "O children of Israel! Indeed we delivered you from your enemy, and We made a covenant with you on the blessed side of the mountain, and We sent to you the manna and the quails."[13] Despite being blessed with ample means of sustenance, the Qur'an declares that, through their wrong-doings, that blessed condition was lost. Without a great deal of explanation, the text immediately asserts that "those who were unjust among them changed it [the law] for a saying other than that which had been spoken to them; so We sent upon them a pestilence from heaven because they were unjust."[14] Israel, according to the Qur'an, "did not do Us any harm, but they did injustice to their souls."[15] Nonetheless, the actions of a segment of the population invoked the wrath of Allah on what appears to be the entire population of Israel.

In beginning its litany of statements denouncing Israel, which, in turn, provides justification for its demise, the Qur'an acknowledges that Allah alone had kept his part of a bilateral covenant with the nation. "O children of Israel! Call to mind My favor which I bestowed on you and be faithful to [your] covenant with Me, I will fulfill [My] covenant with you; and of Me, Me alone, should you be afraid."[16] Muhammad goes on to remind them of their former lofty position saying, "O children of Israel! Call to mind My favor which I bestowed on you and that I made you excel the nations."[17] Later, Musa is referred to again, in establishing a rationale for condemning Israel. "And when Musa said to his people: O my people! Remember the favor of Allah upon you when He raised prophets among you and made you kings and gave you what He had not given to any other among the nations. O my people! Enter the holy land which Allah has prescribed for you and turn not on your backs for then you will turn back losers."[18] However, some among them did turn back losers. Again, without a great deal of elucidation, the Qur'an does not expound on the specifics of what they were guilty of committing. Perhaps it is more important to see that the Qur'an uses the example of Israel to discourage Allah's followers from straying from their covenant with him.

To that end, the Qur'an frequently uses events that occurred during the era of Moses and other times in Jewish history to remind the followers of Islam that even the puritans' lofty status is not guaranteed. One way Muhammad accomplished this feat was to point out that the children of

Israel had failed in keeping up their part of the bilateral covenant. The Qur'an uses their sense of loss to prick a consequential sense of guilt to which, he assumed, Muslims could relate. As the Qur'an explains through questioning, "Ask them about the town which stood by the sea; when they exceeded the limits of the Sabbath, when their fish came to them on the day of their Sabbath, appearing on the surface of the water, and on the day on which they did not keep the Sabbath they did not come to them; thus did We try them because they transgressed."[19]

The Qur'an uses other figures from the Torah to show how Allah had bestowed blessings and punishments on the children of Israel. These people were given their positions through the sovereign, but somewhat variable, will of Allah. It is important to recall that in Islam, Allah's grace is not entirely free (as one would see in the context of Calvinism). The thoughts and deeds of single individuals, small groups, and nations can cause Allah to switch from sending blessings to leveling punishments on the entire town or nation. For a time, at least, Allah grants forgiveness to some nations if they repent and submit to the teachings of the Prophet. Here again, Israel provides the Qur'an with a fertile example: "Have you not considered the chiefs of the children of Israel after Musa, when they said to a prophet of theirs: Raise up for us a king, [that] we may fight in the way of Allah. He said: May it not be that you would not fight if fighting is ordained for you? They said: And what reason[s] have we that we should not fight in the way of Allah, and we have indeed been compelled to abandon our homes and our children. But when fighting was ordained for them, they turned back, except a few of them, and Allah knows the unjust."[20] The children of Israel were apparently forgiven for that transgression, for the Qur'an then moves on to explain how Allah empowered the children of Israel to vanquish their enemy. During the heat of battle, David (*Dawood*) slew Goliath (*Jalut*). "Allah," Muhammad wrote, "gave him [David] kingdom and wisdom, and taught him of what He pleased. And were it not for Allah's repelling some men with others, the earth would certainly be in a state of disorder; but Allah is gracious to the creatures."[21] Allah's grace, according to the Qur'an, was offered to Israel for several more centuries. It is important to point out here that many Jews and Christians believe that in Ezekiel 36–39, the Bible speaks of the rebirth of

Israel. In a speech at the Nazi extermination camp called Auschwitz, on January 27, 2010, Israeli Prime Minister Benjamin Netanyahu invoked the words in Ezekiel 37:11–12: "Then He said unto me: These bones are the whole House of Israel. They say, 'Our bones are dried up, our hope is gone; we are doomed.' Prophecy, therefore, and say to them: Thus said the Lord God: I am going to open your graves and lift you out of your graves, O My people, and bring you to the land of Israel."[22]

According to the Qur'an, however, Israel reached the end of its grace period when it rejected the message of Jesus (*Isa*) as told in the Gospel of Jesus. In Surah 3, the text describes the virgin conception of Mary (*Marium*), and then the text moves on to tell us that Jesus had a divinely appointed mission to remind the children of Israel of the truths in the Torah (*Taurat*). The Qur'an purports that Jesus said, "[I am] a verifier of that which is before me of the Taurat, and that I may allow you part of that which has been forbidden you, and I have come to you with a sign from your Lord, therefore be careful of [your duty to] Allah and obey me."[23] In the Qur'an, Jesus is an interesting mixture of humanity and special creation, but he is not divine. To Muhammad, Jesus was sent to earth for several purposes, none of which, however, was of his own design. All that he accomplished was through the sovereign will and grace of Allah. In speaking about Jesus' mission, Muhammad wrote: "And [make] him an apostle to the children of Israel: that I have come to you with a sign from your Lord, that I determine for you out of dust like the form of a bird, then I breathe into it and it becomes a bird with Allah's permission and I heal the blind and the leprous, and bring the dead to life with Allah's permission and I inform you of what you should eat and what you should store in your houses; most surely there is a sign in this for you, if you are believers."[24] Jesus, according to Surah 3, was not crucified but simply removed without suffering death, so it follows that there is no way he could have served as a blood sacrifice for the sins of humanity. The historicity of Jesus' crucifixion is verified, however, by the Jewish apologist and historian Titus Flavius Josephus, who wrote an extra-biblical description of the crucifixion of Jesus as well as a firsthand account of the sacking of Jerusalem in 70 CE.[25] Josephus was certainly not a Christian, and, as a Roman citizen, he had no political motives for helping to spread a lie in support of Christianity's claim that Jesus' crucifixion was propitiation for the sins of humanity. Despite

Josephus's work, here is the Qur'an's version of events concerning the "supposed" death of Jesus: "And their saying: Surely we have killed the Messiah, Isa son of Marium, the apostle of Allah; and they did not kill him nor did they crucify him, but it appeared to them so [like Isa] and most surely those who differ therein are only in doubt about it; they have no knowledge respecting it, but only follow a conjecture, and they killed him not for sure."[26] According to the Qur'an, Jesus and Allah sensed that some of the children of Israel did not believe his message. The Family of Imran describes Jesus' departure from earth: "And when Allah said: O Isa, I am going to terminate the period of your stay [on earth] and cause you to ascend unto Me and purify you of those who disbelieve and make those who follow you above those who disbelieve to the day of resurrection; then to Me shall be your return, so I will decide between you concerning that in which you differed."[27]

In showing that Jesus was just a prophet and to be counted among the judging voices of the likes of David, Muhammad declares: "Those who disbelieved from among the children of Israel were cursed by the tongue of Dawood and Isa, son of Marium; this was because they disobeyed and used to exceed the limit [of Allah's tolerance]."[28] Note how the Qur'an refers to Jesus as the son of Mary. It is worth pointing out that this title, which some argue shows how much Muhammad respected Mary, was more likely used to deemphasize Jesus' claim of being the Son of Man, the truth and way, and it was certainly used to refute the church's claim from the fourth century, hammered out at the Council of Nicaea, that Jesus was both god and man. Muhammad was convinced that Jesus, despite granting validity to the gospels, was simply a man acting as a prophet for Allah; anyone who insists that Jesus is divine is a liar. This notion is confirmed by the Qur'an's words later in Surah 18: "And warn those who say that Allah has taken a son. They have no knowledge of it, nor had their fathers; a grievous word it is that comes out of their mouths; they speak nothing but a lie."[29] The Qur'an places Jesus in a conversation with Allah in which Jesus rejects the notion that he had laid claims to deity: "And when Allah will say: O Isa son of Marium! Did you say to men take me and my mother for two gods besides Allah, he will say: Glory be to Thee, it did not befit me that I should say what I had no right to [say]; if I had said it, Thou wouldst indeed have known it; Thou knowest what is in my mind, and I do not know what is in

Thy mind, surely Thou art the great Knower of the unseen things."[30] Jesus, according to the Qur'an, was a Muslim prophet used by Allah to remind the children of Israel of their covenant with him. The children of Israel clearly failed to respond appropriately to Jesus; therefore, he was taken away to be cleansed of their disbelief. In an attempt to further invalidate Christianity, the Qur'an claims that in the post-Jesus era, Jesus' disciples became committed Muslims.[31]

It is worth pointing out that a passage in Matthew projects a different version of Jesus' mission, delineating a contested version of sacred history. Most scholars agree that the Book of Matthew was written before the conclusion of the first century.[32] The Qur'an was not written until the seventh century. Since Muhammad refers to the validity of the Gospel of Jesus, it could logically be concluded that he had read it in its entirety. Apparently he doubted the veracity of this passage:

> When Jesus came into the coasts of Caesarea Philippi, he asked his disciples, saying, whom do men say that I the Son of man am? And they said, some say that thou are John the Baptist; some, Elijah; and others Jeremiah, or one of the prophets. He saith unto them, but whom say ye that I am? And Simon Peter answered and said, Thou art the Christ, the Son of the living God. And Jesus answered and said unto him, Blessed art thou, Simon Barjona: for flesh and blood hath not revealed it unto to thee, but my Father which is in heaven.[33]

On the subject of the disciples, a number of them are reported to have founded various Christian churches, though the Qur'an does not recognize this. Peter, to whom Jesus spoke in the previous passage, founded the Syriac Church[34] and the roots of the Armenian Church were planted by Jesus' apostles Bartholomew and Thaddeus.[35] The Qur'an also does not acknowledge that the disciple Mark laid the foundation for the Coptic Church in Alexandria, Egypt, in 42 CE.[36] Because there is no objective source to confirm Muhammad's declaration that Jesus' disciples were Muslims, acceptance of that claim is strictly a matter of faith. Indeed, history tells us that they were Christians, although there was, and continues to be, disagreement over the nature of Christ, including his divinity and his part in the Trinity. However, much of the disagreement over the nature of Christ was resolved in the Nicean Creed, which resulted from the proceedings of the Council of Nicaea in 325 CE.[37] Nevertheless, none of the early churches founded by Jesus' disciples denied his deity. Regardless of scriptural passages and extra-biblical evidence, puritan Muslims do not believe historical accounts that stand in opposition to the Qur'an, for Muhammad taught that the worship of Jesus was in error and that those who did so, not to mention Jews who rejected Jesus as the messiah altogether, were liars.[38]

This brings up the need to explore the way in which the Qur'an merges Christianity and Judaism into an alliance against Islam, although it does admit that Christians and Jews follow different beliefs and teachings revealed in the same book.[39] Nevertheless, the two are imagined as joined together in opposition to the truth revealed in the Qur'an. The Qur'an puts these words into the mouths of Christian and Jews: "And the Jews and the Christians say: We are the sons of Allah and His beloved ones. Say Why does He then chastise you for your faults? Nay, you are mortals from among those whom He has created; He forgives whom He pleases and chastises whom He pleases: and Allah's is the kingdom of the heavens and the earth and what is between them, and to Him is the eventual coming."[40] Muhammad warned his followers that Christians and Jews will not be pleased with Muslims until they convert to follow one of the other religions.[41] They are not to be trusted: "O you who believe! Do not take the Jews and Christians for friends; they are friends of each other; and whoever amongst you takes them for a friend, then surely he is one of them; surely Allah does not guide the unjust people."[42] In switching to a future tense, the Qur'an declares that the children of Israel were given the book, the Torah and the gospels, but they did not abide by it nor did they follow its guidance. "Most certainly you will make mischief in the land twice, and most certainly you will behave insolently with great insolence."[43]

With respect to geoteleology, the future does not bode well for Christians and the children of Israel. Christians and Jews are to be treated harshly or, at best, coldly, as payment for their disbelief. Because the children of Israel persisted in disobeying Allah by rejecting the admonishments of Jesus, the Qur'an declares: "We said to them: Be [as] apes, despised and hated."[44] The Jews and Christians are not only to be hated by all men, especially the followers of Islam, the Qur'an calls upon Allah to curse and destroy them.

"And the Jews say: Uzair [Ezra] is the son of Allah; and the Christians say: The Messiah is the son of Allah; these are the words of their mouths; they imitate the saying of those who disbelieved before; may Allah destroy them; how they turned away!"[45] Here, the Qur'an sees Christians as an adjunct movement of the children of Israel. Christians and Jews are arguably to be regarded by Muslims as one and the same.

The Qur'an assures Muslims that these false religions are doomed. "He it is Who sent His Apostle with guidance and the religion of truth, that He might cause it to prevail over all religions, though the polytheists may be averse."[46] The future, according to Muhammad, is in the hands of an omniscient Allah. Geographer John K. Wright would have seen this statement as geoteleological in that Allah is making a way for his religion to prevail.[47] To the puritan Muslim, the emerging world of Muhammad will usher in another golden age in which the true religion will prevail over all competing faiths, especially those who claim to be heirs of Abraham.

Summary

These perceptions of the Jewish and Christian faiths, taken together with the prevailing economic and demographic trends in the Middle East, leave little room to speculate about Israel's future. The Jewish community in Palestine has benefited greatly by the immigration of Sephardic and Ashkenazi Jews. Even with a Muslim enhanced natural increase rate of 1.2, the country's current Jewish population is barely replacing itself.[48] Meanwhile, Israel's Christian population is disappearing. In 1946, just two years before the rebirth of Israel, some 13 percent of the population in Palestine lived in small, Christian enclaves. By 2000, the percentage of Christians living there had dwindled to a miniscule 2.1 percent.[49] As Iranian president Ahmadinejad has stated, there is no need for war or atom bombs. Surely he knows that Israel exists on a precarious precipice, and, in time, the weight of millions of Muslims will push it over the edge. Where will it fall? What will be its ultimate fate? Indeed, Israel resides at the core of the imagined theological worlds of over a quarter of the earth's human inhabitants.

Chapter 9

Future Geographies of Islam

Introduction

In this book, special consideration has been given to geographic, especially geotheological, imagery found in the Qur'an. These images provide illumination on how the Qur'an presents Allah in relation to spaces occupied by individuals, communities, and nations. The Muslim holy book also features depictions of the forces of nature and their relationship to perceptions of divine will and human behavior. Qur'anic geotheology, hence, demands adherence to Islam with implications for civic governance. This book has also described the demographic shifts and transitions in and among traditionally Christian nations of Europe, North America, and the countries that make up the Islamic world. In this final chapter, we project these trends into the future to consider how geographic patterns in Islam will change throughout the first half of the twenty-first century.

Islam is creating its own spaces in the United States. In the small town of Perrysburg, Ohio, a large mosque rises above surrounding cornfields. In Minneapolis, Minnesota, Muslim taxi drivers safeguard their microspaces from the evils of alcoholic beverages and those who wish to carry and consume alcohol in taxi cabs. In Hamtramck, Michigan, a former Polish ethnic enclave, calls to prayer are heard in public spaces, and in an airport in Kansas City, wash benches have been installed to allow Muslim workers, including taxi drivers frequenting the airport, the opportunity to wash and prepare for daily prayers. Even in southern Appalachia, Muslims, in some communities like Harlan, Kentucky, compose a significant portion of the population of primary care physicians. These professionals provide a stark contrast to the image that many Americans have regarding Muslims. It is perhaps popular to believe that Islamic followers are either poor Arabs or African American converts. As the Pew report discussed in chapter 1 shows, most American Muslims are middle class. About two-thirds of Islamic immigrants consider themselves racially white, as opposed to African American or Asian. In fact, the world's largest Muslim-dominated country is Indonesia, and it is certainly not an Arab nation. These facts illustrate the spread of Islam throughout the world and its effect on both its followers and inhabitants of the secular world.

Figure 11. The Mosque of Greater Cincinnati. (Photo courtesy of the author.)

The Pew report does not show, however, the future demographic profiles of American and global Islam. To accomplish that important task, we must consider the demographic patterns in other countries. To further assist us in creating a future geography of Islam, it is fitting to consider mobility transition or migration theories like those offered by geographers E. G. Ravenstein and Wilbur Zelinsky. As was shown in chapter 1, current Muslim doubling times around the world suggest that Islam will be the world's largest religion by 2060. Also, it was shown that the vast majority of the forty-six Muslim-dominated countries will double their populations in less than forty-five years. At least twenty-one of those countries will double their populations in as little as thirty-five years. It is important to know that these doubling times consider only natural increase rates; they do take into account the effects that net migration might have on future population estimates.

Given the current Islamic doubling time in the United States (about six years) and the continued high growth rate in most Muslim countries, the Muslim American population could reach 300 million before high school graduates entering college in the decade of 2010 retire from the workforce in the late 2050s. That scenario does not consider the growth in the existing American population or that generated by other immigrant streams coming to America.

Muslim population growth is occurring throughout traditionally Christian countries in western Europe and North America while the resident populations are either slowly growing or are on the decline. While it is tempting to provide theoretical depictions of what society might look like in the 2060s, it is up to the reader to appreciate what the Qur'an has to say about people, lands, and governance, because, despite different traditions in Islamic jurisprudence, all Muslim societies recognize that the Qur'an is not the inspired word of God, as is the case among Christians regarding the Bible; instead, Muslims regard the Qur'an as the word of God as told to Muhammad through the angel Gabriel. Despite this book's observations regarding how Muslim societies are responding demographically to religiously inspired images of self, community, nature, nation, and governance, it must be recognized that there are an undetermined number of people living in Muslim nations and Muslim enclaves in the United States and Europe who do not really believe all that the Qur'an has to say. They, like many who call themselves Christians, are only nominal Muslims. Nevertheless, the ethos that permeates the spatially blurred world of Islamic fundamentalism, or puritanism, deserves a deeper understanding. The geotheological concepts originally coined by John K. Wright offer a clear framework for appreciating the synergistic relationship between religiously inspired images of self, community, nation, and landscapes and the Qur'an's need for Islamic self-rule. The coining and use of the terms geotheokolasis and geotheomisthosis to deepen the application of geotheology in the study of religion, generally, and Islam, specifically, adds to our understanding of the imagined situations in which Allah either punishes people through natural forces or rewards them with lush, water-soaked, and thriving lands.

Table 3. Demographic Profile of Countries with Significant Muslim Populations > 4 % 2009[1]

Country N = 82	Population	Population Density (people/sq. mile)	Doubling Time (years)	Percent Muslim
Afghanistan*	32,738,376	131	27	99
Albania*	3,619,778	342	72	70
Algeria*	33,769,669	36.7	58	99
Azerbaijan*	7,911,974	237	73	93
Bahrain*	718,306	2,797	55	81
Bangladesh*	153,546,901	2,969	34	83
Bosnia and Herzegovinal	4,590,310	89.8	2,400	40
Benin*	8,532,547	199.8	24	24
Brunei*	381,371	187.4	48	67
Burkina-Faso*	15,264,735	144.4	23	50
Cameroon*	18,467,692	101.9	32	20
Chad*	10,111,337	20.8	28	53
Comoros*	731,775	873.4	26	98
Democratic Republic of the Congo	66,514,506	76	23	10
Cote d'Ivoire*	20,179,602	164	33	35
Cyprus	792,604	222.2	150	18
Djibouti*	506,221	57.1	37	94
Egypt*	81,713,517	212.6	42	90
Ethiopia	82,544,838	190.9	22	33
Fiji	931,741	132.1	44	7
France	64,057,790	259.2	171	10
Gabon*	1,485,832	14.9	31	25
Gambia*	1,735,464	449.5	27	90
Georgia	4,630,841	172.1	7,200	10
Ghana	23,382,848	262.2	36	16
Guinea*	9,806,509	103.3	27	85
Guinea-Bissau*	1,503,182	139	35	45
Guyana*	770,794	10.1	75	7
India	1,147,995,898	1,000	46	13
Indonesia*	237,512,355	336.8	55	86
Iran*	65,875,223	104.3	64	98
Iraq*	28,221,181	169.1	28	97
Israel	7,112,359	906.1	49	16
Jordan*	6,198,677	174.6	41	92
Kazakhstan*	15,340,533	14.9	102	47
Kenya	37,953,838	172.7	26	10
Kuwait*	2,596,799	377.4	37	85
Kyrgyzstan*	5,356,869	72.5	44	75
Lebanon*	3,971,941	1005.6	62	60
Liberia	3,334,587	89.7	33	20
Libya*	6,173,579	9.1	32	97
Macedonia	2,061,315	214.8	225	33
Madagascar	20,042,551	89.3	24	7
Malawi	13,931,831	383.5	30	13
Malaysia*	25,274,133	199.2	41	60
Maldives*	385,925	3,331.8	64	99
Mali*	12,324,029	26.2	22	90

Mauritania*	3,364,940	8.5	25	100
Mauritius	1,274,189	1,625.7	88	17
Morocco*	34,343,219	199.3	46	99
Mozambique*	21,284,701	70.3	40	18
Niger*	13,272,679	27.1	24	80
Nigeria*	146,255,306	415.9	35	50
Oman*	3,311,640	40.4	23	75
Pakistan*	172,800,051	574.7	35	97
Palestine*	3,907,883	1,627	no data (likely high)	99
Philippines	96,061,683	834.4	34	5
Qatar*	824,789	186.4	55	78
Russia	140,702,094	21.4	none	10
Rwanda	10,186,063	1057.5	28	5
Saudi Arabia*	28,146,657	33.9	27	100
Senegal*	12,853,259	173.4	28	94
Sierra Leone*	6,294,774	227.6	32	60
Singapore	4,608,167	17,482.2	160	15
Somalia*	9,558,666	39.5	26	99
Sri Lanka	21,128,773	845.3	68	8
Sudan*	40,218,455	43.8	35	70
Suriname*	475,996	7.6	63	20
Swaziland	1,128,814	170	none (AIDS)†	10
Syria*	19,747,586	277.9	33	90
Tajikistan*	7,211,884	130.9	36	90
Tanzania	40,213,162	117.6	32	35
Thailand	65,493,298	331.5	112	5
Togo*	5,858,673	279	26	20
Trinidad & Tobago	1,047,366	529	313	6
Tunisia*	10,383,577	173.1	70	98
Turkey*	71,892,807	241.6	71	99
Turkmenistan*	5,179,571	27.5	38	89
Uganda*	31,367,972	406.8	20	12
United Arab Emirates*	4,621,399	143.2	52	96
Uzbekistan*	27,345,026	166.5	57	88
Yemen*	23,013,376	112.9	21	99

*Member of the Organization of Islamic Conference (OIC); See maps 2 and 3.

†In Swaziland, 26.1 percent of the population is infected with HIV (*The World Almanac and Book of Facts 2009*, p. 821).

The data in table 3 do not tell the entire story of global Islam, especially in regard to places that may be serving as migration entry points for the establishment of enclaves in the United States. Guyana and Trinidad and Tobago are countries in the Western Hemisphere that may well serve as departure points for entry into the United States through the porous southern US border.

Europe also serves as a departure point for transatlantic relocations. Germany is home to a growing Muslim population that currently represents 4 percent of the country's eighty-two million people. In pure numbers, this means that there are 3.28 million Muslims living in Germany. Switzerland, too, has a 4 percent Muslim population. Nearly two million of the people who call the United Kingdom of Great Britain and Northern Ireland home are Muslims. Given the realization that Russia, Italy, and Germany have negative natural increase rates, they will most likely embrace more immigrants, including Muslims, who can provide desperately needed labor. From table 3 and map 3 it is possible to see that France is a major point of entry for Muslim immigrants into western Europe. The proportion of Muslims living in European countries will likely increase over the next few decades and, perhaps, well into the future. The question of whether or not immigrants will continue high fertility rates in their new nations is not easy to answer because of the culturally conservative nature of ethnic enclaves. Historically, because patriarchal power structures dominate most Islamic societies, Qur'anic doctrines regarding gender roles will likely continue to influence the generally high fertility of Muslim women. This situation is not likely to change in the foreseeable future, keeping fertility rates high.

Being situated thousands of miles away from the hearth of Islam, the United States is less than 1 percent Muslim—but that figure is doubling every six years. As we saw in chapter 1, the growth in the Muslim American population is resulting more from immigration than from conversions.

While Indonesia is the world's largest Muslim country, its rate of growth is about half that of Pakistan, Nigeria, and Bangladesh. Those countries will likely have greater populations than Indonesia later in the century. Bangladesh, however, is already densely populated, and its people per square mile figure is more characteristic of an urban population, rather than one made up of subsistence farmers and low-wage earners laboring away in the country's growing cotton textile, tea processing, and garment industries.[2] Nigeria, on the other hand, has had a recent history of religious-based civil wars that, especially in the 1960s, caused a great deal of emigration. Growing population there, along with a meager per capita gross domestic product (GDP) of barely $2,000 suggests that its demographic profile will

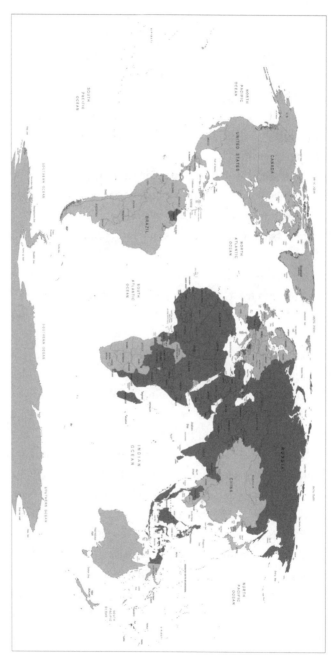

Map 3. Countries with a significant Muslim population > 4% in 2009.
(Map courtesy of Geraldine Allen.)

not change in the near future. This situation is compounded by a low literacy rate of only 30.4 percent, so the social infrastructure is not in place to facilitate demographic sustainability. As we saw in chapter 1, countries with higher literacy rates, especially among women, are not growing as fast as countries with glaring educational inequalities. Educating women and opening doors to their personal growth are tied to reducing population-related pressures and social and environmental problems. For example, Pakistan and its Kashmir region represent potential problems for neighboring India. With India's Muslim population of about 150,000,000, will a desire for Islamic unity destabilize India? This situation could worsen if the Taliban makes political gains in Pakistan. With existing social links among Indian and Pakistani Islamic communities, fundamentalist insurgencies could fester in the Asian subcontinent.

In terms of international linkages among Muslim states, the United Nations is not alone in grouping Islamic countries together. The Organization of Islamic Conference (OIC) is described by Roger W. Stump as an organization dedicated to unifying "local groups adhering to a common religious system within a larger tradition."[3] He also likens it to other international bodies, such as the World Council of Churches (founded in 1948) and the World Buddhist Sangha Council (1966), which endeavor to make tangible the intangible nature of imagined religious communities through actions that can be seen in public places. He observes that there is an implicit territoriality in these organizations. As with sociologists like Ronald Johnstone, scholars often avoid the messy details of theological imagining by making comparisons to other religious systems. Here, Stump follows that comparative and limited approach. Upon closer examination of the immaterial aspects of Islam, as well as the stated goals of the OIC, glaring differences render most comparisons to Christian and Buddhist beliefs about people, lands, and governance devoid of any real meaning. The World Council of Churches and Christian denominations do not have institutional ties to national governments. On the other hand, the OIC does have those connections. The organization describes itself as the second largest inter-governmental organization after the United Nations which has membership of 57 states spread over four continents. The Organization is the collective voice of the Muslim world and ensuring to safeguard and protect the interests of the Muslim world in the spirit of promoting international peace and harmony among various people of the world. The Organization was established upon a decision of the historical summit which took place in Rabat, Kingdom of Morocco on 12th Rajab 1389 Hijra (25 September 1969) as a result of criminal arson of Al-Aqsa Mosque in occupied Jerusalem.[4]

From this statement, it is clear that the imagined world of the Islamic religion is connected to the ruling apparatus of fifty-seven states. There is no separation of religion and state in the OIC, and it is odd that Turkey, a country with no official religion, is a member. The statement also makes it clear that its declaration that Jerusalem is an occupied city suggests hostile views toward Israel as an occupying force. The identification of the city of David as "occupied Jerusalem" has deep political meaning.

Even with different traditions in jurisprudence, languages, and race, these countries regard the Qur'an as the spiritual glue that binds them together. It is important to recall that the Qur'an sees the "nation" as a gracious gift from Allah to help sinful mankind. The need for government rule would not be necessary had man dutifully followed Allah's laws. The goal of Islamic fundamentalists is to create an international caliphate in which there is no distinction between the secular aspects of the state and geotheological notions of the Islamic community. Such a utopian vision includes an age in which Allah no longer has to punish sinful mankind. As we saw in earlier chapters, the Qur'an is overflowing with examples of ways in which a judicious Allah uses the forces of nature, aside from the sword, to reward or punish human behavior. It should be recalled that the Qur'an sees the children of Israel as a fallen and divinely punished people with no justification for being reunited as the modern state of Israel. Iranian president Mahmoud Ahmadinejad certainly holds this view. Given the religious and increasingly political sentiments held against it, Israel, which is surrounded by much larger Islamic countries with populations growing faster than the Jewish element in the region, is in a precarious position. This is especially true if the

United States lessens its support for the state or is otherwise divested of its regional power and influence. The Middle East will most likely continue to simmer, and unless there is an act of God, or Israel politically transforms itself into Palestine, more blood will flow through the streets surrounding Islam's third holiest site.

Looking again at the American homeland, we know that the United States has two basic Islamic communities: immigrants and African American converts. As we saw in chapter 6, a major reason for American Islam's two communities rests with the exaltation of the Nation of Islam's Elijah Mohammad and Wallace Fard Muhammad as prophets, which is heresy to traditional Muslims who hold that Muhammad, Islam's founder, is the last and greatest of Allah's preceding prophets. According to the Pew report released in 2007, the majority of American Muslims are immigrants, and they are mostly middle class. However, from what we know about the chain migration process and the way enclaves form and function in new lands, that socioeconomic description of American Islam is likely to change. Pioneering immigrants pave the way, so to speak, and make it easier for less talented and less able people to follow them. There can be little doubt that Muslim enclaves in Europe and the United States will increasingly resemble the stratified societies of former homelands. Such was the case in the formation of Little Italy and Little China areas in major cities like New York and San Francisco.

Summary

In the final analysis, it is impossible for one book to capture the many hues and tones of any major world religion. This book contributes a new perspective on the interfaces among people, lands, and governance in the increasingly large and influential world of Islam. Particularly important to the body of knowledge on religion that this book intends to make is the notion of geotheology applied to Islam, which has heretofore never been attempted. Many of the geotheological concepts used in this book were coined by John K. Wright, but new subconcepts were added to his useful lexicon. In my earlier work on seventeenth-century Puritan Christianity, I found Wright's ideas helpful, but limited in their capacity to express the relationship between perceptions of how God uses natural forces to either punish or reward sinful, but oftentimes repenting, humanity. In the present work, "geotheokolasis" was introduced as a way to show how the Qur'an describes Allah's use of storms, floods, winds, and fire to punish wayward people. The book also introduces the concept of "geotheomisthosis" to show how the Muslim holy book depicts Allah's control of nature's bounty as well as his use of it to reward people for their dutiful thoughts and behaviors. These concepts can and should be applied to all religions that feature supernatural aspects of the divine.

Finally, and perhaps equally important, *Puritan Islam: The Geoexpansion of the Muslim World* paints a demographic profile of the near future in light of the ecological concept of carrying capacity. Change is occurring in ways that could drastically alter existing cultural landscapes in Africa, Asia, Europe, and North America. It will be interesting to see these changes unfold.

Notes

Introduction

1. C. Allen Joyce, ed., *World Almanac and Book of Facts 2009* (Pleasantville, NY: World Almanac Education Group, 2009), p. 769. This is based on applying the natural increase rate of 1.12 to the Rule of 72. This rule identifies the mathematical reality that when 72 is divided by the natural increase rate, the answer indicates how much time is required, in years, for the population to double in size. (The Rule of 72 is also used in finance to determine the amount of interest that must be earned for an investment to double in value.)

2. See table 1 in chapter 1.

3. Wilbur Zelinsky, "The Hypothesis of Mobility Transition," *Geographical Review* 61 (1971): 219–49.

4. Khaled Abou El Fadl, "Islam and the Theology of Power," *Middle East Report* 221 (Winter 2001): 28–33. See, specifically, the discussion on the demise of the classical tradition on page 31.

5. El Fadl, "Islam and the Theology of Power," pp. 28–33.

6. John K. Wright, "Notes on Early American Geopiety," *Human Nature in Geography* (Cambridge: Cambridge University Press, 1966), pp. 250–88. I coined the term *geotheokolasis*, which is discussed in depth in a later chapter, to represent the synthesis of earth, God, and punishment. Such a use of these words was inspired by the older geographer John K. Wright, who first used *geotheology* to capture the relationship between the worship of God and the worship of spaces.

7. Wright, "Notes on Early American Geopiety," pp. 28–33. Wright's work shows the original use of the concept of geotheology. Geotheology is the relationship between space, including spatially defined places like countries, and the worship of the divine. As later chapters show, geotheology has a number of social and political implications. To see its political implications in a puritan Christian context, refer to Barry A. Vann, *In Search of Ulster-Scots Land: The Birth and Geotheolog-*

ical Imaginings of a Transatlantic People, 1603–1703 (Columbia: University of South Carolina Press, 2008); see also Avihu Zakai, *Exile and Kingdom: History and Apocalypse in the Puritan Migration to America* (Cambridge: Cambridge University Press, 2002).

8. El Fadl, "Islam and the Theology of Power," p. 32. As El Fadl discusses, there arose among some Muslims a desire to rid the faith of the tradition of jurisprudence based originally on the Hadith, which gave an account of the life and deeds of Muhammad. The Hadith was written under the Caliphate of Umar II in the eighth century. Puritan Islam seeks to return to the Qur'an and is disinterested in juris traditions that began evolving in different areas of the geographically expansive Muslim world by the eighth century.

9. A more complete delineation of Muslim and Western demographic trends is given in chapter 1.

10. M. H. Shakir, trans., *The Qur'an: Translation*, 14th ed. (Elmhurst, NY: Tahrike Tarsile Qur'an, 2003). Specifically, see Surah 13:37. In this text, all references from the Qur'an refer to this fourteenth edition. It was originally published by the Habib Esmail Benevolent Trust of Karachi, Pakistan, and later it was reprinted by the World Organization for Islamic Services of Teheran, Iran.

11. Sharon Kehnemui Liss, "GOP Candidates, Supporters Bask in Own Glory following Feisty Debate," Fox News, May 16, 2007, http://www.foxnews.com/ story/ 0,2933,272719,00.html (accessed June 1, 2009). Representative Ron Paul made his observations public during a Republican presidential debate in South Carolina on May 15, 2007.

12. Seyyed Hossein Nasr, *The Heart of Islam: Enduring Values for Humanity* (San Francisco: Harper, 2002).

13. Huston Smith, *The World's Religions: Our Great Wisdom Traditions* (San Francisco: Harper, 1991).

14. Ibid., p. 249. Inside this quote is a passage Smith took from Ameer Ali, *The Spirit of Islam* (London: Christophers, 1923), p. 173.

15. Peter R. Demant, *Islam versus Islamism: The Dilemma of the Muslim World* (West Port, CT: Praeger Books, 2006). Demant sees the current tensions as limited to Islam and Islamism, but he calls for dialogue between the leaders of the West and the leaders of moderate Muslim countries and groups to head off a global crisis.

16. Karen Armstrong, *Battle for God: A History of Fundamentalism* (London: Ballantine Books, 2001), p. xiii; Kelly Knauer, *Middle East: History, Cultures, Conflicts, Faiths* (New York: Time, 2006), pp. 1–10; Adnan A. Musallam, *From Secularism to Jihad: Sayyid Qutb and the Foundation of Radical Islam* (West Port, CT:

Praeger Books, 2005); S. Sayyid, *Fundamental Fear: Eurocentrism and the Emergence of Islamism*, 2nd ed. (London: Zed Books, 2006).

17. Roger W. Stump, *Geography of Religion: Faith, Place, and Space* (Plymouth, UK: Rowan and Littlefield, 2008), p. xvi.

18. Ronald L. Johnstone, *Religion in Society: Sociology of Religion*, 7th ed. (Upper Saddle River, NJ: Prentice Hall, 2004), p. 41.

19. Khaled Abou El Fadl, "Islamic Law and Muslim Minorities: The Juristic Discourse on Muslim Minorities from the Second/Eighth to the Eleventh/Seventeenth Centuries," *Journal of Islamic Law and Society* 22, no. 1 (1994): 141–87. See also El Fadl, "Islam and the Theology of Power," pp. 28–32.

20. Brigitte Gabriel, *Because They Hate: A Survivor of Islamic Terror Warns America* (New York: St. Martin's Press, 2006); see also Bruce Bawer, *While Europe Slept: How Radical Islam Is Destroying the West from Within* (New York: Doubleday, 2006).

21. El Fadl, "Islamic Law and Muslim Minorities." See also El Fadl, "Islam and the Theology of Power," pp. 28–33.

22. Jonathan Brockopp, ed., *Islamic Ethics of Life: Abortion, War, and Euthanasia* (Columbia: University of South Carolina Press, 2003), p. 99.

23. El Fadl, "Islam and the Theology of Power," p. 31.

24. Ibid., p. 33.

25. Colonel B. Wayne Quist and David F. Drake, *Triumph of Democracy over Militant Islamism* (Frederick, MD: Publish America, 2006); Demant, *Islam versus Islamism*.

26. Mevat Hatem, "Gender and Islamism in the 1990s," *Middle East Report* 222 (Spring 2002): 44–47.

27. Stump, *Geography of Religion*, p. 192.

28. Ibid. The Shafii school, for example, is concentrated in Egypt, western Turkey, southeastern Asia, and the east-central coast of Africa. It was founded by an Egyptian named Muhammad al-Shafii in the ninth century. Shafii taught that there are four sources for Islamic law: the Qur'an, the Hadith, the consensus of scholars (*ijma*), and traditions.

29. Brockopp, *Islamic Ethics of Life*, p. 81.

30. Zakai, *Exile and Kingdom*; Vann, *In Search of Ulster-Scots Land*; Barry A. Vann, "Geotheological Imaginings of a Trans-Irish Sea Scottish Community, 1560–1690," *Geographies of Religions and Belief Systems* 2 no. 1 (2007): 21–39.

31. Hibba Abugideiri, "Islam," in *Geography of Religion: Where God Lives, Where Pilgrims Walk*, ed. Susan T. Hitchcock and John L. Esposito (Washington, DC: National Geographic, 2004), p. 340.

32. Surah 2:174.

33. James M. Rubenstein, *The Cultural Landscape: An Introduction to Human Geography*, 7th ed. (Upper Saddle River, NJ: Prentice Hall, 2002), p. 184. There are Muslim activists who argue against a literal interpretation of the Qur'an. See the argument of Konca Kuris in Hatem, "Gender and Islamism," p. 46.

34. Stump, *Geography of Religion*, p. 189.

35. Ibid., p. 189.

36. Zakai, *Exile and Kingdom*; Wright, "Notes on Early American Geopiety"; Vann, *In Search of Ulster-Scots Land*.

37. M. Price and C. Whitworth, "Soccer and Latino Cultural Spaces: Metropolitan Washington *Futbol* Leagues," in *Hispanic Spaces, Latino Places: Community and Diversity in Contemporary America*, ed. D. Arreola (Austin: University of Texas Press, 2004), pp. 167–86; Paul L. Knox and Sallie A. Marston, *Human Geography: Places and Regions in Global Context* (Upper Saddle River, NJ: Pearson Prentice Hall, 2007), pp. 204–205. For a reference to ethnic enclaves, see William A. Schwab, *Sociology of Cities* (Englewood Cliffs, NJ: Prentice Hall, 1992), p. 388.

38. Schwab, *Sociology of Cities*, p. 382.

39. Herbert Gans, *Urban Villagers: Groups and Class in the Life of Italian-Americans* (New York: Random House, 1965).

40. Abraham Maslow, "A Theory on Human Motivation," *Psychological Review* 50 no. 4 (1943): 370–96.

41. Ibid.

42. Émile Durkheim, *Elementary Forms of Religious Life* (Oxford: Oxford University Press, 2001). Originally published in 1912, this text offers an extensive look at Durkheim's study on how religion plays a role in creating social identity.

43. Surah 4:97–100.

Chapter 1: An Emerging Muslim World

1. Bryan Sykes, *The Seven Daughters of Eve* (London: Bantam Books, 2001). Studies on human DNA prove that the Near East and the eastern Fertile Crescent, including Northeastern Africa, is the source of all modern humans.

2. Spencer Wells, *Deep Ancestry: Inside the Genographic Project* (Washington, DC: National Geographic, 2006).

3. Jerome Fellman, Arthur Getis, and Judith Getis, *Human Geography: Land-*

scapes of Human Activities (Boston: McGraw Hill, 2007), pp. 503–508. Population data, including projections, for this section are taken from this source.

4. William A. Schwab, *Sociology of Cities* (Englewood Cliffs, NJ: Prentice Hall, 1992), p. 388.

5. Ibid.

6. Robert Famighetti, ed., *World Almanac and Book of Facts 1995* (Mahwah, NJ: Funk and Wagnalls, 1995), p. 767.

7. William A. McGeveran Jr., ed., *World Almanac and Book of Facts 2006* (New York: World Almanac Education Group, 2006), p. 779.

8. Office of National Statistics, "Census 2001" (London, UK).

9. Simon Naylor and James R. Ryan, "Mosque in the Suburbs: Negotiating Religion and Ethnicity in South London," *Social and Cultural Geography* 3, no. 1 (2002): 39–50.

10. Dennis Conway, "Step-Wise Migration: Toward a Clarification of the Mechanism," *International Migration Review* 14, no. 1 (1980): 3–14. The step-wise migration process is discussed at length in Conway's work.

11. Schwab, *Sociology of Cities*.

12. Rich Morin, ed., "Muslim Americans: Middle Class and Mostly Mainstream," (Washington, DC: Pew Research Center, May 2007). View the report at http://pewresearch.org/pubs/483/muslim-americans (accessed July 4, 2008). For an estimate close to 5 million, see McGeveran, *World Almanac*, p. 714.

13. Barry A. Kosmin, Egon Mayer, and Ariela Keysar, *American Religious Identification Survey 2001* (New York: The Graduate Center of the City University of New York, 2001), p. 13.

14. Alisher Ilkhamov, "Uzbek Islamism: Imported Ideology or Grassroots Movement?" *Middle East Report*, no. 221 (Winter 2001): 40–46. The quote is taken from page 46.

15. Ibid., p. 46.

16. James M. Rubenstein, *Cultural Landscape: An Introduction to Human Geography*, 7th ed. (Upper Saddle River, NJ: Prentice Hall, 2002), p. 272.

17. Khaled Abou El Fadl, "Islamic Law and Muslim Minorities: The Juristic Discourse on Muslim Minorities from the Second/Eighth to the Eleventh/Seventeenth Centuries," *Journal of Islamic Law and Society* 22, no. 1 (1994): 32. For an excellent discussion on the Hadith and the role of jurisprudence in Islamic history, see Frederick Mathewson Denny, "Islamic Theology in the New World: Some Issues and Prospects," *Journal of the American Academy of Religion* 2, no. 4, (1994): 1069–1084.

18. El Fadl, "Islamic Law," p. 32.

19. Qur'an, Surah 4:97.

20. Surah 4:100.

21. Surah 16:110.

22. Surah 4:150.

23. Ilkhamov, "Uzbek Islamism," pp. 41–45.

24. Surah 4:144.

25. Surah 4:140.

26. Surah 4:148.

27. Nicolas Blanford, "Shia Crescent Pierces Heart of Arab World," *Times of London*, July 17, 2006, http://www.timesonline.co.uk/tol/news/world/middle_east/article688836.ece (accessed September 21, 2010). King Abdullah's identification of this area as the Shia Crescent was made in December 2004. There are other countries with sizable Shiite populations. Bahrain is 70 percent Shia and some 5.6 million Afghans are also Shiites. See William McGeveran Jr., ed., *World Almanac and Book of Facts 2006* (New York: World Almanac Books), pp. 750, 756.

28. Barry A. Vann, *In Search of Ulster-Scots Land: The Birth and Geotheological Imaginings of a Transatlantic People, 1603–1703* (Columbia: University of South Carolina Press, 2007). This work shows how seventeenth-century Christian Puritans, too, formed imagined communities. The concept of imagined communities was first used by Benedict Anderson in his *Imagined Communities: Reflections on the Origins and Spread of Nationalism* (London: Verso, 1983).

29. Surah 5:33.

30. Jaqueline Beaujeu-Garnier, "The Contribution of Geography," cited in Chris Philo, "History, Geography, and the Still Greater Mystery of Historical Geography" in *Human Geography: Society, Space, and Social Science*, Derek Gregory, Ron Martin, and Graham Smith, eds. (Minneapolis: University of Minnesota Press, 1994), p. 255.

31. Jerome D. Fellman, Arthur Getis, and Judith Getis, *Human Geography: Landscapes of Human Activities*, 9th ed. (New York: McGraw-Hill, 2007), pp. 86–88. This provides an excellent summary of E. G. Ravenstein's "laws."

32. Ibid., p. 87.

33. Ibid., p. 89.

34. Brigitte Waldorf, "Determinants of International Return Migration Intentions," *Professional Geographer* 47, no. 2 (1995): 125–36. See Waldorf's discussion on the relationship between intended stay and return migration. To read about trans-Irish Sea migrations in the seventeenth century, see also Barry A. Vann, "Presby-

terian Social Ties and Mobility in the Irish Sea Culture Area," *Journal of Historical Sociology* 18, no. 3 (September 2005): 227–54.

35. Nil Demet Güngör and Aysit Tansel, *Determinants of Return Intentions of Turkish Students and Professionals Residing Abroad: An Empirical Investigation* (Bonn, Germany: Institute for the Study of Labor, 2005).

36. Surah 4:100.

37. Ibid.

38. Wilbur Zelinsky, "The Hypothesis of Mobility Transition," *Geographical Review* 61 (1971): 219–49.

39. Huw Jones, "Evolution of Scottish Migration Patterns: A Social-Relations-of-Productions Approach," *Scottish Geographical Journal* 102, no. 3 (December 1986): 151–64.

40. Fellman, Getis, and Getis, *Landscapes of Human Activities*, pp. 503–508. Population projections for this section are taken from this source.

41. C. Alan Joyce, ed., *World Almanac and Book of Facts 2009* (Pleasantville, NY: World Almanac Education Group, 2009), pp. 729–835. Data in table 1 is gathered from this source. The figures reflect only those countries in which at least 50 percent of their respective populations claim adherence to Islam. Doubling time is calculated by using the Rule of 72, which identifies the mathematical reality that when 72 is divided by the natural increase rate, the answer indicates how much time is required, in years, for the population to double in size.

42. McGeveran, *World Almanac*, pp. 798, 802. In the case of Maldives, its economy depends heavily on the labor supplied by immigrants from surrounding poor countries.

43. Ibid., pp. 750–850. All of the data in this section, unless otherwise stated, are taken from this source.

44. Ibid.

45. Tony Manolatos, "Mosques Call to Prayer Signal Hamtramck Change," *Detroit News*, February 23, 2005, http://www.detnews.com/2005/religion/0503/03/B01-98280.htm (accessed July 4, 2009).

Chapter 2: Puritans Views of Self and Community

1. The *Jyllands-Posten*, September 30, 2005. The twelve cartoons (from various illustrators) depicting Muhammad first appeared in this Danish newspaper.

2. Pope Benedict XVI, "Meeting with the Representatives of Science: A Lec-

ture of the Holy Father," September 12, 2006, http://www.vatican.va/holy_father/
benedict_xvi/speeches/2006/september/documents/hf_ben-xvi_spe_20060912
_university-regensburg_en.html (accessed September 21, 2009). This event refers to
comments made by Pope Benedict XVI on September 12, 2006, nearly one year
after the publication of the Muhammad cartoons. In a speech delivered in his native
Germany, the Pope quoted the fourteenth-century Byzantine emperor Manuel II
Paleologus who argued that early Islam spread through violence and that anything
new introduced by Muslims was "evil and inhuman."

3. Qur'an, Surah 14 and Surah 17.

4. Surah 17:16; Surah 13:30–35. These verses show how Allah deals with
nations in dispensing rewards and punishments.

5. In this instance, one must exclude evil. That is the purview of the Satan
and the *shayatin* (evil ones).

6. Surah 16:22–23.

7. Surah 16:53.

8. Surah 16:93.

9. Surah 18:29.

10. Gordon Marshall, *Presbyteries and Profits: Calvinism and the Development of
Capitalism in Scotland* (Oxford: Oxford University Press, 1980), p. 88. Max Weber's
thesis was published in *Protestant Ethic and the Spirit of Capitalism* (New York: Routledge Classics, 2001).

11. Marshall, *Presbyteries and Profits*, p. 88.

12. Lorriane Boettner, *Reformed Faith* (Philipsburg, NJ: Presbyterian and
Reformed Company, 1983).

13. Surah 3:129.

14. Surah 3:131.

15. Surah 16:106.

16. Surah 13:31.

17. Surah 13:34.

18. Surah 3:26.

19. Surah 8:39–41.

20. Barry A. Vann, "Learning Self-Direction in a Social and Experiential Context," *Human Resource Development Quarterly* 7, no. 2 (Summer 1996): 121–30. For a
good discussion on this psychological condition, consult this source.

21. Surah 3:31–32.

22. Calvinists point to Eph. 1 and Rom. 8 in the Bible to support this view of
salvation.

23. Arminians are likely to temper Eph. 1 with John 3:16.

24. R. C. Sproul, "We are Capable of Obedience: Pelagius" in R. C. Sproul, *Willing to Believe: Controversy over Free Will* (Grand Rapids: Baker Books, 1997), pp. 33–48. This offers a well-written comparison of Pelagianism and Calvinism.

25. Surah 16:112.

26. Surah 4:47.

27. Surah 3:56.

28. Surah 8:29.

29. Surah 2:174.

30. Surah 6:156.

31. Surah 9:108.

32. Surah 2:22.

33. Barry A. Vann, *In Search of Ulster-Scots Land: The Birth and Geotheological Imaginings of a Transatlantic People* (Columbia: University of South Carolina Press, 2008).

34. Surah 4:171; and Surah 5:73. The Qur'an clearly rejects the Trinity doctrine.

35. Surah 2:213; Surah 16:9, 93.

36. Sproul, *Willing to Believe*, 88.

37. D. James Kennedy, *Why I Believe: In the Bible, God, Creation, Heaven, Hell, Moral Absolutes, Christ, Virgin Birth, Christianity* (Nashville: W. Publishing Group, 2005).

38. Surah 6:6; Surah 9:89; Surah 13:35.

39. Ferdinand Tönnies, *Gemeinschaft and Gesellschaft* (Lansing: Michigan State University Press, 1957). For an excellent discussion of the concept, see William Schwab *Sociology of Cities* (Englewood Cliffs, NJ: Prentice Hall, 1992), pp. 336–338. To retain a connection with their rural heritage, mothers and fathers in these places often sent their children to be educated in the ways of the desert nomad. Even Muhammad was sent to live with a Bedouin family east of Mecca, near Taif. See Hibba Abugideiri, "Islam," in Susan Tyler Hitchcock and John L. Esposito, *Geography of Religion: Where God Lives, Where Pilgrims Walk* (Washington, DC: National Geographic Society, 2004), p. 337.

40. Surah 7:38.

41. Surah 18:59.

42. George Braswell, *What You Need to Know about Islam and Muslims* (Nashville: Broadman and Holman, 2000), p. 63.

43. Bible, Matt. 6:5–7. In this text, all references to the Bible are derived

from the King James Study Bible published in Nashville, TN by Thomas Nelson Publishers.

44. It is helpful to think of these symbols as centripetal forces that pull Muslims toward the center, toward the fundamentals of Islamic beliefs.

45. Ergun Mehmet Caner and Emir Fethi Caner, *Unveiling Islam: An Insider's Look at Muslim Life and Beliefs* (Grand Rapids: Kregel, 2002), p. 122.

46. Ibid.

47. Surah 49:15.

48. Surah 3:28.

49. Surah 49:13.

50. Caner and Caner, *Unveiling Islam*, p. 125.

51. Ibid.

52. Surah 2:183.

53. James Rubenstein, *Cultural Landscape: An Introduction to Human Geography* 7th ed. (Upper Saddle River, NJ: MacMillan, 2002), pp. 191–92, 202. Medina, which means "the city of the Prophet," and Jerusalem are the second and third most holy sites in Islam, respectively.

54. Eph. 1.

Chapter 3: Puritans' Perception of Unbelievers

1. The schism occurred in 1054. Protestantism forms a third major division of Christianity. It could also be argued that, since Henry VIII's separation from Catholicism in 1534 occurred because of nontheological reasons, his church, which now leads a world-wide body of allied groups called Anglicanism, is a fourth division.

2. Brian Murphy, "Pope Urges Tolerance in Turkey," *Christian Post*, November 30, 2006, http://www.christianpost.com/article/20061130/23761.htm (accessed September 18, 2009).

3. Peggy Noonan, "Pope Benedict XVI," *Time*, April 30, 2006, http://www.time.com/time/magazine/article/0,9171,1186689,00.html (accessed September 18, 2009).

4. Ibid.

5. Karen Armstrong, *Battle for God: A History of Fundamentalism* (London: Random House Publishing, 2001), p. 3.

6. Ibid. For a similar perspective, see Paul Johnson, *A History of the Jews* (London: Harper Perennial, 1987), p. 229.

7. Kelly Knauer, *Middle East: History, Cultures, Conflicts, Faiths* (New York: Time, 2006), p. 6.

8. Jimmy Carter, *Palestine: Peace Not Apartheid* (New York: Simon and Schuster, 2006).

9. Jimmy Carter, introduction to *Middle East: History, Cultures, Conflicts, Faiths* by Kelly Knauer (New York: Time, 2006).

10. Ibid.

11. Media Matters, "Rosie O: Don't Fear Terrorists, They're Just Moms and Dads," WorldNet Daily, November 12, 2006, http://www.wnd.com/news/article .asp?ARTICLE_ID=52919 (accessed September 23, 2009). A full discussion of O'Donnell's comments made in November 2006 can be found here.

12. Ibid.

13. Khaled Abou El Fadl, "Islam and the Theology of Power," *Middle East Report* 221 (Winter 2001): 28–33. This particular topic is discussed on page 31.

14. Ibid. *Muharibs* often resorted to terrorist acts.

15. Ibid.

16. It must be pointed out that there are an untold number of people claiming membership in religious communities, whether they are Christian, Muslim, or Jewish, who really do not deeply believe in their faiths. Here I am referring to the puritan and Islamist person as a believer.

17. Surah 6:155–57.

18. Surah 7:177.

19. Surah 9:113.

20. Surah 48:29.

21. Surah 10:15.

22. Surah 10:7–8.

23. Surah 10:37.

24. Ishaq Zahid, "Allah in the Bible?" *Islam 101: American Edition* (blog), http://www.islam101.com/religions/christianity/aibible.htm (accessed June 4, 2011). This work is cited in Ergun Mehmet Caner and Emir Fethi Caner, *Unveiling Islam: An Insider's Look at Muslim Life and Beliefs* (Grand Rapids, MI: Kregel), p. 202.

25. Knauer, *The Middle East*, p. 11. Zionism began as a nineteenth- and twentieth-century movement among American and European Jews to "re-create" a Jewish homeland in Palestine. The movement has received support from certain Christian denominations, especially Dispensationalists. For excellent works on Jewish Zionism, see Arthur Hertberg, *The Zionist Idea: Historical Analysis and Reader* (New York: Jewish Publication Society of America, 1997). For a look at how Dispensationalist writers in support of

Zionism view Israel, see John Hagee, *Jerusalem Countdown: A Warning to the World* (San Antonio, TX: Frontline, 2006).

26. Surah 62:5–7. In the Bible, in Matt. 4:2–7, Satan tells Jesus to invoke death by falling from a height that would presumably kill him.

27. Surah 5:13.

28. Surah 5:14.

27. Caner and Caner, *Unveiling Islam*, p. 202. Although they are polemicists, Caner and Caner provide an excellent discussion on these two opposing perceptions of Jesus. See specifically pages 200 through 234.

28. Surah 5:73–75.

29. Surah 2:111, 113.

30. Surah 5:12–13.

31. Surah 4:171.

32. Surah 109:1–6.

33. Surah 2:120.

34. Surah 5:51.

35. Surah 2:120.

36. Surah 5:51.

37. Data are taken from William McGeveran, ed., *The World Almanac and Book of Facts 2006* (New York: A Division of World Almanac Education Group, 2006), pp. 775–841.

38. Hibba Abugideiri, "Islam," in *Geography of Religion: Where God Lives, Where Pilgrims Walk*, eds. Susan T. Hitchcock and John L. Esposito (Washington, DC: National Geographic, 2006), pp. 330–395.

39. Communication Department of the European Commision, "European Monitoring Center on Racism and Xenophobia," Europa, http://europa.eu/legislation _summaries/other/c10411_en.htm (accessed September 10, 2009).

40. Surah 4:100.

41. Surah 5:18.

42. Surah 2:211.

43. In Arabic, a *mullah* is a Muslim man educated in Islamic law; an *imam* is a leader in Islamic worship; and a *sheik* is an honorific title usually given to a revered wise man.

44. Surah 9:100.

45. Surah 4:100.

46. Surah 9:101.

47. Surah 9:112.

48. Matthew 7:1.

49. Surah 9:113.

50. Surah 2:86.

51. Surah 2:212.

52. Surah 8:15. Muhammad uses the word "marching" as a way to describe the disbeliever preparing for war against the faithful.

53. Surah 60:9.

54. Surah 60:1–2.

55. Surah 16:104–105.

56. Surah 60:7.

57. Roger W. Stump, *Geography of Religion: Faith, Place, and Space* (New York: Rowan and Littlefield, 2008), pp. 188–89.

58. Ibid.

59. Surah 2:148.

60. Surah 2:284.

61. Surah 16:106–107.

62. Surah 16:108–109.

63. Surah 16:95.

64. Omar Sinan, "Al-Qaida No. 2 Berates Moderate Arabs," Associated Press, *Washington Post*, December 30, 2006, http://www.washingtonpost.com/wp-dyn/content/article/2006/12/30/AR2006123000715.html (accessed August 4, 2009).

65. Ibid.

66. Barry A. Vann, *In Search of Ulster Scots Land: The Birth and Geotheological Imaginings of a Transatlantic People, 1603–1703* (Columbia: University of South Carolina Press, 2008), pp. 23, 150, 202n. Geoeschatology captures the relationship between end-times scenarios and space, including imagined space.

67. Barry A. Vann, *Rediscovering the South's Celtic Heritage* (Johnson City, TN: Overmountain Press, 2004), pp. 126–30.

68. Surah 13:30.

69. Surah 13:33–34.

70. Surah 16:63.

71. For reference to this passage in the Christian New Testament, see Luke 18:25.

72. Surah 7:40.

73. Surah 7:50. Here again, Muhammad borrows from Jesus. In Luke 16:19–31, Jesus tells the story of the rich man in hell and his requests to Abraham to have the poor beggar named Lazarus quench his thirst.

74. Surah 6:93.

75. Surah 3:10. For additional Qur'anic references to the fiery destiny of unbelievers, see also Surah 5:10, 86 as well as Surah 21:98.

76. Surah 3:151.

Chapter 4: The Sanctity of Allah's World

1. Surah 7:38.
2. Surah 6:73.
3. Surah 6:1–3.
4. Surah 6:13.
5. Surah 5:120.
6. Surah 16:10–11.
7. Surah 16:49.
8. Surah 2:281.
9. Surah 25:10–11.
10. Surah 9:109.
11. Surah 7:179.
12. Surah 15:43–45.
13. Surah 15:26–29.
14. Surah 35:33–36; Surah 56:11–50. Muhammad makes his promise of virgins to believers who make it to paradise.
15. Surah 18:39.
16. Khaled Abou El Fadl, "Islamic Law and Muslim Minorities: The Juristic Discourse on Muslim Minorities from the Second/Eighth to the Eleventh/Seventeenth Centuries," *Journal of Islamic Law and Society* 22, no. 1 (1994): 141–87. See also his "Islam and the Theology of Power," *Middle East Report* 221 (2001).
17. Ayman Al-Zawahiri, "Letter from al-Zawahiri to al-Zarqawi," Washington, DC: Office of Homeland Security, July 9, 2005, http://www.globalsecurity.org/security/library/report/2005/zawahiri-zarqawi-letter_9jul2005.htm (accessed May 5, 2008).
18. Ibid.
19. Surah 9:17–19, 100–101. The city was formerly named Yathrib.
20. Surah 9:19; Surah 17:1; Surah 24:36.
21. Al-Zawahiri, "Letter."
22. Ibid.

23. Surah 6:6; Surah 17:7; Surah 14:19–20.
24. Surah 16:1. See also Surah 9:19–20.
25. Muhammad is unclear as to why they were banished from the garden.
26. Surah 9:72.
27. Surah 9:73.
28. Surah 9:113.
29. Henry Campbell Black, *Black's Law Dictionary*, 6th ed. (Saint Paul, MN: West Publishing), p. 33.
30. Surah 6:59.
31. Surah 14:19–20.
32. Surah 18:40–41.
33. Surah 10:26–27.
34. Surah 10:73.
35. Surah 2:22.
36. Surah 3:198.
37. Surah 10:14.
38. Surah 10:12.
39. Surah 10:14.
40. Surah 10:13.
41. Surah 10:65.
42. Surah 13:11–13.
43. Surah 2:266.
44. Barry A. Vann, *In Search of Ulster-Scots Land: Birth and Geotheological Imaginings of a Transatlantic People, 1603–1703* (Columbia: University of South Carolina Press, 2008), p. 120. Samuel Rutherford, a Scottish Puritan minister who advocated theocracy in the seventeenth century, was noted for using seafaring and fishing metaphors in his letters and sermons.
45. Surah 10:22–23.
46. Surah 69:10–12.
47. Surah 18:42–44.
48. Surah 15:80–84.
49. Surah 7:138–155. See also Bible, Exodus 32.
50. Surah 7:155.

Chapter 5: Toward a Theocratic Nation

1. Barry A. Vann, *In Search of Ulster-Scots Land: The Birth and Geotheological Imaginings of a Transatlantic People, 1603–1703* (Columbia: University of South Carolina, 2008); Paul Kengor, *God and George W. Bush: A Spiritual Life* (New York: Regan Books, 2004). With respect to Islam, see Roger W. Stump, *Geography of Religion: Faith, Place, and Space* (New York: Rowan and Littlefield, 2008), pp. 188–216.

2. Avihu Zakai, *Exile and Kingdom: History and Apocalypse in the Puritan Migration to America* (Cambridge: Cambridge University Press, 2002); Vann, *In Search of Ulster-Scots Land*. For a recent work on how former presidents Reagan and Carter viewed America's divine role, see Bob Slosser, *Reagan Inside Out* (Waco, TX: Word Books, 1984).

3. William A. McGeveran Jr., ed., *World Almanac and Book of Facts 2006* (New York: World Almanac Education Group, 2006), p. 787. Data for 1995 were taken from Robert Famighetti, ed., *The World Almanac and Book of Facts 1995* (Mahwah, NJ: Funk and Wagnalls), p. 775.

4. "UN at a Glance," *United Nations*, http://www.un.org/en/aboutun/index.shtml (accessed May 10, 2010). Countries that do not share membership in the UN are Taiwan, Vatican City, Western Sahara, and Kosovo.

5. *Organization of the Islamic Conference*, http://www.oic-oci.org/ (accessed October 27, 2009).

6. McGeveran, *World Almanac 2006*, p. 785; Famighetti, *The World Almanac 1995*, p. 773.

7. Surah 16:84.

8. Surah 16:85.

9. Surah 53:53–54, 56–57.

10. Surah 18:59.

11. Surah 10:13.

12. Surah 16:112.

13. Surah 17:16.

14. Surah 14:19.

15. Surah 14:23. There are numerous references in the Qur'an to gardens with flowing rivers as rewards for good behavior.

16. Surah 17:57–58.

17. Ergun Caner and Emir Fethi Caner, *Unveiling Islam: An Insider's Look at Muslim Life and Beliefs* (Grand Rapids, MI: Kregel Publications, 2002).

18. "History," *Nation of Islam*, http://www.noi.org (accessed May 21, 2008).

19. Ibid.
20. Surah 49:13.
21. Surah 2:13.
22. James D. Tracy, *Europe's Reformations, 1450–1650* (New York: Rowan and Littlefield, 1999); Vann, *In Search of Ulster-Scots Land*. This notion is similar to views held by some Reformation-era Christians who believed that there were two kingdoms: one kingdom was spiritual and the second was secular. Some Protestant Church officials then argued that the civil magistrate was to abide by the superior authority of the Church. Also see, Ferdinand Tönnies, *Community and Society: Gemeinschaft und Gesellschaft*, ed. and trans. Charles Price Loomis (East Lansing: Michigan State University Press, 1957). A community that needs the formal structure of government to police human behaviors due to their self-interests is no longer in a *Gemeinschaft* state. It has become a society, *Gesellschaft*.
23. Surah 3:96.
24. Surah 2:128–29.
25. Surah 16:36.
26. Surah 16:37.
27. Surah 16:39.
28. Surah 11:48–49.
29. Surah 7:38.
30. Surah 7:34.
31. Surah 10:47, 49.
32. Surah 16:63
33. Surah 15:4.
34. Surah 15:5.
35. Surah 10:13.
36. Chris Park, *Sacred Worlds: An Introduction to Geography and History* (London: Routledge, 1994), p. 109.
37. Ibid.
38. Surah 10:68–70.
39. Surah 10:70.
40. Surah 10:73.
41. Surah 4:133.
42. Surah 4:138.
43. Surah 3:109.
44. Surah 16:41.
45. Surah 3:103.

Chapter 6: American Islam's Two Communities

1. Rami Nashashibi, "IMAN (Inner City Action Network): Showing the Way," http://www.mana-net.org/pages.php?ID=activism&NUM=5 (accessed May 26, 2009).

2. Richard Morin, ed., "Muslim Americans: Middle Class and Mostly Mainstream," Pew Research Center, May 22, 2007, http://pewresearch.org/assets/pdf/muslim-americans.pdf (accessed May 31, 2007). The issue mentioned first is mostly the result of the NOI's teaching that Wallace Fard Muhammad and Elijah Muhammad were prophets. The issue of assimilation may also play a role in the different Muslim communities' isolation from each other. According to the Pew Research report, about two-thirds of Muslim immigrants consider themselves to be white, as opposed to black or Asian.

3. David Horowitz, "Aminah Beverly McCloud," *The Professors: The 101 Most Dangerous Academics in America* (Washington, DC: Regnery Publishing, 2006), pp. 263–65.

4. Ibid.

5. Morin, "Muslim Americans."

6. Robert Davis, *Christian Slaves, Muslim Masters: White Slavery in the Mediterranean, the Barbary Coast, and Italy, 1500–1800* (New York: Palgrave MacMillan, 2004).

7. Morin, "Muslim Americans," p. 1.

8. Ibid., p. 2

9. Ibid., p. 6.

10. Morin, "Muslim Americans."

11. Ergun Mehmet Caner and Emir Fethi Caner, *Unveiling Islam* (Grand Rapids, MI: Kregel, 2002), p. 166. For a deeper look at the Nation of Islam, see Vibert L. White, *Inside the Nation of Islam: A Historic and Personal Testimony by a Black Muslim* (Orlando: University of Florida Press, 2001).

12. James Rubenstein, *Cultural Landscape: An Introduction to Human Geography*, 7th ed. (Upper Saddle River, NJ: Prentice Hall, 2002), p. 217.

13. Surah 3:67.

14. Surah 2:130–32.

15. Surah 3:33.

16. Surah 4:54.

17. Rachel Zoll, "Rival Muslim Groups Converge on Chicago," Associated Press, *Washington Times*, August 30, 2003, http://www.washingtontimes.com/news/2003/aug/29/20030829-113811-6563r/ (accessed May 29, 2008).

18. Horowitz, *The Professors*, pp. 33–34. Bagby offered his refutation in an interview for a University of Kentucky student newspaper conducted by Eric Lindsey, *Kentucky Kernel*, November 10, 2006.

19. University of Kentucky College of Arts and Sciences, "Islamic Studies," http://www.as.uky.edu/IslamicStudies/faculty.html (accessed June 2, 2009).

20. Andrea Stone, "There is No One Kind of Muslim" (includes an interview with Ihsan Bagby), in *Islamic Bulletin* 12, January 27, 1994, http://www.islamicbulletin.com/newsletters/issue_12/islam.aspx (accessed September 21, 2010).

21. Alexander Rose, "How Did Muslims Vote in 2000?" *Middle East Quarterly* 8 no. 3 (Summer 2001): 13–27.

22. Zoll, "Rival Muslim Groups."

23. William A. McGeveran Jr., ed., *World Almanac and Book of Facts 2006* (New York: World Almanac Education Group, 2006), p. 620.

24. Ihsan Bagby, "Executive Summary," in *A Portrait of Detroit Mosques: Muslim Views on Policy, Politics, and Religion* (Clinton Township, MI: Institute for Social Policy and Understanding, 2004), http://ispu.org/files/PDFs/detriot_mosque_exec_summary.pdf (accessed September 21, 2010).

25. Morin, "Muslim Americans," p. 45.

26. Ibid., p. 38.

27. Ibid., p. 2.

28. Ibid., p. 30.

29. Ibid., p. 5.

30. Ibid.

31. Ibid., p. 3.

32. Quoted in Zoll, "Rival Muslim Groups."

33. Quoted in ibid.

34. For a more thorough reading of this organization, visit its website at http://www.ispu.org.

35. For a complete look at the research projects supported by the ISPU, see http://www.ispu.us.

36. Benjamin R. Barber, *Jihad vs. McWorld* (New York: Ballantine Books, 1996), p. 206.

37. Adolf Hitler, quoted in *Inside the Third Reich: Memoirs by Albert Speer* (New York: MacMillan, 1970), p. 114.

38. Muslim American Society, http://www.masnet.org/freedomfoundation.asp (accessed September 21, 2010).

39. Ibid.

40. Ibid.

41. Morin, "Muslim Americans," p. 18.

42. Muslim Alliance of North America, http://www.mana-net.org/index.php (accessed September 12, 2008).

43. Siraj Wahhaj, "Offering an Islamic Perspective on the Great African Diaspora," http://www1.cuny.edu/portal_ur/news/cuny_matters/2003_march/islamic.html (accessed September 12, 2009).

Chapter 7: The Incommensurability of Liberalism and Puritan Islam

1. Wilbur Zelinsky, "Hypothesis of Mobility Transition," *Geographical Review* 61 (1971): 219–49. His mobility transition model argues that when an area exceeds its carrying capacity, residents will leave in search of a new place to live.

2. Anthony Giddens, *Sociology*, 4th ed. (Cambridge: Cambridge University Press, 2001), p. 562.

3. See Barry A. Vann, *In Search of Ulster-Scots Land: The Birth and Geotheological Imaginings of a Transatlantic People, 1603–1703* (Columbia: University of South Carolina Press, 2008).

4. Muslim American Society, http://www.masnet.org/freedomfoundation.asp (accessed July 5, 2008).

5. Matt. 22:21.

6. Surah 6:157.

7. Surah 14:19–20.

8. Surah 3:151.

9. Surah 8:12.

10. Surah 5:33.

11. Surah 8:65.

12. Khaled Abou El Fadl, "Islam and the Theology of Power," *Middle East Report* 221 (Winter 2001): 28–33. See specifically the discussion on the demise of the classical tradition on pages 31–33.

13. Surah 8:17.

14. Michelle Malkin, "Myth of Muslim Hate Crime Epidemic," *Capitalism Magazine*, August 17, 2003, http://www.capmag.com/article.asp?ID=3030 (accessed July 20, 2008). Makin is a conservative commentator; for a liberal perspective, see Tanya

Schevitz, "FBI See Leap in Anti-Muslim Hate Crimes: 9/11 Attacks Blamed for Bias—Blacks Most Frequent Victims," *San Francisco Chronicle*, November 26, 2002, http://www .sfgate.com/cgi-bin/article.cgi?f=/c/a/2002/11/26/MN224441.DTL (accessed May 8, 2008).

15. John Gibson, *The War on Christmas: How the Liberal Plot to Ban the Sacred Christian Holiday Is Worse Than You Thought* (New York: Sentinel, 2005). Gibson's work provides a conservative and biased view on the movement. The popular media, including television, has discussed this issue at some length. In reality, it is more likely that the decline in the use of Christian symbols in the market place is the result of companies marketing their products to an increasingly diverse population of consumers. It simply makes sense to them to use symbols that have a wider appeal.

16. Randy Hall, "Hate Crimes Bill Opposed by Religious Zealots, Activists Say," CNSNews.com, July 7, 2008, http://www.cnsnews.com/news/article/31304 (accessed August 4, 2008).

17. Susan Jones, "CAIR Views Conservative Commentary as Incitement," CNSNews.com, July 03, 2007, http://forums.somd.com/politics/105769-cal-thomas-vs-cair.html (accessed August 6, 2008).

18. Surah 9:31, 34.

19. Vann, *In Search of Ulster-Scots Land*, p. 117.

20. Nahid Angha, "Women in Islam," International Association of Sufism (IAS), July 7, 2007, http://ias.org/articles/Women_in_Islam.html (accessed August 8, 2008). The abbreviation "swa" is used after mentioning the Prophet. In English, it translates to, approximately, "may Allah honor him and grant him peace."

21. Ibid.

22. Elizabeth Joseph, "Polygamy—The Ultimate Feminist Lifestyle," Islam for Today, May 1997, http://www.islamfortoday.com/polygamy3.htm (accessed August 15, 2008).

23. Ibid.

24. Giddens, *Sociology*, p. 689.

25. Joseph, "Polygamy."

26. Islam for Today, http://wwwislamfortoday.com (accessed August 15, 2008).

27. Kelly Knauer, *Middle East: History, Cultures, Conflicts, Faiths* (New York: Time, 2006), p. 29.

28. Knauer, *Middle East*, p. 29. For a discussion on Muhammad's wives see, Ergun Mehmet Caner and Emir Fethi Caner, *Unveiling Islam: An Insider's Look at*

Muslim Life and Beliefs (Grand Rapids, MI: Kregel Publications, 2002), pp. 40–41, 56–60. See also Surah 4:3.

29. Knauer, *Middle East*, p. 29.

30. Ibid.

31. Caner and Caner, *Unveiling Islam*, p. 135. It is likely that, at the time Anas wrote this, Muhammad had not yet married his twelfth and final wife, which explains Anas only mentioning eleven wives.

32. Surah 4:11.

33. Surah 4:34.

34. Knauer, *Middle East*, p. 29.

35. Surah 2:223.

36. Caner and Caner, *Unveiling Islam,* p. 137.

37. Surah 4:34.

38. Surah 4:56.

39. Surah 4:3.

40. Woodrow Wilson International Center for Scholars, *Best Practices: Progressive Family Laws in Muslim Countries* (Washington, DC: The Rand Corporation, 2005), p. 8. While countries like Iran have set minimum age requirements for marriages, they are difficult to enforce.

41. Ibid.

42. Caner and Caner, *Unveiling Islam*, p. 135.

43. Knauer, *Middle East*, p. 29.

44. James Rubenstein, *The Cultural Landscape: An Introduction to Human Geography*, 7th ed. (Upper Saddle River, NJ: Prentice Hall, 2002), pp. 287–90.

45. Ibid., p. 289.

46. Ibid.

47. Ibid., p. 288.

48. Surah 8:22.

49. Surah 8:23.

50. Surah 4:25.

51. Surah 11:77–83. See also Surah 26:165–67.

52. Surah 26:165–66.

53. Al-Fatiha, http://www.al-fatiha.org (accessed September 21, 2010).

54. Ibid.

55. Jennifer Carlile, "Homosexual and Passionate about Islam: Britain's Gay Muslims' Struggle with Sexuality, Religion, and Discrimination," MSNBC, July 6, 2006, http://www.msnbc.msn.com/id/13712248/ (accessed August 16, 2008).

56. Ibid.

57. Ibid.

58. Tom Boellstorff, "Between Religion and Desire: Being Muslim and Gay in Indonesia," *American Anthropologist* 17, no. 4 (2005): 575–85.

59. Ibid.

60. Surah 16:36.

Chapter 8: Puritans' Perception of the State of Israel

1. William A. McGeveran Jr., ed., *World Almanac and Book of Facts 2006* (New York: World Almanac Education Group, 2006), p. 797. The 2002 Gaza population estimate was 1,225,911 people concentrated on a land area of 140 square miles. The population density was 8,756 people per square mile. By 2007, the population figure had grown to 1,482,405, which represents a 21 percent increase in just five years. To see this increase, see C. Alan Joyce, ed., *World Almanac and Book of Facts 2008* (New York: World Almanac Education Group, 2008), p. 786.

2. Douglas Brinkley, ed., *Reagan Diaries* (New York: HarperCollins Publishers, 2009), pp. 294, 414–15, 508.

3. Council on Foreign Relations, "Hamas," http://www.cfr.org/publications/8968 (accessed August 28, 2008).

4. Alfred Sipa, "People Who Mattered: Mahmoud Ahmadinejad," *Time*, December 16, 2006, http://www.time.com/time/magazine/article/0,9171,1570714,00 .html (accessed August 29, 2008).

5. McGeveran Jr., *World Almanac 2006*, pp. 426–51, 750–850.

6. James Rubenstein, *The Cultural Landscape: An Introduction to Human Geography*, 7th ed. (Upper Saddle River, NJ: Prentice Hall, 2002), pp. 232–34.

7. See table 1 in chapter 1.

8. Surah 5:12; Surah 7:159–71.

9. Surah 3:3–4.

10. Surah 27:23.

11. Surah 7:160.

12. Surah 7:160.

13. Surah 20:80.

14. Surah 7:162.

15. Surah 7:160.

16. Surah 2:40.

17. Surah 2:47.

18. Surah 5:20–21.

19. Surah 7:163.

20. Surah 2:246.

21. Surah 2:251.

22. Benjamin Netanyahu, "Address by PM Netanyahu at Auschwitz Concentration Camp," Israel Ministry of Foreign Affairs, January 27, 2010, http://www.mfa.gov.il/MFA/Government/Speeches+by+Israeli+leaders/2010/Address_PM_Netanyahu_at_Auschwitz_27-Jan-2010.htm (accessed March 26, 2010).

23. Surah 3:50.

24. Surah 3:49.

25. Titus Flavius Josephus, *Antiquities of the Jews*, trans. William Whiston (1737). Available online at http://www.sacred-texts.com/jud/josephus/index.htm #aoj (accessed June 7, 2011).

26. Surah 4:157.

27. Surah 3:55.

28. Surah 5:78.

29. Surah 18:4–5.

30. Surah 5:116.

31. Surah 3:52.

32. Sarah Lawall and Maynard Mack, eds., *Norton Anthology of World Masterpieces: The Western Traditions*, 7th ed. (New York: W. W. Norton and Company, 1999), p. 961.

33. Matt. 16:13–17.

34. Eusebius of Caesarea, *Chronicon*. In Acts 11:36, in Antioch, the disciples were first given the name Christians.

35. This is a tradition held by the Armenian Orthodox Church.

36. Coptic Church, http://www.coptic.net/EncyclopediaCoptica/ (accessed August 29, 2008).

37. Owen Chadwick, *A History of Christianity* (New York: St. Martin's Press, 1995), p. 61.

38. Surah 18:5.

39. Surah 2:113.

40. Surah 5:18.

41. Surah 2:120.

42. Surah 5:51.

43. Surah 17:4.

44. Surah 7:166.

45. Surah 9:30.

46. Surah 9:33.

47. John K. Wright, "Notes on Early American Geopiety," in *Human Nature in Geography* (Cambridge: Cambridge University Press, 1966). To see how others have used the concept of geoteleology, see Avihu Zakai, *Exile and Kingdom: History and Apocalypse in the Puritan Migration to America* (Cambridge: Cambridge University Press, 2002); see also Barry A. Vann, *In Search of Ulster-Scots Land: The Birth and Geotheological Imaginings of a Transatlantic People, 1603–1703* (Columbia: University of South Carolina Press, 2008).

48. McGeveran, *World Almanac 2006*, p. 791.

49. Kelly Knauer, *Middle East: History, Cultures, Conflicts, Faiths* (New York: Time Books, 2006), p. 34.

Chapter 9: Future Geographies of Islam

1. C. Alan Joyce, ed., *World Almanac and Book of Facts 2009* (Pleasantville. NY: World Almanac Education Group, 2009), pp. 729–835.

2. Ibid., p. 735.

3. Roger W. Stump, *Geography of Religion: Faith, Space, and Place* (Lanham, MD: Rowan and Littlefield, 2008), p. 253.

4. Organization of Islamic Conference, http://www.oic-oci.org/ (accessed August 2, 2009).

Bibliography

Abugideiri, Hibba. "Islam." In *Geography of Religion: Where God Lives, Where Pilgrims Walk*, edited by Susan T. Hitchcock and John L. Esposito, 330–95. Washington, DC: National Geographic, 2004.

Ali, Ameer. *The Spirit of Islam*. London: Christophers, 1923.

Anderson, Benedict. *Imagined Communities: Reflections on the Origins and Spread of Nationalism*. London: Verso, 1983.

Angha, Nahid. "Women in Islam." International Association of Sufism, July 7, 2007. http://ias.org/articles/Women_in_Islam.html.

Armstrong, Karen. *Battle for God: A History of Fundamentalism*. London: Ballantine Books, 2001.

Bagby, Ihsan. *A Portrait of a Detroit Mosques: Muslim Views on Policy, Politics, and Religion*. Clinton Township, MI: Institute for Social Policy and Understanding, 2004. http://ispu.org/files/PDFs/detriot_mosque_exec_summary.pdf.

Barber, Benjamin R. *Jihad vs. McWorld*. New York: Ballantine Books, 1996.

Bawer, Bruce. *While Europe Slept: How Radical Islam Is Destroying the West from Within*. New York: Doubleday, 2006.

Beaujeu-Garnier, Jaqueline. *The Contribution of Geography*. Ibadan, Nigeria: Ibadan University Press, 1952.

Benedict, XVI. "Meeting with the Representatives of Science: A Lecture of the Holy Father." September 12, 2006. http://www.vatican.va/holy_father/benedict_xvi/speeches/2006/september/documents/hf_ben-xvi_spe_20060912_university-regensburg_en.html.

Blanford, Nicolas. "Shia Crescent Pierces Heart of Arab World." *Times of London*, July 17, 2006. http://www.timesonline.co.uk/tol/news/world/middle_east/article688836.ece.

Boellstorff, Tom. "Between Religion and Desire: Being Muslim and Gay in Indonesia." *American Anthropologist* 17, no. 4 (2005): 575–85.

Boettner, Loraine. *Reformed Faith*. Philipsburg, NJ: Presbyterian and Reformed Company, 1983.

Braswell, George. *What You Need to Know about Islam and Muslims*. Nashville: Broadman and Holman, 2000.

Brinkley, Douglas, ed. *Reagan Diaries*. New York: HarperCollins Publishers, 2009.

Brockopp, Jonathan, ed. *Islamic Ethics of Life: Abortion, War, and Euthanasia.* Columbia: University of South Carolina Press, 2003.

Caner, Ergun Mehmet, and Emir Fethi Caner. *Unveiling Islam: An Insider's Look at Muslim Life and Beliefs.* Grand Rapids, MI: Kregel, 2002.

Carlile, Jennifer. "Homosexual and Passionate about Islam: Britain's Gay Muslims' Struggle with Sexuality, Religion, and Discrimination." MSNBC, July 6, 2006. http://www.msnbc.msn.com/id/13712248/.

Carter, Jimmy. *Palestine: Peace Not Apartheid.* New York: Simon and Schuster, 2006.

———. Introduction to *Middle East: History, Cultures, Conflicts, Faiths,* by Kelly Knauer. New York: Time, 2006.

Chadwick, Owen. *A History of Christianity.* New York: St. Martin's Press, 1995.

Conway, Dennis. "Step-Wise Migration: Toward a Clarification of the Mechanism." *International Migration Review* 14, no. 1 (1980): 3–14.

Council on Foreign Relations. "Hamas." http://www.cfr.org/publications/8968.

Davis, Robert. *Christian Slaves, Muslim Masters: White Slavery in the Mediterranean, the Barbary Coast and Italy, 1500–1800.* New York: Palgrave MacMillan, 2004.

Demant, Peter R. *Islam versus Islamism: The Dilemma of the Muslim World.* West Port, CT: Praeger Books, 2006.

Denny, Frederick Mathewson. "Islamic Theology in the New World: Some Issues and Prospects." *Journal of the American Academy of Religion* 2, no. 4 (1994): 1069–84.

Durkheim, Émile. *Elementary Forms of Religious Life.* Oxford: Oxford University Press, 2001.

El Fadl, Khaled Abou. "Islam and the Theology of Power." *Middle East Report* 221 (Winter 2001): 28–33.

———. "Islamic Law and Muslim Minorities: The Juristic Discourse on Muslim Minorities from the Second/Eighth to the Eleventh/Seventeenth Centuries." *Journal of Islamic Law and Society* 22, no. 1 (1994).

Communication Department of the European Commission. "European Monitoring Center on Racism and Xenophobia." Europa, http://europa.eu/legislation_summaries/ other/c10411_en.htm.

Famighetti, Robert, ed. *World Almanac and Book of Facts 1995.* Mahwah, NJ: Funck and Wagnalls, 1994.

Fellman, Jerome, Arthur Getis, and Judith Getis. *Human Geography: Landscapes of Human Activities.* New York: McGraw-Hill, 2007.

Gabriel, Brigitte. *Because They Hate: A Survivor of Islamic Terror Warns America.* New York: St. Martin's Press, 2006.

Gans, Herbert. *Urban Villagers: Groups and Class in the Life of Italian-Americans.* New York: Random House, 1965.

Gibson, John. *The War on Christmas: How the Liberal Plot to Ban the Sacred Christian Holiday Is Worse Than You Thought.* New York: Sentinel, 2005.

Giddens, Anthony. *Sociology.* 4th ed. Cambridge: Cambridge University Press, 2001.

Güngör, Nil Demet, and Aysit Tansel. *Determinants of Return Intentions of Turkish Students and Professionals Residing Abroad: An Empirical Investigation.* Bonn, Germany: Institute for the Study of Labor, 2005.

Hagee, John. *Jerusalem Countdown: A Warning to the World.* San Antonio, TX: Frontline, 2006.

Hall, Randy. "Hate Crimes Bill Opposed by Religious Zealots, Activists Say." CNSNews.com, July 7, 2008. http://www.cnsnews.com/news/article/31304.

Hatem, Mevat. "Gender and Islamism in the 1990s." *Middle East Report* 222 (Spring 2002): 44–47.

Hertberg, Arthur. *The Zionist Idea: Historical Analysis and Reader.* New York: Jewish Publication Society of America, 1997.

Hitchcock, Susan, and John L. Esposito, eds. *Geography of Religion: Where God Lives, Where Pilgrims Walk.* Washington, DC: National Geographic, 2004.

Horowitz, David. *The Professors: The 101 Most Dangerous Academics in America.* Washington, DC: Regnery Publishing, 2006.

Ilkhamov, Alisher. "Uzbek Islamism: Imported Ideology or Grassroots Movement?" *Middle East Report* 221 (Winter 2001): 40–46.

Johnson, Paul. *A History of the Jews.* London: Harper Perennial, 1987.

Johnstone, Ronald L. *Religion in Society: Sociology of Religion.* 7th ed. Upper Saddle River, NJ: Prentice Hall, 2004.

Jones, Huw. "Evolution of Scottish Migration Patterns: A Social-Relations-of-Productions Approach." *Scottish Geographical Journal* 102, no. 3 (December 1986): 151–64.

Jones, Susan. "CAIR Views Conservative Commentary as Incitement." CNSNews.com, July 03, 2007. http://forums.somd.com/politics/105769-cal-thomas-vs-cair.html.

Joseph, Elizabeth. "Polygamy—The Ultimate Feminist Lifestyle." Islam for Today, May 1997. http://www.islamfortoday.com/polygamy3.htm.

Josephus, Titus Flavius. *Antiquities of the Jews.* Translated by William Whiston. 1737. Available online at http://www.sacred-texts.com/jud/josephus/index.htm#aoj.

Joyce, C. Alan, ed. *World Almanac and Book of Facts 2009.* Pleasantville, NY: World Almanac Education Group, 2009.

Kengor, Paul. *God and George W. Bush: A Spiritual Life*. New York: Regan Books, 2004.

Kennedy, D. James. *Why I Believe: In the Bible, God, Creation, Heaven, Hell, Moral Absolutes, Christ, Virgin Birth, Christianity*. Nashville: W. Publishing, 2005.

Knauer, Kelly. *Middle East: History, Cultures, Conflicts, Faiths*. New York: Time, 2006.

Knox, Paul L., and Sallie A. Marston. *Human Geography: Places and Regions in Global Context*. Upper Saddle River, NJ: Pearson Prentice Hall, 2007.

Kosmin, Barry A., Egon Mayer, and Ariela Keysar. *American Religious Identification Survey 2001*. New York: The Graduate Center of the City University of New York, 2001.

Lawall, Sarah, and Maynard Mack, eds. *Norton Anthology of World Masterpieces: The Western Traditions*. 7th ed. New York: W. W. Norton and Company, 1999.

Liss, Sharon Kehnemui. "GOP Candidates, Supporters Bask in Own Glory Following Feisty Debate." Fox News, May 16, 2007. http://www.foxnews.com/story/0,2933,272719,00.html.

Malkin, Michelle. "Myth of Muslim Hate Crime Epidemic." *Capitalism Magazine*, August 17, 2003. http://www.capmag.com/article.asp?ID=3030.

Manolatos, Tony. "Mosques Call to Prayer Signal Hamtramck Change." *Detroit News*, February 23, 2005. http://www.detnews.com/2005/religion/0503/03/B01-98280.htm.

Marshall, Gordon. *Presbyteries and Profits: Calvinism and the Development of Capitalism in Scotland*. Oxford: Oxford University Press, 1980.

Maslow, Abraham. "A Theory on Human Motivation." *Psychological Review* 50, no. 4 (1943): 370–96.

McGeveran, William A., Jr., ed. *World Almanac and Book of Facts 2006*. New York: World Almanac Education Group, 2006.

Media Matters. "Rosie O: Don't Fear Terrorists, They're Just Moms and Dads." WorldNet Daily, November 12, 2006. http://www.wnd.com/news/article.asp?ARTICLE_ID=52919.

Morin, Rich, ed. "Muslim Americans: Middle Class and Mostly Mainstream." Washington, DC: Pew Research Center, May 2007. http://pewresearch.org/pubs/483/muslim-americans.

Murphy, Brian. "Pope Urges Tolerance in Turkey." *The Christian Post*, November 30, 2006. http://www.christianpost.com/article/20061130/23761.htm.

Musallam, Adnan A. *From Secularism to Jihad: Sayyid Qutb and the Foundation of Radical Islam*. West Port, CT: Praeger Books, 2005.

Muslim Alliance of North America. http://www.mana-net.org/index.php.

Muslim American Society. http://www.masnet.org/freedomfoundation.asp.

Nashashibi, Rami. "IMAN (Inner City Action Network): Showing the Way." http://www.mana-net.org/pages.php?ID=activism&NUM=5.

Nasr, Seyyed, Hossein. *The Heart of Islam: Enduring Values for Humanity.* San Francisco: Harper, 2002.

Naylor, Simon, and James R. Ryan. "Mosque in the Suburbs: Negotiating Religion and Ethnicity in South London." *Social and Cultural Geography* 3, no. 1 (2002): 39–50.

Netanyahu, Benjamin. "Address by PM Netanyahu at Auschwitz Concentration Camp." Israel Ministry of Foreign Affairs, January 27, 2010. http://www.mfa.gov.il/MFA/Government/Speeches+by+Israeli+leaders/2010/Address_PM_Netanyahu_at_Auschwitz_27-Jan-2010.htm.

Noonan, Peggy. "Pope Benedict XVI." *Time Magazine,* April 30, 2006. http://www.time.com/time/magazine/article/0,9171,1186689,00.html.

Office of National Statistics. "Census 2001." (London, UK).

Park, Chris. *Sacred Worlds: An Introduction to Geography and History.* London: Routledge, 1994.

Philo, Chris. "History, Geography, and the Still Greater Mystery of Hisotrical Geography." In *Human Geography: Society, Space, and Social Science.* Edited by Derek Gregory, Ron Martin, and Graham Smith. Minneapolis: University of Minnesota Press, 1994.

Price, M. and C. Whitworth. "Soccer and Latino Cultural Spaces: Metropolitan Washington *Futbol* Leagues." *Hispanic Spaces, Latino Places: Community and Diversity in Contemporary America.* Edited by D. Arreola. Austin: University of Texas Press, 2004.

Quist, Wayne B. and David F. Drake, *Triumph of Democracy over Militant Islamism.* Frederick, MD: Publish America, 2006.

Ravenstein, E. G. "The Laws of Migration." *Journal of the Statistical Society of London* 48, no. 2 (June 1885): 167–235.

Rose, Alexander. "How Did Muslims Vote in 2000?" *Middle East Quarterly* 8, no.3 (Summer 2001): 13–27.

Rubenstein, James M. *The Cultural Landscape: An Introduction to Human Geography.* 7th ed. Upper Saddle River: Prentice Hall, 2002.

Sayyid, S. *Fundamental Fear: Eurocentrism and the Emergence of Islamism.* 2nd ed. London: Zed Books, 2006.

Schevitz, Tanya. "FBI See Leap in Anti-Muslim Hate Crimes: 9/11 Attacks Blamed for Bias—Blacks Most Frequent Victims." *San Francisco Chronicle,* November 26, 2002. http://www.sfgate.com/cgi-bin/article.cgi?f=/c/a/2002/11/26/MN224441.DTL.

Schwab, William A. *Sociology of Cities*. Englewood Cliffs, NJ: Prentice Hall, 1992.

Sinan, Omar. "Al-Qaida No. 2 Berates Moderate Arabs." Associated Press, *Washington Post*, December 30, 2006. http://www.washingtonpost.com/wp-dyn/content/article/2006/12/30/AR2006123000715.html.

Sipa, Alfred. "People who Mattered: Mahmoud Ahmadinejad." *Time*, December 16, 2006. http://www.time.com/time/magazine/article/0,9171,1570714,00.html.

Slosser, Bob. *Reagan Inside Out*. Waco, TX: Word Books, 1984.

Smith, Huston. *The World's Religions: Our Great Wisdom Traditions*. San Francisco: Harper, 1991.

Speer, Albert. *Inside the Third Reich: Memoirs by Albert Speer*. New York: MacMillan, 1970.

Sproul, R. C. *Willing to Believe: Controversy over Free Will*. Grand Rapids, MI: Baker Books, 1997.

Stone, Andrea. "There Is No One Kind of Muslim." *Islamic Bulletin* 12, January 27, 1994. http://www.islamicbulletin.com/newsletters/issue_12/islam.aspx.

Stump, Roger W. *Geography of Religion: Faith, Place, and Space*. Plymouth, UK: Rowan and Littlefield, 2008.

Sykes, Bryan. *The Seven Daughters of Eve*. London: Bantam Books, 2001.

Tönnies, Ferdinand. *Community and Society: Gemeinschaft und Gesellschaft*. Edited by Charles Price Loomis. East Lansing: Michigan State University Press, 1957.

Tracy, James D. *Europe's Reformations, 1450–1650*. New York: Rowan and Littlefield, 1999.

United Nations. "UN at a Glance." http://www.un.org/en/aboutun/index.shtml.

University of Kentucky College of Arts and Sciences. "Islamic Studies." http://as17.as.uky.edu/academics/departments_programs/MCLLC/MCLLC/Islamic/Pages/default.aspx.

Vann, Barry A.. "Geotheological Imaginings of a Trans-Irish Sea Scottish Community, 1560–1690." *Geographies of Religions and Belief Systems* 2, no. 1 (2007): 21–39.

———. *In Search of Ulster-Scots Land: The Birth and Geotheological Imaginings of a Transatlantic People, 1603–1703*. Columbia: University of the South Carolina Press, 2008.

———. "Learning Self-Direction in a Social and Experiential Context." *Human Resource Development Quarterly* 7, no. 2 (Summer 1996): 121–30.

———. "Presbyterian Social Ties and Mobility in the Irish Sea Culture Area." *Journal of Historical Sociology* 18, no. 3 (September 2005): 227–54.

———. *Rediscovering the South's Celtic Heritage*. Johnson City, TN: Overmountain Press, 2004.

Wahhaj, Siraj. "Offering an Islamic Perspective on the Great African Diaspora." http://www1.cuny.edu/portal_ur/news/cuny_matters/2003_march/islamic.html.

Waldorf, Brigitte. "Determinants of International Return Migration Intentions." *Professional Geographer* 47, no. 2 (1995): 125–36.

Weber, Max. *Protestant Ethic and the Spirit of Capitalism*. New York: Routledge Classics, 2001.

Wells, Spencer. *Deep Ancestry: Inside the Genographic Project*. Washington, DC: National Geographic, 2006.

White, Vibert L. *Inside the Nation of Islam: A Historic and Personal Testimony by a Black Muslim*. Orlando: University of Florida Press, 2001.

Woodrow Wilson International Center for Scholars. *Best Practices: Progressive Family Laws in Muslim Countries*. Washington DC: Rand Corporation, 2005.

Wright, John K. *Human Nature in Geography*. Cambridge: Cambridge University Press, 1966.

Zahid, Ishaq. "Allah in the Bible?" *Islam 101: American Edition* (blog). http://www.islam101.com/religions/christianity/aibible.htm.

Zakai, Avihu. *Exile and Kingdom: History and Apocalypse in the Puritan Migration to America*. Cambridge: Cambridge University Press, 2002.

Zelinsky, Wilbur. "The Hypothesis of Mobility Transition." *Geographical Review* 61 (1971): 219–49.

Zoll, Rachel. "Rival Muslim Groups Converge on Chicago." Associated Press, *Washington Times*, August 30, 2003. http://www.washingtontimes.com/news/2003/aug/29/20030829-113811-6563r/.

Index